GOD WITH US

Critical Issues in Christian Life and Faith

God
with Us

CRITICAL ISSUES
IN CHRISTIAN LIFE
AND FAITH

John Breck

ST VLADIMIR'S SEMINARY PRESS
CRESTWOOD, NEW YORK 10707

Library of Congress Cataloging-in-Publication Data

Breck, John, 1939-
    God with us : critical issues in Christian life and faith / John Breck.
        p.   cm.
    ISBN 0-88141-252-X (alk. paper)
    1. Orthodox Eastern Church—Doctrines.   2. Christian ethics—Orthodox
Eastern authors.   3. Bioethics.   4. Bible—Hermeneutics.   5. Orthodox
Eastern Church—Liturgy.   6. Christian life—Orthodox Eastern authors.
I. Title.

BX323.B735 2003
241'.0419—dc21

                                                        2003049824

ST VLADIMIR'S SEMINARY PRESS
575 Scarsdale Road
Crestwood, NY 10707
1-800-204-2665

ISBN 0-88141-252-X

Printed in the United States of America

for VESELIN KESICH
agapētos synergos
WITH GRATITUDE

Contents

III. OF GOD AND OURSELVES

Introduction

A LIFETIME AGO IT SEEMS NOW—the beginning of the Orthodox Holy Week 1966—my wife and I boarded a bus with our infant son and made the six-hour journey from Geneva to Paris. With other theological students, most of whom were single, we settled into a run-down little hotel near the park Buttes-Chaumont in the 19th arrondissement, the city's poor northeast corner. After too short a night in a room with too many people, I got up and dressed, then made my way to our Holy Week destination, the Saint Sergius Institute in the rue de Crimée.

There, for the first time, I entered an Orthodox church. The previous ten days had provided us with a theological and liturgical introduction to Orthodox Christianity. They gave little idea, though, of what I would experience in that astonishingly beautiful place.

Morning light streamed in through the dusty, stained glass windows. Life-sized images of saints covered the walls and columns, the details obscured by a cloud of incense that hung palpably in the air. A small crowd of men and women, and a few children, stood immobile, or moved quietly about, lighting candles before icons. A reader finished what I took to be a series of psalms. From behind the icon screen a priest's voice intoned a litany. And the all-male choir, invisible in the right wing of that sacred space, responded.

How long did I stay listening to those hymns, those prayers? Maybe for a moment, maybe forever. The words that come to mind can't describe it. I was in awe of its majesty and solemnity, its power and beauty. This was no mere "esthetic appreciation," and there was nothing at all sentimental about it. This was simply the purest, fullest, most "spiritual" worship I had ever known: praise, thanksgiving and glory offered to the One who has placed in the depths of every person's being a terrible and wonderful yearning for Himself.

In that place, filled with sacred smoke, with the presence of saints and angels, and with the tears of the faithful, I was a total stranger. I understood not a word of what was being chanted, sung, and celebrated, although I could follow tentatively with a translated service book.

Beauty, though, conveys its own special message. Beauty touches the heart to reveal its own special truth. In the beauty of that place, I knew I had come home.

Every once in awhile we are awed by beauty. It's all too rare a happening, but when it does occur, it comes as pure gift.

It can be as simple as an autumn leaf, or a child's face upturned in wonder. Or a silent moment spent with the person you love most in this world. Or a group of Russian Christians singing ancient Slavonic melodies—music of power and heartbreaking loveliness, that expresses, as only such music can, the heart's insatiable longing for God.

My first encounter with that music in a framework of worship was a revelation. It confirmed one of the most basic intuitions of the Church, expressed by the Latin phrase *lex orandi lex est credendi*: worship expresses theology, the essence of the faith, just as theology provides the content of worship. The two are inseparable. Theology that does not come to expression in worship is sterile, reduced to an intellectual exercise with no ultimate purpose. Worship without theology, on the other hand, is, in St Paul's words, "a noisy gong or clanging cymbal," empty of content, devoid of truth and therefore meaningless.

In my previous experience—the tradition in which I grew up—these two domains of worship and theology usually were separated, sometimes rigorously so. Even within a particular church service, theology tended to be limited to the sermon, while the hymns and prayers were conceived so as to express pious emotion or to offer a psychological uplift. As a result, both worship services and seminary classes left me feeling profoundly dissatisfied.

All of that changed, however, with the discovery of "Orthodoxy," a shorthand term for the "One, Holy, Catholic, and Apostolic Church." There worship and theology are fully integrated. There the "rule of prayer" is one with the "rule of faith."

Nearly four decades have passed since that first encounter with Orthodox Christianity. Prior to our move to Europe in 1965, in order to begin graduate work, I had attended a "nondenominational" Protestant seminary with an enviable academic reputation. Once we passed the fourth-century Cappadocian Fathers and arrived at St Augustine, however, every course from Patristics to Systematic Theology led us straight up the Western branch of Christendom, through Anselm and on to the Reformers (with only the briefest mention of Aquinas and other medieval Roman Catholic luminaries). It was a Protestant perspective in a Protestant world. All I knew of the Orthodox Church was that the local Greek deli owner went to one of that name somewhere across town. A New Testament professor of mine did once recommend that I read some homilies by John Chrysostom, to learn something of ancient patristic approaches to Scripture. He never followed up on the suggestion though, and frankly neither did I, at least not for several years. As for names such as Maximus the Confessor, John of Damascus, Symeon the New Theologian, or Gregory Palamas, they were never mentioned, either in class or outside of it.

Little wonder, then, that I reacted with reluctance and some skepticism when the late Greek theologian and director of the Ecumenical Institute of the World Council of Churches (Bossey), Nikos Nissiotis, invited me one day to attend a seminar held each year at the Institute. The purpose of the seminar was to introduce non-Orthodox theological students to Orthodoxy. That I went at all was in retrospect a miracle. We were living in Germany at the time, where I was learning the language and attending doctoral seminars.

My wife had given birth to our first child scarcely three months earlier. It was her intuition that this would be an important step for us, and her willingness to undertake a two-week session in the unknown while nursing our baby enabled me to set foot for the first time in an Orthodox church. That venture began for both of us a journey that seems even now barely to have begun. And not a day goes by that I don't thank God for setting us, gently and firmly, on this pathway that has brought to us and our two sons a dose or two of heartache and an abundance of joy.

During the last three years or so, I have written brief articles for several Internet sites, particularly *Beliefnet.com*, *Christianity.com*, and the Web-page of the Orthodox Church in America (*www.oca.org*). Those articles, like the courses I have offered in various theological seminaries, have focused primarily on two broad areas: ethics, specifically bioethics that deals with issues at the beginning and end of life; and New Testament, with emphasis on hermeneutics, or principles of biblical interpretation.

Some kind readers of the Internet have told me that those columns have been of use to them in several ways, from personal meditation to sermon preparation, and they have asked that they be made available in print. This present collection is drawn largely from those articles. Some of them have been thoroughly revised and updated; others remain more or less as they originally appeared; and still others have been added in an attempt to provide continuity and to develop particular themes.

My aim has been to discuss critical moral, biblical, and general theological "issues" in a way that is relevant to the lives of Christian people today, while remaining faithful to the sacred tradition of the Orthodox Church. Although some chapters are more technical than others, I have tried to make them accessible to any reader who is interested in Christian morality and biblical interpretation. Some themes, such as abortion, the status of the embryo, and innocent suffering, I return to several times, attempting to explore them from a variety of perspectives.

Because a few of these writings are controversial, they will

inevitably elicit disagreement in certain quarters, maybe even passionate disagreement. But that's all to the good, if they succeed in
provoking reflection that will provide better answers than I can
offer to the challenges we as Orthodox Christians are currently facing, both within Christendom and within a hostile and increasingly
anti-Christian world.

That world, however, belongs to God, who creates, loves, and
redeems it. The most striking aspect of Christian faith is its conviction—based on revelation but also on personal experience—that
this God is *with us*, as both sovereign Lord and merciful Father. In
the Person of His eternal Son, God took upon Himself our "flesh"
(Jn 1:14), our fallen nature, thereby restoring that nature to its original purity, innocence, and wholeness. He assumed our mortality,
our death, by assuming our humanity through His Incarnation in
the womb of the Virgin Mary. By descending through the Cross into
the realm of death, He destroyed death's power by His Resurrection. As the God-Man, He ascended with our humanity into heaven,
to manifest to all of creation the glory He shared with the Father
from all eternity. Finally, the Father and the exalted Son together
sent into the world the Spirit of Truth (Jn 14:26), who is also the Paraclete: our Advocate before the throne of judgment and Comforter
in a world of militant unbelief. By virtue of the Spirit's presence
with us, we receive the baptismal grace of a new birth "from above,"
by which we are incorporated into the Body of Christ, the Church,
and nourished by the Body of Christ in the Holy Eucharist.

Thereby the God who is with us—Father, Son, and Spirit—creates the conditions for the resurrection, ascension, and glorification
of all those who unite themselves to Him in faith and in love. And
thereby He frees us from an otherwise meaningless existence,
whose end is corruption and annihilation. In the language of the
Church Fathers, "God became man that man might become God by
grace." This is the Church's teaching on *theōsis*, or the "deification,"
of the human person. In the most simple yet profound terms, it
declares that God shares fully in our life, in order that we might
fully share in His.

What distinguishes Christianity from every other form of religious faith is this knowledge that God *comes to us*, that God is ever present with us. "Religions" involve a quest of the soul for the Transcendent, an inner movement towards a reality that lies beyond ordinary life and experience. In Christ and the Spirit, on the other hand, God comes to us precisely in the ordinariness of our daily routine. He participates fully in our struggles, our joys, our suffering, and our death. This God, unlike the God or gods of religion, is present and acting within our world, including in the most intimate details of our life. His will and His hand are guiding us and all of creation toward ultimate fulfillment and providing all things with ultimate meaning. This God, as the Scriptures declare, is *Emmanuel*, "God with us."

The bedrock of authentic Christianity is this unshakable conviction that God is present with us, that the One who is infinitely beyond all that exists is nevertheless intimately concerned and involved with every aspect of our reality. It is this conviction that enables us within the Church to raise questions and reach specific conclusions regarding the most significant matters we face, including ethical issues of life and death, and the interpretation of God's self-revelation in the Holy Scriptures. And hence the title of this book.

This collection is divided roughly into three parts. The first deals with ethical issues of contemporary interest, including manipulation of human embryos for purposes of cloning; and matters surrounding death and the process of dying: suicide, the taking of one life to spare another, and euthanasia. Part two focuses on the Bible and liturgical celebration. It begins with some practical advice on reading Holy Scripture in a way that conforms to the approach and vision of the Orthodox Church Fathers. Several chapters then offer examples of the function and importance of Scripture in the Church's celebration throughout the liturgical year. The third part takes up contemporary theological issues, beginning with some words about the tragic events of September 11, 2001, and moving on to a variety of doctrinal and pastoral questions.

There is nothing complete or definitive about the reflections offered here. They are brief meditations—mostly serious, but sometimes tongue-in-cheek—on selected subjects that seem to have particular relevance for the difficult matter of living a Christian life in this new millennium.

It is my hope that these little chapters might serve as a catalyst for further reflection on these and similar issues, to be undertaken by our clergy but also by interested laypersons, both individually and in small study groups. They will serve their purpose well if they raise some pertinent questions and encourage a quest for answers that address important pastoral needs of the Church, and do so to the glory of God.

My thanks go in particular to three people who encouraged and gave direction to various facets of this project in its earlier stages: Frederica Mathewes-Green, George Papageorge, and V. Rev. Alexander Garklavs. Over the past few years I have come to cherish their friendship as much as I have appreciated their help and guidance. Protopresbyter Robert Kondratick, Chancellor of the Orthodox Church in America, and David Lucs of the chancery staff, have provided invaluable help and support, without which much of this material would never have been produced. My gratitude goes to them as well.

This book is dedicated, with special affection and appreciation, to my friend, mentor and former colleague, Veselin Kesich, Professor of New Testament Emeritus at St Vladimir's Orthodox Theological Seminary.

—Father John Breck
Feast of Theophany 2003

I

Moral Issues

1
Moral Crises and Christian Responsibility

*I*N THE SPHERE OF MORALITY Christians of all confessional traditions today are facing a vast number of "crises": critical issues that require serious and concerted reflection to determine appropriate courses of action that are consistent with the demands and promises of the gospel.

Part I of this book focuses on areas of particular moral or ethical concern, especially in the field known as "bioethics." These are issues dealing primarily with the beginning and end of human life. They include technological procedures developed in connection with fertilization (medically assisted procreation), genetic engineering (manipulation of human gametes, cloning), and life support (care for premature neonates, accident and disease victims; treatment of the terminally ill), together with ancillary issues such as abortion and euthanasia, including "physician-assisted suicide."

This present chapter is little more than a listing of some of the various problems and possibilities resulting from rapid developments over the past years in this new field of bioethics. Its purpose is to raise questions that demand close attention, in part to determine appropriate limits that should be imposed on the use of newly developed technologies that have changed traditional approaches to life and death. Later on, we will return to some of these issues and look at them in more detail.

Extraordinary recent advances in biomedical technologies are forcing us to expand ever further the very notion of "bioethics." Increasingly life and death issues include problem areas such as the relation between the "sanctity of life" and the "quality of life"; moral judgments we pass on various economic, political and social systems; the nature and limits of national defense in an age of terrorism and weapons of mass destruction; the ever increasing gap between the rich and the poor within our own country and around the world; and even such matters as gun control and suicide.

Because they involve human behavior and have a direct impact on human life and values, we should include as well such problems as alcoholism and drug abuse; pornography in the media and especially over the Internet; the dissolution of the nuclear family; violence and sexual exploitation in films and video games; the negative effects of commercialism and competition (the Enron/WorldCom syndrome and corporate greed in general); the lack of adequate medical insurance and deficiencies in health care, together with the overall spiritual poverty in this country that lies behind illness and dysfunction at many levels of social life, including life within the Church.

These are all essentially bioethical issues. Although many of them have been with us for a long time, there is a growing urgency today to highlight in the sphere of public debate perspectives that are informed by the Christian Gospel. For the Orthodox, that means the Gospel as read and interpreted in the light of Holy Tradition.

Orthodox Christians have usually been reluctant to seek common ground with members of other churches. This is due in part to the historical isolation in which the Orthodox find themselves. It is also due to fear that Orthodoxy, with its specific ethos, high theology and intense liturgical life, will become assimilated into the amorphous mass of American "denominations."

Roman Catholic moral theologians have been in the forefront of ethical reflection for decades, and their Protestant counterparts are not far behind. These traditions could benefit greatly from an Orthodox perspective on the many issues we have named. And we

Orthodox certainly could benefit from mutual exchanges of ideas, experiences, and apprehensions, as we seek to make the voice of the Church heard in this increasingly pluralistic and militantly secular society.

When it comes to issues of life and death, those who call on the name of Jesus Christ as Lord and Savior need to reflect and to work together. Bioethics is too vast a domain for the voice of any one tradition to make itself heard effectively. As difficult as it may be for many Orthodox (and those of other confessions, for that matter) to carry on serious and prolonged reflection beyond the bounds of their own tradition, such a concerted effort today is indispensable. To some, it may seem a threat: succumbing to the "heresy of ecumenism." To others, who trust in the indestructible truth and power of Orthodox Christianity, it will provide a forum for much that is positive, including both learning from others and witnessing to our own faith.

In the face of a growing number of moral crises, this kind of concerted effort, grounded in mutual respect and mutual desire to discern God's will, is nothing less than our Christian responsibility. May God grant us the wisdom and determination to assume it, with unqualified faithfulness to Orthodox tradition and with genuine concern for the health and welfare of all of His people.

2
The Beginning of Human Life

*I*N ORDER TO SAY ANYTHING at all about issues such as abortion, euthanasia, and other practices concerning the beginning and end of human life, we need to have a clear understanding of what the limits of life really are. There has been endless debate over this question, especially since the passage of *Roe v. Wade* in January 1973. When, in fact does human life begin: at conception (meaning fertilization) or at some later point, such as implantation, quickening, birth, or even beyond?

The human embryo comes into existence with the fusion of the nuclei of a sperm and an ovum. No one questions the fact that from this moment on there is "genetic individuality." That is, the twenty-three chromosomes of one gamete unite with their counterparts of the other, to produce a genetically unique individual. The question is, is that individual entity "human," and if so, can it be qualified as "personal"?

A great deal of ethical reflection today tends to deny that either adjective can be applied appropriately to the zygote, the cell in its initial stage of development formed by the union of the two gametes. Many, including basically "pro-life" Christians, will acknowledge the human *potential* of the early embryo, yet they will refuse to accord it human status during the period when it moves through the fallopian tubes on its way to implantation in the wall of the mother's uterus. This entity, they hold, should be called a "pre-embryo." They find its lack of distinctively human or personal characteristics demonstrated by the fact that at this stage the embryo can twin and even recombine. Moreover, each cell of the growing embryo is characterized by "totipotency," that is, each one contains the genetic information and developmental capacity to become a complete individual being.

Other ethical perspectives hold more radical views. Some maintain that an embryo cannot be considered human because the nervous system is not yet integrated. Others hold that the fetus is not truly human—and in any case does not constitute a "person"—until either it can be felt moving in the mother's womb (quickening) or it comes to term at birth. Still others argue that even a newborn child must prove itself worthy of being granted the social status of "person" by demonstrating good health, potential intelligence, a capacity for meaningful relationships, and an absence of genetic anomalies: otherwise society has no obligation to nurture it and sustain its existence. According to these criteria, autistic and Down syndrome children, as well as those with serious physical disabilities, forfeit all claim to life.

These perspectives represent what is termed "delayed animation" as contrasted with "immediate animation," the view that human life begins with formation of the zygote. Delayed animation has been unequivocally rejected by Orthodox moral theologians since at least the fourth century. Following Tertullian, St Basil the Great (†379) insisted that abortion at any point constitutes murder, "and we do not ask whether the fetus was formed or unformed" (*Canonical Letters* 2 and 8). Instinctively, Orthodox Christians have sensed that genetic uniqueness constitutes the beginning of new life. As it is often stated: there is no point other than fertilization at which we can say, "Life begins here and now."

Even if we accept fertilization as the beginning of human life, though, is this tantamount to saying that the zygote is "personal"? Empirically, the position seems absurd and groundless. Can a one-celled, or eight-celled, or even an implanting embryo be reasonably attributed the status of "person"?

If the Orthodox insist that it can, it is for one reason only. Genetic uniqueness is merely the physical or physiological counterpart to a deeper and more significant reality, which is creation of a spiritual being in which soul and body are thoroughly integrated, one with the other. We are created—from the outset of individuated existence—in the image of God. That created being qualifies as "personal" not only because it possesses the capacity to develop into a complete human being. It is personal because at every stage of human existence it bears and manifests the very image of the *personal* God. One is always a bearer of the divine image, whether as an embryo or as a terminally ill patient in deep coma. Therefore at any and every stage of existence, one is essentially a "person," reflecting the "being in communion" of the Three Persons of the Holy Trinity. This is the God who brings all reality into being and sustains human life as it progresses toward its intended goal, the "likeness of God."

While proponents of abortion and euthanasia may see the matter differently, the perspective of the Church from apostolic days to the present has opposed willful destruction of life at any stage precisely because it bears the divine image and thereby possesses eternal value. To our eyes, an embryo may be a bit of tissue with no more intrinsic worth than a single hair or a mole. The Church's attitude toward "life from the beginning," however, has been shaped by the conviction that God, and not we ourselves, determines authentic "personhood." He brings human life into existence and grants it a status the psalmist recognized as "little less than God" (Ps 8).

That status is grounded in God's love for His human creature at every stage of the growing process, from conception to the grave and beyond. It may sound improbable to say that "God loves an embryo." But it is a truth that has always been known by the Church—and by countless pregnant women as well.

3

A Consistent Life Ethic

S HORTLY BEFORE THE ELECTION of G.W. Bush, I was talking with a journalist friend who had been born and raised in Paris. He had just finished a six-month stay in the United States, listening to many of us and writing articles on his experience. "Though we admire you Americans more than you think," he said, "what strikes us most is the odd—may I say crazy?—inconsistency in the way you take sides on issues of life and death."

He went on to give a few examples, beginning with current politics. On the one hand, he pointed out, the Republicans oppose abortion yet heartily support the death penalty. And their front runner in the upcoming presidential election is clearly in the pocket of the National Rifle Association, despite the fact that American children are committing mayhem in the classroom with readily available handguns. The Democrats, on the other hand, have taken the high ground on the question of gun control. But their candidate belongs heart and soul to the pro-abortionists, to the point that he sees nothing wrong (nothing barbaric) with partial-birth abortions.

One party, in other words, is pro-life regarding the unborn, pro-death for society's violent undesirables, and pro-gun because of some specious interpretation of the Constitution. The other party takes just the opposite stand, crying for "abortion rights" even when the issue is infanticide, yet arguing against the death penalty because of its inherent injustice, and waging war with the NRA, maybe because of its hopes for a voters' backlash in the wake of recent killings of children by both grown-ups and other kids.

"What gets me," he concluded, "is the inconsistency inherent in the respective positions of both parties. It seems to me that it would make more sense if at least one major political party in the country held to a really consistent 'pro-life' philosophy, as we try to do in Europe."

I couldn't argue with him, since I've been troubled by the same inconsistency myself. What has bothered me all the more, though, is the realization that the problem isn't limited to political parties. It infects the thinking of a great many Christians as well, including many Orthodox.

We Orthodox are by nature "conservative," hopefully in the true sense of that word. We feel called by God to preserve—to conserve—the faith of our Fathers (and Mothers), which multitudes of saints and martyrs have transmitted as the tradition of the One, Holy, Catholic, and Apostolic Church. And this is all to the good.

But in this country especially, that conservative bent has often embraced the platforms of conservative political parties as a matter of principle. Many Orthodox Christians vote Republican. This is because they see the party of Lincoln as the one that defends individual rights, family values, and the life of the unborn. They point with dismay (and sometimes with undisguised glee) at Democrats who violate those values. When they are questioned about the inconsistency in being pro-life regarding abortion while defending both capital punishment and the "right" to bear deadly weapons, they usually reply by invoking the innocence of the unborn and the (presumed) guilt of those destined for the chair or a lethal injection.

In the case of the Democrats the matter is a little more coherent, but not much. Their concern for the rights of the already born takes precedence over other values, including the rights of a child *in utero*. Because gun violence violates a person's rights as decisively as anything else, they favor serious gun control. And the matter of rights extends to criminals as well, especially given the undisputed fact that a sentence of capital punishment is often influenced by racism or a lust for vengeance. But they are no more consistent in their political philosophy than the Republicans, a fact those Orthodox who vote Democratic need to come to terms with.

The question is, what image of the human person lies behind these positions? Orthodoxy holds that every human being, without exception, is created in the image of God and bears the Divine Image from conception to the grave. The human person, therefore, is of infinite value, because he or she—at any stage of growth and development—is precious in the sight of God. This includes the guilty as well as the innocent, abortionists as well as the aborted, gun dealers as well as social workers, sinners as well as saints.

The late Catholic Cardinal Joseph Bernardin was honored in part because of his insistence on what is called a "consistent life ethic." This perspective acknowledges the wrong in sinful and anti-social acts, and it prescribes appropriate punishment. But it refuses to acknowledge the right of the State, any more than that of the individual, to take another person's life—just as it refuses to sanction abortion, and just as it peacefully militates against the gun culture that has wreaked such destruction in American cities, homes, and schools.

After I put my French friend on the plane, I stopped off at the local Piggly Wiggly to pick up some groceries. In one aisle there was a woman, obviously pregnant, holding the hand of a three-year old. Next to her was, I suppose, her husband. He was dressed in jeans and wore a Home Depot cap. Bulging from his hip, only partially hidden by his jacket, was a pistol. They were shopping. And like so many in the state where I live, he was exercising his legal right to carry a concealed weapon. Even in the Piggly Wiggly.

On my way home, I couldn't stop praying for the twin blessings of sanity and consistency. And I couldn't stop wondering either how many more children have to be aborted, how many more have to be shot down, before either sanity or consistency finally takes hold.

4

Manipulation of the Human Person

S INCE THE BEGINNING OF 2002, the media have focused with a single-minded intensity on the continuing threat of terrorism at home, in Israel, and elsewhere. As a result, our attention has been drawn away from what is potentially a more dangerous threat to our well-being: the virtually uninhibited manipulation and destruction of human embryos in the interests of a "new eugenics."

Embryonic stem cell research began in earnest in early 1999. It has been driven by the potential capacity of stem cells to develop into every tissue and organ in the human body.

Of equal concern are the increasing pressures to patent human genes, segments of DNA that carry the code of human life. Not surprisingly, the driving force behind these initiatives is economic: they promise virtually limitless profits to the burgeoning biotech industry that provides most of the research funding. Although present emphasis is on the medical potential—ultimately building new organs to replace old ones and eliminating various genetic anomalies—the marketplace is already pressuring specialists to create "designer babies" with preselected characteristics, including, via the wizardry of cloning, another person's genetic make-up.

Where does the Orthodox Church stand on this issue, which involves manipulation of human life at its most basic level? Although neither Scripture nor patristic teaching speaks to the matter directly, together they offer a vision that addresses it very clearly. That vision offers precious insight into the meaning and value of the human *person*.

Orthodox anthropology—the doctrine of the human person—begins with the Genesis affirmation that every human being is created "in the image and likeness of God." However the term "image" is to be defined; it implies what theologians today call "being-in-communion." The human person is not an isolated entity but a member of a community. And the primary and primordial community is that of the Church, the Body of the risen and glorified Lord, Jesus Christ.

The ultimate model for the ecclesial community is God Himself: the eternal life-in-communion of Father, Son and Holy Spirit. "Be perfect," Jesus instructs His followers, "as your heavenly Father is perfect." That perfection, as God expresses it, consists above all in self-sacrificing love, offered as a free gift to the other: to the other Persons of the Holy Trinity, and to the created world, particularly to human persons.

In order for us to reflect the perfection of the Trinity, we cannot avoid engaging in an ongoing struggle against the tendencies of our darker side, what the ascetic tradition calls the "passions." Accordingly, many of the Church Fathers will make a distinction between "image" and "likeness," defining "likeness" as the goal of that ascetic struggle, the "unseen warfare" of the soul. Just as every human being is created in the divine "image," so every one is called to assume the divine "likeness." The image, in other words, refers to our nature, the "givenness" of human life that we all share. The likeness, on the other hand, constitutes the goal toward which each "person" or particular human being is called to strive. That goal is described by the Fathers as *theōsis*, a Greek word meaning "deification." It signifies that the purpose and end of human life is to participate eternally in the life of God, in his "energies," or attributes, such as justice, truth, mercy, beauty, and love.

Orthodoxy is well known for its "high christology," its conviction that Jesus of Nazareth is no less than the God-Man, the eternal Son of the Father, who "without change became man and was crucified" in order to work out our salvation. Equally "high," though, is Orthodox anthropology: its understanding of the eternal value of the human person. However much it may stress the reality of human sin, Orthodox Christianity also acknowledges that the chief aim of human existence—towards which every person is called to strive and struggle—is to glorify God and to enter into eternal and joyful communion with the Persons of the Holy Trinity.

What does this imply with regard to our original question concerning the manipulation and commercial exploitation of human genetic material and human embryos?

Above all, it means that no manipulation of the human person, on the macro or micro level, can be accepted unless that manipulation is for strictly therapeutic purposes that will serve the best interests of the person concerned. This necessarily excludes experimentation using viable human embryos (who, in God's eyes are fully personal, bearers of the divine image, and not merely "blobs of tissue"), just as it excludes the patenting of human genes for commercial ends.

Already physicians are complaining that certain recently developed diagnostic tests involving genes (e.g., for Alzheimer's disease) are not available to them because patents on the procedures are held by private corporations. In America we used to express shock at the way Japanese companies virtually "owned" their employees. The risk today is infinitely greater: that commercial interests will literally "own" us, insofar as they control the use of our DNA.

In 1998, the Holy Synod of the Orthodox Church in America called for a moratorium on experimentation leading toward the cloning of human beings. This appeal was renewed in the fall of 2001, with the bishops' statement condemning embryonic stem cell research and human cloning in general. Now that the first stage of the human genome project has been completed, that appeal needs to be expanded to cover any and all manipulation of human genetic material for commercial purposes that do not include clear and acceptable therapeutic results. And legislation definitely should be enacted to prohibit the patenting of human genes.

This newly acquired knowledge concerning genetics, with its extraordinary potential for good or ill, must be kept in the public domain. Orthodox Christians should insist on this point, through the media and by any other means at their disposal. Otherwise we face the very real risk of succumbing to a new and insidious form of slavery, in which our genetic heritage is literally owned by interests—commercial or governmental—other than our own. Similarly, we need to make clear our unequivocal opposition to the manipulation and destruction of human embryos, particularly since *adult* stem cells, together with those harvested from placentas and umbilical cords, have proven to have as great a therapeutic potential as their embryonic counterparts.

The human person, created in the image of God and called to progress toward the divine likeness, is unique and of infinite value. Any attempt to reduce the person to a reservoir of genetic components or to reproduce that person through cloning, is an offense not only against human rights and human dignity. It is above all an offense against the God who creates and loves each person, and calls each one without exception to share forever in His divine life.

5

*Election Dilemma, 2000**

W HEN THIS COLUMN APPEARS, the presidential election will have been decided and we'll be in for at least four years of something I don't much like. This election, more than any in memory, has forced all of us into an ethical dilemma with unavoidable and undesirable consequences. No matter how we voted, no matter who is sitting in the White House right now, a fundamental principle of the Gospel has been seriously violated.

The dilemma is this: Whichever presidential candidate wins, whichever party controls Congress, some form of uncontrollable violence will receive official sanction. Republicans will support unrestrained possession of handguns and semi-automatic weapons, while the Democrats will work to remove all restrictions on abortion, and particularly so-called partial-birth abortion. Winners will include the NRA or NARAL. Losers, I'm afraid, will be the same as they have always been: school children and their devastated families, or newborn infants who are victims of infanticide.

Most of us have read the arguments used to defend both weapon possession and unrestricted abortion: the Second Amendment to the Constitution, the inadequacy of police protection in a dangerous society, the joys of hunting (to shoot down whom or what?),

*This chapter and the one following it were written shortly before the presidential election at the turn of the new century. They are reproduced unchanged, since their point depends in part on the uncertainty at that time regarding the outcome of the vote.

"guns don't kill people, people kill people," and so on; then again: "a woman's right to choose" (death for her baby?), "Whose body is it, anyway?," together with feigned concern for the mother's health—even pro-abortion medical professionals admit that partial-birth abortions are never required for therapeutic purposes.

The way I list these arguments, of course, makes me as guilty as their proponents of using language to vent feelings and attitudes. The long and short of it is, I just can't buy either set of reasonings: those that treat murderous assault weapons as sporting equipment or those that treat human life as rubbish.

The irony is that this little diatribe I've put forth has no conclusion, no resolution. All I can do is state my opinion that major planks of each party's platform—even if they have been largely hushed up and considered unofficial—are not only politically unwise and morally perverse, but they reflect a grave sickness in the heart and gut of American society.

Do we really want to live in a country where law and order is preserved by vigilantism? And do we really believe that vigilantes, or average home-owners for that matter, can defend their lives and property more effectively if they are armed to the teeth? Wouldn't it make more sense to beef up our police forces, providing better training, requiring tougher standards, offering higher pay, and thereby replacing the undesirable elements with guardians of the peace who are qualified, efficient, and judicious? I know: this doesn't address the real issue, which is the macho thrill so many people get out of handling a .357 Magnum or pulling the trigger on an Uzi. But it might help neutralize the reckless notion that you and I can do it "better than the cops."

Then again, do we really want to live in a society where the legal rights of the mother take precedence in any and all cases over the very life of her unborn child? Especially when the option to destroy that child's life involves the gruesome procedure called "partial-birth abortion"? To make the point, let's review the procedure one more time (ad nauseam, right, but sometimes that's the only way to get something across).

Partial-birth abortions work like this. The live baby is in the birth canal, then his or her body is turned so as to emerge feet first. The delivery continues until only a portion of the head remains in the canal. The child is rotated so as to expose the back of the neck. The physician forces scissors into the skull to make an opening. A hose is inserted and a vacuum pump sucks out the brain. The skull collapses or is crushed, and the remainder of the corpse is extracted.

The whole procedure is nothing more than a way to avoid a charge of infanticide in the brutal killing of an unwanted child. And no one seems to care that the infant feels excruciating pain. (Have you ever contemplated the effects of a saline abortion? Or the widely used procedure called D&E, dilatation and evacuation, in which the child is dismembered with forceps before being removed piece by piece from the womb?)

More kids shot down on playgrounds, in the streets and in their own homes. More babies murdered in the delivery room. Some choice.

But now that choice has been made, and "we the people" have to live with it. Some of us, in any case, will die with it. And that's a shame.

"Suffer the little children to come unto me," Jesus said. Suffer indeed.

6

The Great Disconnect

A CCORDING TO MY DICTIONARY, "disconnect" is a verb. Its noun form is "disconnection." The idea behind both is the severing of a connection or relationship. More generally, the terms can imply a break in logic, as in "to disconnect from reality" through false reasoning.

A few years ago people started using the verb form as a noun, to express this last idea. A "disconnect" doesn't hang together. It can imply a fractured relationship: "Jim and his wife—a total disconnect!" It can signify detachment from reality, as when a teenager remarks about parents, "They're on disconnect!" Or it can suggest mental incompetency, an inability to reason coherently: "Alzheimer's creates a massive disconnect."

The noun "disconnect" possesses its own special energy. Substitute "disconnection" for it in the examples above, and you'll see what I mean.

There's a profound disconnect, it seems to me, in the surprisingly articulate and substantive acceptance speech the Democratic presidential candidate (to avoid naming names) made not long ago. Whatever your political inclinations, you could hardly fault him on specifics and the way he spelled out his party's and his own vision for the future. What troubles me is the lack of logic—the "total disconnect"—in his treatment of "life" issues.

First we heard an impressive litany of proposals for supporting and defending everything from affirmative action to universal medical care, particularly for children. Children, in fact, were a major focus of the proposals, as the candidate homed in on problems of health, education, and general welfare. He is a family man who takes obvious pride in his own children, just as he reflects "family values" that in recent years have been trampled into the dust. His proposed programs would offer extraordinary benefits and safeguards to America's children, without concern for their gender, class or race—as long as they have made it out of the womb.

The disconnect came when he affirmed in strident terms his support for "a woman's right to choose." We have heard so much on both sides of the abortion issue, that to raise it once again risks annoying, if not infuriating, pro-life as well as pro-choice people. Without going into details of abortion procedures, as pro-life groups are wont to do, it's worth giving a moment's thought to the implications of that August speech and to the pro-choice agenda in general.

How is it that a sincere and well-meaning person can argue so eloquently and compassionately for education, universal medical care, and other benefits for the young, yet support abortion on demand, including the inhumane procedure of infanticide known as partial-birth abortion? How can someone defend with such conviction and passion the rights and needs of our children, yet draw an absolute line at (total) emergence from the womb?

Were my children any less human persons than they are now when they were still in their mother's body, or when all but one small portion of their anatomy was "born"? Were yours? Were you?

I look at my now grown "boys"—long since become young men—and I marvel at the life that is theirs. Not just biological existence, but life in the biblical sense. Not only distinct and distinctive personalities, but "persons," unique and inexpressibly precious. Each of them sees the world and relates to it in a special way. Day by day each one contributes something to it, through laughter, humor, sympathy, reflective observations, music, creative energy, and acts of kindness.

All children do this, insofar as we offer them the space and encouragement to do so. There's nothing unusual in that. The Columbines of our society are demonic aberrations, not the norm. Our children—like ourselves, though that is harder to admit and maybe to recognize—are creatures of infinite value. They have the capacity to offer the gift that transforms any soul from a simple individual into a fully mature "person": the gift of disinterested love. And we can only love them in return.

There are reasons, sometimes very good—if inevitably tragic—reasons, why a woman feels compelled to resort to an abortion. In all of those times she needs our support, understanding and love rather than our condemnation. This is not where the disconnect lies, whatever the circumstances that lead to her decision.

The disconnect lies in public policy that rightly defends the newly born yet allows the almost-born to be destroyed. The disconnect, in other words, lies in the irrational and immoral way we have allowed the principle of the mother's "rights" to take absolute precedence over the reality of the child's very life. Human life does not begin at birth, any more than it begins with adolescence or with the first Social Security check. It begins—as the ancient Fathers of the Church knew, long before embryologists came on the scene—at conception.

Until that truth is acknowledged, public policy will continue to operate in a mode of profound disconnect. And we will continue, with legal sanction and social approval, to engage in a massacre of the innocents.

7

Ova for Sale

*T*HE AD IN THE LOCAL PAPER shows two pretty, smiling faces. The young women are relaxed and happy. The message is that they are doing something both good and easy. And their smiles ask, "Won't you help?"

It's an ad for "egg" donations. "Being an egg donor," the first line reads, "can be the nicest thing you'd ever do for someone you'll never know." It's inviting, practically seductive. Especially since donors are compensated two to three thousand dollars "for their time and trouble."

What's wrong with this picture? Why should anyone question the motives or ends of the entire process that leads some women to make anonymous donations of their ova, especially if it will help infertile women who deeply desire to bear and raise children?

There are lots of reasons, really. The most obvious is the problem of *selling* ova or sperm. We are so accustomed to a capitalist approach to life in general that most of us no longer sense the demonic dynamic at work here: the commercialization, and consequent cheapening, of human reproductive material.

Then again, the question must be asked: who determines the criteria by which prospective donors will be chosen? The ad (and most like it, for they are legion these days) declares that every effort will be made to match donors with recipients appropriately, and so the sponsors seek a variety of donors, of "all aptitudes, interests, physical characteristics, and ethnicity." On the surface the proposal seems eminently just, fair, and, certainly, politically correct. But indeed, what's wrong with this picture?

When Orthodox ethicists get together to talk about matters like this, the consensus is unambiguous. A basic rule of thumb to which all of us adhere as a matter of faith is that there should be no "third party" in the work of procreation. When I mentioned this to one of our parishioners, she assumed it meant foregoing gynecologists, obstetricians, and midwives. What it rejects, rather, is any procedure that involve third party genetic material—sperm or ova—donated anonymously or otherwise. (To some Orthodox theologians it also excludes such practices as artificial insemination and *in vitro* fertilization, but that's another issue.)

The reasoning behind this position is the same that leads the Orthodox to reject surrogate mothering, whether the surrogate is impregnated by the man's sperm or serves simply as an incubator for an embryo that was fertilized in a petri dish and transferred to her uterus. It has to do with the intimacy of the sexual act that leads to procreation. Indeed, this is why we refer to the entire process as "procreation" rather than "reproduction." Copy machines reproduce; people procreate.

This is not merely a semantic quibble. Procreation, whether recognized as such or not, involves participation in God's ongoing work of creation. Just as He works out our salvation in part through our intercession for one another, so He relies on the loving relationship of husband and wife to bring forth new life. Husband and wife, and not just any couple—unmarried, homosexual, or other—because their loving union is essentially a spiritual reality. It is a relationship created within the framework of the Church, the community of faith, where the spouses receive God's blessing according to accepted tradition and make a formal, public commitment that begins with the wedding ceremony and endures into eternity.

Does the Church, then, feel any compassion at all for women who for some unavoidable reason are unable to bear children without resorting to donor gametes? Of course it does; we all do. The point is, however, that the possibility of bearing children is a gift, one that involves sacrifice and pain as well as joy and fulfillment.

When a couple finds themselves in the difficult, often heart-rending circumstance of irreversible sterility, Orthodox spiritual guides will embrace the couple with full understanding and sincere compassion. But they will also urge the couple to accept the barrenness as an expression of God's (often inscrutable) will. And more often than not they will counsel the couple to consider seriously the possibility of adoption.

A growing number of Orthodox Christians, with or without children of their own, are finding adoption to be a joyful and blessed solution to their very natural longing to have and raise a child. Many find their heart's answer here in the United States. Many others seek elsewhere: Russia, Romania, Korea, Guatemala . . . The possibilities are endless, and the needs are overwhelming.

"The nicest thing you'd ever do for someone you'll never know" may not be to provide gametes, especially not at a price. It may be, instead, to provide the material, emotional and other forms of support that will allow a woman who would otherwise abort her child to bring it to term, then place it for adoption. If this were done, there would be no need for "egg donors." And we would be well on the way to bringing sanity to a social order that spends billions to develop new procreative technologies, yet every year destroys the lives of 1.3 million unborn children.

8

The Embryo and the Bible

C HRISTIAN ANTHROPOLOGY is firmly grounded in the Old Testament understanding of the origin and destiny of the human person. It makes its greatest departure from Hebrew teaching with its proclamation of Christ's incarnation, resurrection, and ascension. These momentous events provide the conditions for the general resurrection of humankind "at the last day" and for the glorification or deification (*theōsis*) of those who dwell "in Christ."

The ancient Hebrews nevertheless understood that we are created "in the image and likeness of God" (Gen 1:26–27). Our life-breath is the Breath of God Himself (Gen 2:7). This divine "inspiration," identified by the Church Fathers as either the soul or the Spirit of God, animates human life from its beginning, that is, from what we would call fertilization or conception. Therefore the psalmist can declare: "Thy hands have made and fashioned me" (Ps 118/119:73), and "For Thou didst form my inward parts, Thou didst knit me together in my mother's womb" (Ps 138/139:13). Job reminds God that His hands have fashioned him "from clay" and "knit [him] together with bones and sinews" (10:8–11). God creates the "heart" of all persons, and He animates them with His own life-breath (Isa 33/34:15; Ps 32:15; etc.).

The Septuagint or Greek translation of Exodus 21:22 makes a distinction between the "formed" and "unformed" fetus (we might say, between the fetus and the embryo). Yet both live by virtue of God's indwelling Breath, or Spirit. And they do so from the moment of creation, that is, from fertilization.

New Testament authors took up these basic notions and developed them into a distinctively Christian view of the human person. If Rebecca's twins could struggle with one another in their mother's womb (Gen 25:21ff), John the Baptizer could, from his own mother's womb, recognize and rejoice in the presence of Jesus, borne in the womb of Mary (Lk 1:44). These are not "fetuses"; they are conscious, sentient human beings who relate to one another as persons.

A great many other passages from Hebrew and Christian Scriptures could be cited to make the point that God animates His human creatures from the beginning of their existence and sustains them throughout the period of their earthly life. One of the most interesting is found in the Wisdom of Solomon 15:11. Here the author speaks of those who fail "to know the One who formed them and inspired them with active souls and breathed a living spirit into them." For those who do know God, Christian witnesses will later affirm that inspiration, or in-breathing of the life principle, is the necessary condition for achieving their ultimate purpose. If God creates the soul together with the body, as Christian tradition affirms, it is so that the human person might participate from the very beginning in God's own life.

For the sake of convenience—and perhaps also to camouflage what really happens in an abortion—we make a distinction between "embryo," "fetus," and "child."

From a Biblical perspective, these distinctions or divisions in the human growth process are artificial. In reality, there is complete continuity from one stage to the next. The act of creation itself produces a living, "ensouled" human being, a bearer of the divine image, whose entire existence is given for one fundamental purpose: to grow in holiness from conception, through maturity, and to physical death, to full participation in God's very being, His own personal existence.

"As for man," St Irenaeus declared, "it was necessary for him to be created; then having been created, to grow; and having grown, to become an adult; and having become an adult, to multiply; and having multiplied, to become strong; and having become strong, to be glorified; and having been glorified, to behold the Lord." (*Against Heresies* IV.38)

9

The Embryo and the Church Fathers

E ARLY CHURCH THEOLOGIANS of both Latin and Greek tradition
puzzled over the status of the human embryo almost as much
as we do today. Despite their lack of detailed scientific knowledge
in the area of embryology, their conclusions were often marked by
a surprising degree of insight.

Many of both traditions, for example, tended to distinguish—
largely on the grounds of the Septuagint rendering of Exodus
21:22–24—between the "formed" and "unformed" fetus. Tertullian,
Jerome, Augustine, and other Latin Fathers held the unformed
fetus to be fully human; but they recognized two basic stages in
embryonic development: from mere life to full "humanity" once
the growing child has acquired its complete "form." Some Eastern
thinkers made a similar distinction (Origen, Ephrem the Syrian,
and Cyril of Alexandria).

In the Preface to his treatise *On First Principles*, Origen (†254)
laments the fact that Church teaching until his time had not clearly
taught whether the soul is created (or, to his mind, "transferred,"
since he believed the soul is preexistent) at conception, or has
another origin, whether it is begotten or unbegotten, given from
within or infused from without. While his conclusions were generally rejected by the Church, they provoked an extraordinary
amount of reflection on the nature of the soul, its relation to the

physical body, and the moment at which soul and body are united in the newly created human being.

The basic question raised by the Fathers of East and West concerned "animation." Most representatives of Latin (Western) tradition held to a belief in "delayed animation," arguing that the soul is created, or enters the body from without, at some point after fertilization. Their Greek counterparts tended to argue for "immediate animation," holding that the soul is created together with the body. Orthodox teaching, grounded in Greek tradition, generally holds to the latter. It considers an embryo to be "ensouled" from the moment of conception, when the sperm and ovum unite to form a new being. It is this conviction—that the zygote itself is fully "ensouled"—that leads Orthodox theologians to qualify the embryo as "a person."

Although Tertullian could distinguish between a "formed" and an "unformed" fetus, he recognized that the soul exists together with the body from the very beginning, that is, from fertilization. The same is true for the Greek (Eastern) Fathers: Irenaeus, Clement of Alexandria, Gregory of Nyssa, Maximus the Confessor, John of Damascus, and many others.

However we may regard the process of fetal development, Orthodox Christianity continues to affirm "immediate animation." It holds unequivocally to the view that the zygote—the one-celled product of fertilization—is already an "ensouled" being. For this reason, it also insists that the zygote is, from the very beginning of its existence, a personal being, bearer of the image of God.

This conviction underlies the increasingly unpopular Orthodox view that the growing child—as zygote, embryo, fetus, or newborn—deserves the same measure of legal protection as any adult human being.

It is interesting to note that defenders of immediate animation tend to reject a (typically Latin) theory regarding the fate of deceased embryos or fetuses. Whether that death results from a miscarriage or an abortion, most Eastern witnesses affirm that those who die in the womb, because they are innocent of any sin or willful rejection of God, will be welcomed by Him into the kingdom of heaven. Although unbaptized, they will not await judgment in some state of limbo (Tertullian), nor will they be condemned to eternal punishment (Augustine), or be deprived of union with God (Aquinas).

The Fathers, then, are divided as to the fate of deceased embryos. Those of Latin tradition tend to shape their understanding in terms of God's justice; those of Eastern tradition, in terms of God's compassion. There are certainly elements of truth in both positions.

Yet to those parents who have lost a child under any circumstances, it is safe to say that with God justice *is* compassion. God has created us for life—all of us. Therefore, we may understand Jesus' invitation, "Let these little ones come unto me," to include even the very little, even the littlest of all.

10

Clone Human Embryos?

*A*NYONE WHO HAS SEEN a loved one wither away under the effects of Parkinson's disease or disappear into their own darkness because of Alzheimer's, can only hope and pray that these tragic and devastating illnesses soon will be curable. Genetic engineering and particularly the cloning of human stem cells promises just such cures, and many more besides. Who can reasonably oppose the research needed to discover those cures?

This is perhaps the chief moral issue, and dilemma, of our day. As we all now know, Great Britain recently legalized human cloning. It is the first country to do so, but it surely will not be the last. Scientists and philosophers in a number of Western countries are insisting that the "new medicine," which will grow out of the successful sequencing of the human genome, will offer heretofore undreamt of possibilities for healing disease, preventing epidemics, correcting genetic defects, and prolonging human life. To realize this medical utopia, though, will ultimately require experimentation on literally millions of human embryos.

Those who oppose the research on moral grounds are dismissed as retrograde: mindless reactionaries who—like pro-life people in general—are out of step with the needs and demands of modern society and especially of "today's woman." To their way of thinking, however, the exalted roles of child-conceiving, child-bearing, and motherhood are seriously threatened by pressures that will lead to the fabrication of embryos-on-demand. They are acutely aware that little Adam Nash was conceived from a genetically selected embryo and brought into the world so that the stem cells from his umbilical cord could be used to relieve or even cure the Fanconi anemia that afflicted his older sister. The ineluctable slope, it seems, is getting slipperier and slipperier.

Just how, as members of the Body of Christ, are we to evaluate these developments? The problem with the Nash baby is the same as with the cloning of embryos, although to a lesser degree. We hardly can raise objections to using blood from an umbilical cord, especially since Adam was not at all harmed by the procedure. The problem, however, concerns the selective process that takes the determination of gametes out of the realm of "natural selection" and places it into the realm of conscious manipulation.

There is a question we need to ask ourselves, one that will seem naive or irrelevant to many people, including many Christians: What is God's role in the process of human procreation?

Orthodox Christians, in any case, are convinced that God is directly and intimately involved in literally every aspect of human existence and experience. The hairs of the head are all counted, the lilies of the field are arrayed, the birds of the air are nourished, and all by the hand of God. These poetic images are taken very seriously. They mean that everything that occurs in our life and experience is known by God and, in some fashion, comes under God's sovereignty. This truth is well expressed by a prayer many Orthodox Christians say each morning: "Teach me to treat all that comes to me throughout the day with peace of soul and with firm conviction that Thy will governs all. . . . In unforeseen events, let me not forget that all are sent by Thee."

If indeed we take these words seriously, then this means that God is also directly and intimately involved in the process of human procreation. And this means that we must leave the choice—the "natural selection"—of which sperm and ovum unite in the process of fertilization to the unconscious movements of the human body—movements that are ultimately directed by God.

There is no greater mystery in this life than the creation of new life that bears the divine image. And by definition, any and every "mystery" or "sacrament" derives from God and is to be offered up to God as a sacrifice of praise.

The legal cloning of human embryos in the United States, at least for the time being, is restricted to the production of stem cells for purposes of medical research. A recent British decision, reported by *The Washington Times/*Associated Press on January 23, 2001, stated the following: "Like all other embryos used in research, the clones created under the new regulations would have to be destroyed after 14 days, and the creation of babies by cloning would remain outlawed."

The point, however, is that those embryos, too, are "babies." Hundreds of thousands already have been created and destroyed for the sake of scientific research. Whatever the motives of the medical teams, whatever the promises of the "new medicine," we mustn't forget that one most basic, if inconvenient, truth: Those embryos, too, are babies.

11
Will Human Clones Have Souls?

*T*HIS QUESTION IS PRODUCING a great deal of anxiety these days, especially since Great Britain, and more recently Holland, have legalized research that will inevitably lead to the widespread cloning of human beings.

Some people, including at least one bishop who has spoken out on the subject, argue that human clones will not "have souls" in any conventional sense. This, they argue, is because the embryo was conceived apart from "an act of love."

This kind of reasoning, as sincere as it may be, is simply false. The emotional or affective state of the parents at the time of intercourse, prior to conception, has no direct bearing at all on the status of the embryo. If an ensouled human being only can be produced by two people who engage in the sexual act out of genuine love for one another, either there would be far fewer people on earth than there are now, or most of the world's population would be less than human because they possess no soul. Can we really hold that every child conceived by rape, incest, conjugal violence, or simple indifference is ipso facto deprived of a soul?

If we frame a question the wrong way, it is impossible to give it a correct or even a reasonable answer. Behind the question, "Will human clones have souls?", there lurks a very unorthodox notion of what "the soul" really is. Origen, we remember, was condemned in part for teaching the preexistence of souls: spiritual entities that become "incarnate" in particular physical bodies. Christian anthropology rejected that kind of dualistic notion a millennium and a half ago, but the idea persists, even in the minds of some people who are responsible for preserving and transmitting authentic Orthodox doctrine.

From a biblical perspective a person does not "have" a soul, in the sense that the soul is an independent entity that enters or is "infused" into a physical body at some specific moment: at conception, at implantation, at birth, or whenever. The human person, rather, is characterized as a "living being" (Gen 2:7), which means a "living soul." Soul is the transcendent aspect of our being. Although we speak of the "separation of soul and body" at physical death, the soul is still not to be considered an entity distinct from the body. (More accurately, it is distinct from the "flesh," which "is dust and returns to dust"). In other words, we do not "have" a soul; we "are" soul. Soul is the transcendent, animating principle of our entire being.

Would a clone, then, "have a soul"? On the one hand, that is a false question, since once again a person "is" rather than "has" a soul. But is that true of cloned individuals? The question must be answered in the affirmative, for the following reasons.

Firstly, as we noted, the affective state of the parents at the time of intercourse has no bearing on the status of the embryo. A person need not be conceived "by an act of love" in order to be a complete person (although, as we now recognize, the emotional state of the mother during the pregnancy certainly affects the child growing within her). Personhood is conveyed by God. Even there where genetic anomalies or environmental factors deform the growing embryo, the image of God remains intact. The child remains a fully human person throughout its life both inside and outside the womb.

Then again, cloning is in effect the artificial production of identical twins. "Cloning" occurs *in utero* prior to implantation of the embryo, when a number of blastomeres or embryonic cells break off from the main cluster. Since each cell can express the full complement of DNA, each cell is "totipotent," capable of forming a complete human being. And occasionally those cells will recombine. In any case, whether the mother gives birth to a single child or to "identical twins," the result is the birth of one or more "ensouled" persons. And we know from common experience that "identical twins" are hardly "identical." This is because our personal identity is determined by far more than the genetic material contained in our chromosomes.

Cloned human beings will in fact be even less similar to the "original" than identical twins are to each other. This is because clones share only the DNA of the host nucleus. Unlike identical twins, they are not shaped by the same maternal mitochondria, nor do they share the same environmental conditions during the period of gestation.

We can conclude, therefore, that cloned human beings will indeed "have"—or, rather, "be"—souls. Despite what we must judge to be the grotesque way in which they are conceived, they will be as fully human, personal, and "ensouled" as a child conceived *in utero.*

The moral problem with human cloning, then, lies less with the person thus created than with the manipulation of human gametes and human embryos used to produce the clone in the first place. Already countless thousands of embryos have been destroyed toward this end. Even if we can affirm that a cloned human being is an ensouled person and bearer of the divine image, this does not excuse our silence, since silence will inevitably be read as tacit support. Human cloning is fundamentally immoral, and voices within the Church must condemn it as such.

This is in part because of the famous "slippery slope." In February 2001 researchers in San Francisco announced that they had produced mice, a quarter of whose brains were composed of human cells. Presently, they are working to produce a strain of mice whose brain cells are entirely human. The greatest danger with the mad rush to clone human beings is that, along the way, we will create ever more sophisticated chimeras: animals with human genetic material and anthropoids that are part human, part something else.

Then the question will have to be raised again, Do such creatures have souls? That question only God can answer: the God from whose hands we willfully have snatched the power to create ourselves in our own very fallen image.

12

"Therapeutic" Cloning?

*I*N ENGLAND, EARLY IN 2001, those who make earth-shaking decisions did so by legalizing euthanasia. Although safeguards are
supposedly in place, there is little doubt that this pierces yet
another massive hole in the battered dike that is holding back a
flood tide of "convenience murders."

Something similar is afoot in the area of human cloning,
although the issue is being handled more gingerly and with more
effective propaganda by those who stand to profit the most from its
legalization. The "medical-industrial complex" has managed to convince the media, which has subsequently convinced the public,
that there is a clear scientific and moral distinction to be made
between "reproductive" and "therapeutic" forms of cloning. Reproductive implies "making babies"; therapeutic means merely "creating tissue."

Now England has declared that it wants to ban the former but
allow the latter. This is because most people still wince at the idea
of preselecting our children's genetic traits. Any protocol that can
be successfully labeled "therapeutic," however, is virtually guaranteed today to be accepted by the general public. This is, after all, a
therapeutic age. Whether we attempt to get ourselves fixed by self-
help groups or spend hours enjoying a deep massage, we thrive on
therapy. Who dares call it into question?

If I do so here, it is because the entire issue is based on deception. In fact, *all "therapeutic" cloning is by its very nature reproductive.*

The cloning process itself, insofar as it involves humans and other higher organisms, requires that we create and destroy embryos: large numbers of embryos (it took nearly three hundred "tries" just to produce the famous sheep Dolly). This is true whether we have in mind "therapeutic" or "reproductive" ends. To utilize embryonic tissue for therapeutic purposes, we need to create that tissue in the first place. And whatever end we may have in mind, therapeutic or reproductive, the process by which those embryos are created is the same, the manipulation is the same, and the moral consequences are the same. To pretend otherwise is naively to deceive ourselves or maliciously to deceive other people.

So when we hear journalists, scientists, or business people trying to reassure us that the cloning process would be restricted to therapeutic ends, and that they themselves would never accept its use for reproductive purposes, we might keep one point in mind. In the final analysis, there's no real distinction either between "physician assisted suicide" and "active euthanasia." Although the methods employed may be slightly different, they are in effect the same thing: they both terminate a human life. They may appear to serve life insofar as they put a limit to suffering. But they both kill.

The same is true with cloning. It may appear to produce or enhance life. But whose life? Certainly not the lives of the countless human embryos who will be sacrificed in the process.

13

Abortion: Tragic and Inevitable

*I*F HUMAN LIFE AND INDIVIDUATED personal existence begin at fertilization, then the Church cannot condone the taking of that life while it is in the womb anymore than it can once it is born. This is a conviction that goes back to early apostolic times (Didachē 2:2; Ep. Barnabas 19:5) and is grounded in Old Testament tradition (Ps 139:13–16; Isa 49:1,5; Jer 1:5; cf. Gal 1:15f).

This conclusion is based on the Church's understanding of the "sacredness" or "sanctity" of life. The human person, endowed with a soul or essential spiritual dimension from conception, possesses the quality of "sacredness." A bearer of the image of God, the person exists in communion with both God and other people, a communion which is to reflect the communion-in-love that unites the three Persons of the Holy Trinity. The human person reflects the Divinity. This is true even when sin has so tarnished the divine image that it is unrecognizable and totally obscured. Orthodoxy holds that this image is eternal and therefore indelible. It remains intact, even in the most hardened heart and most corrupted soul. If not, then genuine repentance would be impossible.

It is the image of God within us, then, that provides us with the quality of "sacredness." Like the image itself, that quality characterizes our existence from conception through death and into life beyond.

Abortion destroys the life of a human person, whatever its stage of development. This is why the Fathers of the Church impose upon the mother and the abortionist the penalty for murder (normally, ten years of excommunication).

This said, however, we have to ask about exceptions. Orthodox moral theologians generally admit only one exception to the prohibition of abortion. This is when the continued pregnancy or imminent birth seriously jeopardizes the life of the mother. Even this allowance can be questioned, however, for lack of clear support in the patristic tradition. Nevertheless, because of the mother's existing relationships of love and responsibility for other members of her family, it seems pastorally and morally reasonable to give priority to her life over that of her unborn child.

Other exceptions, accepted as grounds for abortion by many Christians but rejected in principle by most Orthodox, include rape, incest, and serious genetic defects borne by the child. Studies have shown that, in general, rape and incest victims, with the proper love and support, can bring their child to term and then, if necessary, give it up for adoption. Everything, of course, hinges on the qualification, "proper love and support." In any event, this recourse tends to reduce the effects of what is now recognized to be the "post-abortion syndrome" that weighs heavily on "post-abortive women," sometimes to the point that it pushes them to commit suicide. Most importantly, the possibility of giving up a child for adoption offers life to the child.

As for genetic defects, the Church's response is that this child is given by God into the hands of the parents to be protected, nurtured, and loved, irrespective of the "defects" it might bear. Some defects, certainly, are so severe that medical intervention amounting to an abortion might be necessary, but again, to safeguard the mother's own life. If the newborn child manifests life-threatening genetic anomalies or otherwise suffers from conditions that are clearly incurable (anencephaly, for example) and will bring on imminent death, then everything should be done to ensure that the infant will die with as much love and comfort as possible.

In today's world these prescriptions might well sound rigid and doctrinaire, the product of an extreme "pro-life" philosophy. Their justification, though, is not provided by rules, by what is permitted and what is not. It is provided rather by a single set of convictions:

that God is sovereign over both life and death, that His love extends to every created being and especially to every bearer of His divine image, and that He gives life into our hands—our own life and that of our unborn children—for us to cherish, protect, nourish, and love without limit or qualification.

Then He asks of us the ultimate commitment: that we take that life and offer it back to Him as a living sacrifice of thanksgiving and praise. Our children do not "belong" to us; they belong to the Father of us all.

Nevertheless, there will always be abortions, as there always have been. It is both fruitless and cruel, though, to respond by condemning the woman who feels driven to make that tragic choice. To condemn the mother and ignore the responsibility of the father, as so often happens, represents a gross injustice. To condemn a teen-aged girl who, out of desperation, opts for an abortion is to violate a fundamental principle of love, extended to saint and sinner alike. To condemn victims of rape and incest for ridding themselves of the product of sexual violence—even when that "product" is a living human being—is as pointless as it is heartless. There are indeed times when a woman is forced to make a choice she never intended and never wanted to make. Whatever the reasons behind her decision, the role of the Church is clear.

That role is to educate our young people with spiritual direction that is faithful to Holy Tradition. But we must never forget that this tradition itself is grounded in Christ's command to love both neighbor and enemy: demonstrated by His love and forgiveness to the adulteress (Jn 8:3–11), as well as to His own murderers (Lk 23:34).

God will judge us all, according to His own standards, His own will. Our place is to inform, guide, and support, with boundless compassion, all those who find themselves in a state of acute moral crisis. Indeed, we all find ourselves there, from time to time. In the aftermath of abortion, as in every other such crisis, the rule of thumb can only be to "do unto others as we would have God do unto us."

14
Abortion: Let's Talk about It!

O UR LOCAL WOMEN'S PAPER is smart, chic, and humorous. It publishes fiction and commentary that's usually intelligent, frequently poignant, and occasionally inspiring. At times it also sets my teeth on edge.

There's a lot of talk these days about being caught up in the cultural wars. Insofar as those wars involve women's "rights," this paper takes a stance that's anything but ambiguous. It comes down foursquare for every woman's right to choose, in any and all circumstances, the fate of a child she may have conceived. If she wants to abort that child, at any stage of the pregnancy, she should be free to do so. This right seems self-evident. Any opposing view that suggests a child *in utero* should be granted legal protection represents not only a heresy but an absurdity. How can a zygote or an embryo or a fetus have any claim to protection that supersedes the mother's right to rid herself of the unwanted growth within her?

The fact that we have lapsed into cultural warfare, rather than cultural dialogue, over this issue is due in large part to the polarization that has occurred around it. To "pro-lifers," their adversaries are self-centered, morally challenged people who deny the obvious humanity—not to say personhood—of unborn life, merely to guarantee their own comfort. Abortion on demand, in other words, is a matter of sheer expediency.

To "pro-choicers," a naive attribution of "personhood"—or even of humanity—to an embryo or fetus results from a religious fanaticism that puts some skewed, abstract principle above the reality of a woman's life and represents the worst kind of invasiveness into the most personal and private realm of her existence.

In fact, the great majority of women who opt for abortions do so out of motivations that are far less callous, far less egocentric, than many pro-life activists would like to admit. For many "post-abortive women," the experience both before and after the fact is traumatic and depressing. Many feel that they had absolutely *no* choice other than to abort their child. As a result, they react to the typical "pro-choice" line with derision or with tears.

As for responsibility, women are often torn between being responsible either toward their unborn child, or else toward their parents who cannot accept their unmarried daughter's pregnancy, or toward a husband who doesn't want any more kids, or toward themselves in cases where poverty or emotional trauma make unbearable the idea of another mouth to feed, another life to care for and deal with.

Personal responsibility in the abortion issue is not as clear cut as many would have it. Responsibility to whom, when she finds herself caught between conflicting demands?

Those of us who are decidedly "pro-life" need to question the caricatures to which we've become all too accustomed. We need to share, insofar as we can, the pain and anguish so many women go through when they opt to terminate a pregnancy. And those on the other side need to open their minds to the obvious: that unborn life is still life. It is fully human life, and it deserves the care and protection we owe to any human being at any stage of his or her development.

Whatever our position on the issue, we need to stop the verbal overkill and begin to talk, with mutual respect and openness. We need to talk, but also to listen.

The churches have been largely silent on this issue. Some have felt it their calling to denounce abortion, yet they give little attention to the plight of the mother (and virtually none to the responsibility of the father). Others offer varying degrees of support to abortion proponents, particularly those who speak in the interests of victims of rape and incest. While both sides claim to represent truth in the matter, on each side that truth is only partial, in that it focuses either on the child or on the mother. Both the child and the mother, however, have a rightful claim on our attention and our care.

That claim leads us beyond the level of "reproductive rights" and the "status of the embryo." It obliges us to set the entire issue in a theological and pastoral framework, where respect for the life and welfare of the person is extended with equal compassion and equal effectiveness to all parties concerned: to the unborn child, but also to the woman from whom that child receives life.

It seems imperative, then, that the churches (yours and mine) provide, at the local level, a forum for genuine dialogue concerning abortion and the significance of prenatal life, a dialogue that to all parties involved is responsible, respectful, and compassionate. In today's atmosphere, if they don't, there is little chance that anyone else will.

15

The Adoption Option

*T*HE LITTLE ROMANIAN GIRL was handicapped. She was not only "visually challenged" but cross-eyed, with no chance of recovering sight in the most damaged eye. And that eye looked, oddly and unwaveringly, straight at her nose.

Like a scrawny puppy in a run-down pet shop, she waited in the dilapidated orphanage, hoping someone would see something other than the most obvious. Each time potential parents came through, she prayed they would look beneath the surface and find *her*.

The Moroccan hospital was staffed with too few nurses, the blankets were thin and worn. They were as dirty as the shivering children they only partially covered. A gaunt, malnourished little boy rocked back and forth in his crib, looking vacuously at us as we passed by. A nurse told us he hadn't cried in months. Checking back a year later, we discovered that he had died. Not from hunger or cold or disease. Just because he had never been loved.

Neighbors down the street from us tried for several years to adopt a baby from an American orphanage. They had no luck. The bureaucracy was too much and their patience was too limited. One day I saw the young wife pushing a stroller up the street, a beatific smile lighting her face. Strapped in the seat was a little Korean girl, round faced, very Asiatic, and adorable. Some eighteen months later she had a baby brother, also Korean. When we talked, the mother mentioned that their attempts to adopt a non-white child in the United States led nowhere, because some sociologists had decided that "racial mixing" wasn't a good idea.

Several women connected with the seminary where I taught created an adoption agency, with the hope of providing Orthodox homes for "available" children. They didn't have much success because, as one of them explained, with all the abortions in the country, there just aren't that many children who in fact are available.

On one level, that's true. And strict adoption regulations (that vary widely from state to state) have hampered many well-intentioned people who have longed to take a child or two into their home and provide them with the love and nurture they would otherwise never have. But what can you do when well-meaning but short-sighted bureaucrats, social workers, and judges throw up insurmountable roadblocks, pretending it's "in the interests of the child"?

To avoid an unhealthy situation—one of potential abuse—is certainly in the child's interests. But it's also in the child's interest to be hugged, played with, properly educated, and loved.

The world is full of adoptable children. To leap the adoption hurdles, here or abroad, however, requires not only patience and hard work; it also requires a deep and genuine yearning to share one's life with a child, even if that child bears genes that are not our own, or may harbor tendencies toward illness that will only become evident in later years.

Leaping those hurdles also requires money, and that hinders a great many potential parents. Yet there are many people—married and single—who live right around the poverty line and have nevertheless made a home for someone else's children. Sometimes they are the children of their children, or of a sibling or of a neighbor. Sometimes they are kids of another race or culture. In any case, without money but with an abundance of love, care, and affection, they can thrive.

So many abortions in this country! It's our most deplorable and tragic national scandal. Perhaps something would change if laws were modified to facilitate the adoption process yet ensure adequate screening of potential parents. Perhaps something would change if the stigma still attached to unwanted pregnancies, in and outside marriage, was lessened and replaced by a communal and ecclesial effort to help and support pregnant women, so they might bring their child to term and place it for adoption.

In the meantime, if you have ever considered adopting a child, or have tried and encountered frustration, there is one place you might want to turn. It is the Hogar Rafael Ayau Orphanage in Guatemala City, run by a small group of deeply dedicated Orthodox nuns, with the help of hundreds of compassionate lay people. The address is Hogar Rafael, 16 Calle 3-61, Zona 1, Guatemala City 01001, Guatemala; Tel (011) 502-232-1789; Fax (011) 502-232-3080; e-mail: homeayau@ufm.edu.gt.

These sisters have had remarkable success in both raising and placing orphaned children. Be in touch. Offer help, financial and otherwise, if you can. Perhaps you'll find that the child you help today could be yours tomorrow.

16
Down Syndrome at Pascha

MARIE ("MASHA" TO THOSE CLOSE TO HER) had all the symptoms and characteristics of what we used to call "mongolism." She was in her mid-thirties when I got to know her, more than three decades ago. She died a few years back, well into her sixties, far beyond the age when most Down people have succumbed to a variety of congenital defects. Throughout her long life she remained a child with a child's innocence and mischievousness, irascibility, and stubbornness. A true child.

People stared at her on the street, mildly repulsed by her squat figure, slanting eyes, and wide forehead, as though Trisomy 21 were somehow self-willed, a bad or at least unfortunate choice she had made for herself while still in the womb. Her mother, by God's grace, was a saint, who laughed and played, taught and prayed with her only child, to the point that Masha could say her prayers and converse fluently (for a four-year old) in her native Russian and in the French of her classmates at the special school she attended on the outskirts of Paris. She also learned to pray in German. And when my wife and I visited her family, with a big, satisfied grin, she greeted us in English—extraordinary for a Down syndrome person. But Masha herself was extraordinary, simply because she was deeply loved and blessed with exceptional care and understanding.

I first caught sight of Masha in the Russian Orthodox Church of St Sergius, located in Paris' 19th arrondissement, then a poor working quarter of the city. The old wooden church, purchased by émigrés from the days of the October Revolution, was adorned from floor to ceiling with magnificent sacred images, depicting the whole of salvation history. It was Holy Friday, and people milled around before the afternoon vespers service, lighting candles, venerating icons, and whispering quietly to one another. The sense of anticipation was palpable.

A few minutes later the service ushered us into the awesome mystery of the crucified God. Ancient Slavonic hymns resonated throughout the church with power and poignant beauty. Finally the central Royal Doors of the iconostasis opened. The priest and several laymen, with the intensity of the moment etched on their faces, came forth into the center of the nave, carrying the *epitaphion,* or large image of the crucified Lord, wrapped in the shroud of a dead man. Their solemn procession brought them to the center of the church where, before a large wooden cross, they laid the image on a low table, placed a Bible and a cross upon it, and heaped it high with flowers. All the while the choir repeatedly sang the traditional and magnificent hymn known as "The Noble Joseph," commemorating the actions by which this converted Pharisee took Jesus' body down from the cross, anointed it with precious oils, wrapped it in fine linen, and laid it in a tomb.

The scene was indescribably beautiful. It was more than a simple commemoration. Through that service we relived the terror of the disciples and the ineffable sorrow of the faithful women. We stood with Joseph and Nicodemus as they took Jesus' broken body down from the tree. We shared Joseph's wonder as we sang, "How shall I bury Thee, O my God? How can I wrap Thee in a shroud? What songs can I sing for Thine Exodus, O Compassionate One? I magnify Thy Passion, I glorify Thy burial and Thy holy Resurrection, crying: O Lord, glory to Thee!"

At the close of the service the faithful, packed into every corner of the church, came forward to venerate the image of Christ. At some point Masha appeared. As on every Holy Friday, she was dressed entirely in black. Her face was streaked with tears, her head was bowed, and her arms hung down at her sides. As she approached the shroud, she slowly made the sign of the Cross three times, prostrated herself before it, and for a moment kept her head to the floor. Then she rose, kissed the face then the feet of Christ, and finally she venerated the Bible and the cross.

I watched others as they watched her. Most of the people there knew her well. They knew that every Holy Friday she lived the tragic mystery of the Passion as most of us never can. She walked with Christ, she conversed with Him. She was present with Him—and He with her—just like the women who sat opposite the tomb, shedding anguished tears and hoping for a miracle.

Those people knew, too, that the following evening, Masha would also exult in the glory of Christ's Resurrection. With the myrrh-bearing women, she would come to the tomb, discover it empty, encounter the Risen One, and rejoice beyond all rejoicing. For that parish community, Masha was one of the myrrhbearers. She brought the truth and reality of the Resurrection to the heart and consciousness of anyone who took the time to look with wonder and thanksgiving at her unique way of sharing in and bearing witness to the Lord's death and resurrection. She incarnated the hymnography of the feast, and by doing so she became what each of us is called to be: a living icon, a sacred image that reflects the boundless, self-giving love of God.

Masha was a gift. And few in that community doubt that she intercedes for us now before the Throne of Grace.

Today, many years later, the Mashas of the world are disappearing. Their value is weighed according to different standards and found wanting. Through genetic screening they are identified before birth, and many parents think the obvious solution is abortion. It's a true massacre of the innocents.

Some parents of Down syndrome children, like columnist George Will, champion their worth. The question bears raising again: Do we really want a world where there are no Down syndrome children? What immeasurable gift would we lose if we never saw a Masha in humble worship before the shroud of Christ?

17

Rage!

*F*ULLY 25 PERCENT OF AMERICAN WOMEN report having been the object of some form of domestic violence. A man allegedly murders his "best friend," buries then disinters the body, and cuts it into a dozen pieces before reburying it. Young adolescents enter their school armed to the teeth and randomly shoot to death one schoolmate after another. Another youngster, expelled from class, goes home, gets a gun, returns to school, and kills his "favorite" teacher. A driver on a California freeway is cut off by someone in a hurry, pulls a gun and fires, seriously wounding the other driver. A drunk air traveler brutalizes a female flight attendant, then tries to force his way into the cockpit with the aim of crashing the plane. A couple of teens, defending "traditional social morality," beat a gay boy to death. A divorced father murders his wife and child before leading police on a harrowing chase. And, so it goes.

This is not terrorism. This is rage.

America has no monopoly on rage that leads to mayhem. In Germany a Mercedes owner shot and killed another driver because the man spat on his car. The jury acquitted the owner, by the way, claiming it was "a crime of passion." Then there are England's football fans. And Africa's internecine genocide. And Latin America's penchant for making enemies, including nuns, "disappear." Ad infinitum.

Psychologists today talk about "abandonment rage." It seems that a young child, seriously abused or neglected by a parent, senses the abuse as abandonment. Because the child doesn't dare speak out, especially if he or she has known physical violence, the anger is internalized and becomes either depression or rage, or both. As the child grows older, the sense of abandonment can lead to a pathology of rage, particularly when alcohol or other drugs are involved. And rage contains a high degree of energy that often can be diffused only by violence.

Anger is a normal and often healthy response to frustration, injustice, betrayal, and so on. In itself it is not necessarily wrong or sinful. "Be angry but do not sin," the apostle Paul admonishes. Then he adds, "do not let the sun go down on your anger"! (Ephesians 4:26). If we find the sun setting again and again on our anger, then there is a good chance we are dealing with rage. As a pathology that threatens both the enraged person and those around him/her, rage needs to be identified for what it is: an serious illness that needs to be cured.

All too often priests hear parishioners confess repeated anger and have no clue that the penitent is caught up in a pathology of rage. Wives and children often bear the brunt of repeated verbal and physical violence coming from the spouse or parent, with no idea that the problem is profoundly psychological and spiritual—and that they, the victims, are not to blame. Prisons are full of people whose antisocial behavior has resulted from unchecked and uncontrollable rage.

The phenomenon is so widespread today that we are morally obligated to educate ourselves about it, learn to detect it, and distinguish it from occasional outbursts of anger. Then we need to take appropriate steps to diffuse it and to get professional help for the perpetrator and for his or her wounded targets.

Perhaps we need to begin with ourselves and with those closest to us, since we are morally responsible for one another. There are simple questions we can ask ourselves. Does my anger get out of hand? Is it chronic? Or triggered by events that seem to overwhelm me? Is it destructive of my own life and well-being, or of others whom I love or with whom I am obliged to live in close contact (the boss, coworkers, a neighbor)? Is it mixed with irrational fear? Does it make me react in ways that I would find totally unacceptable if I were on the receiving end? When I am angry, do I still feel in control? Or does the anger tear my guts to shreds?

These are unpleasant questions. But they may help us understand our own unacceptable patterns of behavior, or enable us to identify rage in others, especially when it is directed at us. In any case, both the perpetrator of rage and the victims of it need help. If the rage involves domestic violence, there are hotlines listed in the Yellow Pages, and in severe cases there is 911.

I recall the first time, as a fledgling seminarian, I had to confront the father of a boy in my church youth group. The man was an inch shorter than me and thirty pounds heavier, all muscle. I was scared to death, sure that he would leave the same black and blue marks on me that he regularly left on his son. When I confronted him, I was shaking. To my astonishment, he began to cry. Then he begged me for help.

We need to educate ourselves about the phenomenon of rage and learn from professional therapists how to detect it and how to make appropriate referrals. We also need to pray ceaselessly for those who are caught up in it: for the enraged person and for their victims. We are "members of one another" and responsible for one another. When one person is victimized, we are all victimized. When we enable rage by retreating into silence and inaction, we take an active part in another person's destructive behavior. Before God and the abused victims, we ourselves become as guilty as the perpetrator.

18

Violence against Women

*C*HECK OUT THE STATISTICS ON THE "violence" web sites. Or read the first-person accounts in magazines from *Cosmo* to *The Counselor.* The numbers of abused women in America is appalling. From childhood sexual abuse to rape by strangers, friends, and husbands, women are hardly less victimized today than they were in the sexist, patriarchalist societies of yore.

A recent newspaper alert reads as follows: "The World Wrestling Federation has crossed a line into overt and public violence against women as 'sport.' On April 8, a woman was featured as part of a six-person tag team match. She was slammed in the face by a large male wrestler and dragged around the ring by her hair after the match was over. This 'sport' is widely viewed by children (despite a TV-14 warning) and has already resulted in the slamming death of a young girl by an older boy emulating what he saw on the show."

I haven't been able to verify every detail of this account. At the very least it describes a cultural environment that thrives on humiliating women, a point made every day by most sitcoms and R-rated films.

Many long years have gone by since my grandfather taught me to open doors for "ladies" and to behave around them with deference and courtesy—in other words, to watch my language and act like a "gentleman." The very fact that these two words have to be set off today with quotation marks is a good indicator of how far we've slid into macho indifference, even a blatant dissing of women. The last time I instinctively opened a car door for a female member of our parish, she looked at me as though I were a throw-back, a witless toady playing Walter Raleigh in the age of Eminem.

Granted: antebellum chivalry toward women also went hand in hand with the notion that they should be kept barefoot, pregnant, and in the kitchen. Women were humiliated in that way, too.

Something new has been added in recent years, though, and not just by the WWF. Our culture—what's left of it—is driven by in-your-face aggressiveness (that expression didn't even exist a decade ago), as it is by anything and everything that shatters taboos. Violence shock hasn't begun to run its course, at least not in the realm of sex. And women remain the main targets, the inevitable victims.

Many women hate the last chapter of Proverbs. This is the passage that extols the good, virtuous, hard-working, and thoroughly domesticated "handmaiden." To ambitious, career-oriented females especially, that seems archaic, demeaning, and sexist. What we all tend to forget, however, are the lines of this passage that speak of woman's moral greatness and strength in the midst of a world of degradation, poverty, and want. It's her hand that provides for her household in the most essential ways, her charity that feeds the poor, her wisdom that instructs in the ways of kindness as well as productivity.

No question that it's "patriarchalist," at least as measured by today's standards. But today's standards are not necessarily those of God—or of human beings either, when they have their heads and hearts turned in the right direction.

Violence against women, in whatever form, hurts not only women. It shapes an atmosphere in which the abuse of anyone becomes acceptable, in which the weaker are always at the mercy of the more powerful.

If we tolerate it, we undermine our common humanity. We effectively deny that women, and therefore all of women's offspring, are created in the image of God. This produces not only battered women. It creates an ambience that encourages violence and romanticizes it—in our schools and homes, on the streets, and in corporate board-rooms—and threatens to engulf all of us in its mounting wake.

19

Porn and Profits: Where to from Here?

WITH THE REGISTERING OF *Playboy.com* on the Nasdaq exchange in March of 2000, cyberporn gained a new level of respectability. Recent news publications have pointed out that the decision to provide this kind of commercial legitimacy to an enterprise based on soft-core pornography may well open the way to public acceptance of the more hard-core varieties. Because pornography is already one of America's biggest Big Businesses, the question is, will our economy increasingly be run by purveyors of exploitative and demeaning sex?

Some people have argued that *Playboy* and its philosophy are so mild and vapid that they are hardly worth worrying about. After all, Playboy Enterprises has been listed with the New York Stock Exchange since 1971, and the world is still functioning, more or less. Others point out that although we haven't yet reached cosmic collapse, pornography already governs our culture in ways that are both powerful and insidious. From TV sitcoms to shampoo ads, sexual titillation has proven to be a sure draw. And at the end of the slippery slope there's nothing but the bottom line. So the problem is bound to escalate.

In fact, the statistics are scary. At the end of the last millennium *U.S. News & World Report* noted that some 15 to 20 million surfers were visiting cyberspace porn sites each month; in 1998, $1 billion was spent on access to such sites, a figure expected to triple by 2003;

and studies made by two leading American universities concluded that at least 200,000 Americans are addicted to www.porn. The magazine also mordantly observed that the Child Online Protection Act of a few years back was overturned on grounds of "free speech," although an appeal at the time was pending.

On the whole, the churches have once again maintained an eerie silence over this whole issue. To raise it in today's cultural atmosphere seems either petty, puritanically prudish, or politically incorrect. We've come to the point where we are ashamed to raise our voices against the shameful exploitation of the human person by (literally) stripping more or less consenting women, men, and children of any shred of dignity or personal integrity. In today's America the profit motive seems to justify any degree of self-degradation, including cyber-prostitution. But that's only to be expected in a country where the citizenry willingly lays bare its soul and parades its dirtiest little secrets on "talk shows" pandering to sleazy attitudes and behaviors that are hardly worth dignifying by the traditional term, "passions."

A strange and fascinating country, America. So much talent, energy, generosity, and imagination; so much basic goodness among its most "average" citizens. We lead the world in Nobel Prizes, technology, medicine, space exploration, and charitable donations. Yet we don't seem to care enough about our children to protect them from the violence inherent in pornography, a violence as real a 9 mm. fired off in a middle school homeroom. The abuse of women exploited by porn is really little different from the abuse of our most vulnerable by the trigger-happy. In both cases money couples with thrills to appeal to our rawest instincts. And in both cases we justify them by appealing to "the American way" that protects antisocial extremes in the name of individual rights and free speech. In the end, this country may well go down the tubes because of specious, self-serving interpretations of the First and Second Amendments.

No need to get hyper or melodramatic, though. Do I really think Nasdaq's embrace of *Playboy.com* will cause more rape, incest, or pedophilia? No, not really. But then again, if an article subsequently published in the Romanian version of *Playboy* magazine is any indication, we're in for some rough times. That article described ways a man can beat a woman without leaving telltale marks. The ensuing stir was so great, it seemed that the company might pull its zine off the market once and for all. But when I left Romania shortly thereafter, another edition was already in the kiosks.

The whole affair, in fact, reminds me of a story I heard once. I have no idea if it's true, but it makes the point.

Years ago, it seems, Lake Erie was so polluted that scientists were convinced all life in it had died. Then one day somebody discovered that way down in the murky depths there lived some kind of carp. The fish hadn't died off. It had just mutated to the point that it could live on—in fact, it *had* to live on—the filth and toxic wastes that had accumulated in the bottom sludge. And the scientists concluded that maybe that's what we're doing to ourselves. We probably won't blow ourselves to smithereens with nuclear weapons. More likely, we'll become like that carp: mutated to conform to the polluted atmosphere around us, able to consume nothing more nourishing for the body or soul than the toxic wastes that we gradually have allowed to accumulate at nearly every level of our social life.

With typical American ingenuity and dedication, we pretty well cleaned up Lake Erie. We can do it in other areas of social malaise as well, if we have the foresight, the determination, and the wisdom to do so. Indeed, we owe it to ourselves, just as we owe it to our children. Above all, we owe it to the One who invests our life—and every human life—with unlimited dignity, worth, and love.

20

The Drug of Choice

*D*ANNY WAS WHAT THEY CALL ironically a "double winner": the child of an alcoholic and addicted to alcohol himself. After a long struggle, he made it into recovery. Then he relapsed and hanged himself. He was nineteen.

Dramatic and disturbing as it is, Danny's (true) story is repeated in one form or another every day throughout this country. Alcoholism alone is the third most potent killer in the U.S., behind heart disease and cancer. Aside from permanently damaging the liver, heart and brain, it frequently causes suicidal depression. If alcohol were invented today, someone has pointed out, it would never get past the Food and Drug Administration. But like other entrenched interests of modern enterprise (the tobacco industry, for instance), alcohol production is—with nearly universal social approval—legally destroying the health and well-being of the nation.

Nevertheless, as with tobacco, the tide is beginning to turn. More and more, alcoholism is being accepted for what it is: not the hard-luck consequence of a weak will, nor a sin in and of itself, but an *illness*, a progressive and potentially fatal disease. And its causes are now recognized to be genetic (inherited) as well as environmental (a reaction, for example, to stress at home or on the job).

Alcohol is again becoming the drug of choice of American teenagers. And why not?, since it's cheaper than crack and more available than ice-cream.

But what exactly is alcoholism? In a word, "compulsive" (uncontrolled and uncontrollable) drinking of alcohol that results in serious and long-term harm to the drinker and others. To become an alcoholic doesn't require consuming hard liquor or getting "smashed," "wasted," or whatever. Beer and wine are as addicting as Scotch, and many alcoholics never appear to be drunk. They may be "social drinkers," or their consumption may only occur in periodic binges. But if they *need* to drink—to relax, to escape, to self-medicate, or just to have fun—or if they continue using alcohol in spite of harmful consequences, they are addicted. And if it goes untreated, their addiction will more than likely kill them.

Because it affects the brain, alcoholism produces behavior patterns typical of most drug addiction, such as denial, manipulation of others, rage, memory lapses ("blackouts"), selective remembering (to deny inappropriate behavior), depression, and paranoia. Consequently, it affects others as much as it does the addict. Alcoholism now is recognized as a "family disease," weighing upon everyone closely related to the problem drinker: members of the family, friends, or co-workers. People who are victims of another's alcoholism develop a particular syndrome or set of symptoms and behavior patterns that in many ways parallel those of the alcoholic himself (or herself). Such people are called "co-dependents."

Tragedy is all the more difficult to deal with when it strikes the innocent. The innocent co-dependent victims of an alcoholic's destructive behavior are most often young children. If the symptoms they develop are not properly treated, these young people usually reach adulthood with severe emotional and behavioral handicaps. In such cases they join the legions of ACOA's: Adult Children of Alcoholics. Recent statistics estimate that the child of one alcoholic parent has a 65 percent chance of becoming an alcoholic himself. When both parents are afflicted, the probability rises to 85 percent. And like the disease of alcoholism, the ACOA pathology is progressive: its symptoms invariably worsen with time and, if not treated, it too can be permanently debilitating and even fatal.

Statistics like these, abstract as they are, make it clear that alcoholism needs to be classed as a major bioethical problem or issue. The toll it takes on the spiritual state of a family or other close-knit group of people can be devastating: divorce, domestic violence, depression, suicide. That toll has to be acknowledged and dealt with appropriately, by medical professionals trained to do so, but also by others in the community of faith that surrounds the person or family concerned. As with any illness, treatment needs to incorporate both appropriate therapy and unremitting prayer.

In the next chapter, we will take a brief look at some treatment options. Our focus will be especially on the children of alcoholics, who are so often unwilling victims of a parent's illness and resultant "crazy" behavior.

21

The ACOA's Choice

*D*O YOU RECOGNIZE THE TYPICAL ACOA ("Adult Child of an Alcoholic") characteristics in yourself or in someone close to you? It's a sensitive and intrusive question, but it's one we need to ask, if the multitudes of those who can answer "yes" are to find help. Because, as in the case of alcoholics themselves, one of the chief symptoms of the ACOA syndrome is denial.

Emotionally, the symptoms also include excessive anxiety, fear, rage (uncontrolled outbursts of anger), an inability to trust others, sadness (depression), guilt ("It's my fault"; "I made the mistake"), shame ("I *am* the mistake"), and numbness (repressed or "stuffed" feelings connected with traumatic childhood events).

Behaviorally, ACOAs are typically afflicted with perfectionism coupled with procrastination ("If I don't get started, I can't fail"), crisis-management (if a crisis doesn't exist, an ACOA will create one: there is safety in whatever is familiar, however destructive it may be), manipulation of others (playing on their feelings to get what one wants or needs), problems with intimacy and trust, unable to have fun, extreme self-consciousness often mixed with a highly critical attitude toward others, and compulsive-addictive disorders such as overeating or sexual obsessiveness. Greet an ACOA with "Hi, how are you?", and he'll answer with a big smile, "Fine!" In fact, he's miserable. But in order to survive in childhood, he learned to "put a good face" on the deep well of hurt and pain he carries inside.

Treatment of ACOAs, like that of alcoholics, is complicated by many things, particularly (1) feelings of *isolation* ("No one understands me"; "I'm the only person in the world who feels this way"—whereas in fact chemical dependency creates dysfunction that marks the lives of *most* of those around us, whether in our family or in society at large); (2) *denial* ("My parents aren't really alcoholics"; "I can handle my drinking"); and (3) the *"Don't talk" rule* (embarrassment, shame and the fear of betrayal lead to imposed silence and constant making of excuses for the alcoholic, classic symptoms of "enabling" behavior that keeps the alcoholic in his rut).

Nevertheless, a highly successful program for treatment has been developed in recent years and is available throughout the country. Based largely on the "12-step program" of Alcoholics Anonymous (AA), it includes out-patient as well as in-house care (5 day intensive therapy sessions; unfortunately, the former 28-day program has been nearly eliminated because insurance companies refuse to pay the cost). These are coupled with various forms of group therapy that have proven notably effective.

Chemical dependency, and particularly alcoholism, presently affects tens of millions of Americans. Through programs such as AA, Alanon and Alateen, millions are now in treatment. If you think you or anyone close to you has a problem with mood-altering chemicals (alcohol, street-drugs, prescription drugs, even abuse of over-the-counter medications), then you or they can and should go for an assessment or evaluation at a recognized alcoholism and drug abuse treatment center, where anonymity is preserved and confidentiality is respected. Often these assessments are free of charge. Two useful toll-free numbers to note: the Alcohol Hotline (1–800-ALCALLS), and the Domestic Violence Hotline (1–800–942–6906); or look in the Yellow Pages under "Alcoholism Information and Treatment Centers."

Orthodox Christianity recognizes that each of us is created in the image of God. The whole purpose of our life is to become "like" God: to be so filled with His love, beauty, and perfection that we actually share in His divine life. In this gradual transfiguration of ourselves "from glory to glory" lies the source of the greatest freedom and the deepest joy we can ever know.

Few things hinder that growth and distort the divine image in us more than chemical dependency, whether our own or that of persons close to us. In fact, chemical dependency is a form of suicide. If left unchecked, it leads sooner or later to death.

God calls us to life, joy, and peace through eternal communion with Himself. He has the power to heal even the consequences of addiction—provided there exists within us a deep and genuine desire for change. Like God and mammon, when it comes down to drugs or health, dependency or inner freedom, we can't have it both ways. There is a choice to make. But thanks be to God, there are people out there ready and able to help both addicts and co-dependents in the difficult process of making that choice and sticking to it.

22

Fighting Clergy Burnout

*I*T'S NO SECRET THAT CLERGY of all religious traditions today are plagued by a high level of stress and fatigue. I speak as an Orthodox Christian priest, but these remarks concern virtually anyone who has undertaken full-time pastoral ministry.

Most clergy are overworked and, relative to their congregations, underpaid. Like everyone else, they have children to put through school, medical bills to pay, and mortgages to deal with. To make ends meet, they usually need two salaries. This takes the wife out of the house and places her as well into the stress and strains of the workplace. When husband and wife return home in the evening, they often grab a quick bite to eat, then the pastor hurries off to a parish meeting, a mid-week service or Bible study, or a difficult counseling session with someone in the congregation.

Certain periods in the Church's liturgical year are especially stressful and fatiguing, despite the beauty of the services and the joy in performing them. For an Orthodox priest, Theophany services are the longest of the year. Culminating on January 6 after several days of pre-feast, they commemorate Christ's baptism and include at least two Great Blessings of Water. (The Western Church feast of Epiphany, also celebrated on January 6, focuses on the visit of the Magi to the Christ child.) This intense period of congregational worship is usually followed by a long series of house-blessings that can take days or weeks to complete. Couple this with the usual pastoral chores that arise at any time, and you have a set-up for exhaustion if not for burnout.

There are many reasons why clergy tend to exhaust themselves and finally burn out. Some are compulsive workaholics. They can't relax and enjoy themselves, or take a day off each week, or look forward to a vacation, because some unconscious psychological baggage makes them feel guilty if they do. Others are compulsive people-pleasers. They spend all their time and energy trying to meet others people's needs and expectations, convinced that they are faithfully exercising "ministry." Still others suffer from a martyr complex. They believe that the way to please God and guarantee their own salvation is literally to kill themselves with work.

It's no wonder that the average clergy wife feels abandoned, neglected, ignored—and at the same time put upon to fill a role as taxing as that of her clergy spouse: bake the prosphora (eucharistic bread), direct both choir and church school, run interference on the phone and at the door when the priest is otherwise occupied (or hiding), handle a variety of administrative details in the parish, and much else besides. Then too, she is expected to serve as full-time mother, cook, housekeeper, and, if she has the time, to spend some forty hours a week bringing in another salary.

Divorce rates among Orthodox clergy used to be among the lowest. They have soared in recent years, at least in this country. Although the pastor's role hasn't really changed, the stresses have increased enormously, largely because our clergy have bought into the workaholism and sleep-deprivation of most of their parishioners. And if they have not, then they are made to feel guilty. It's a no-win situation.

Although the situation requires many different and complementary solutions, let me point out just one factor that plays more of a role in clergy stress and distress than we usually recognize. It is the simple fact of too little sleep.

At the end of the 1990s the National Sleep Foundation published an appeal to employers to allow their employees to take a short nap while on the job. It has been found that just a few minutes of sleep after lunch, for example, can reduce stress significantly, while increasing both concentration and memory. Those of us who have had to teach a class in the two to four slot know all too well how much that nap is needed, both for the professor and for the students.

Any effective answer to clergy burnout has to involve everything from personal therapy (where appropriate), to sabbaticals offered our priests with the permission and encouragement of our bishops. (Mutatis mutandis—the necessary changes being made— this is true for the pastors of any church body.)

A good start—while we wait for a Lilly sabbatical grant and pray for a geographical cure in the form of a transfer—would be to take seriously our physical, mental, and spiritual need for adequate sleep. Eight hours per night is still the recommended amount. Any less can be compensated for, at least in part, by a brief siesta. A good rule for that is to lie flat on the rug, use a pillow and light blanket, and doze off, getting up immediately as soon as you wake up. Very quickly you can train yourself to go under for just a few minutes, then awaken fully. After a few seconds shaking off the sleep, you are fully rested and ready to take on, if need be, another six to eight hours of productive activity.

This might sound simplistic, but adequate sleep is also one of the most effective antidotes to depression (it restores seratonin and other neurotransmitters). Neither our parishes nor our families want sleep-deprived and depressed pastors. Nor, if I may dare say so, does God.

This may be just a little step toward health and sanity, but it's an important one. So please (as I say to myself), do give it a try.

23

On Remembering Death

*T*HE YOUNG MOTHER TOOK her newborn daughter into her arms and wept quietly. Off in a corner the doctor was trying to explain to the bewildered father the meaning of "anencephaly." The child was lacking the upper hemispheres of her brain. In a few hours, she would die a natural death. A peaceful one, the doctor assured him, because she had no consciousness and no perception of pain.

—The old man had been comatose for more than two weeks. The stress of seemingly endless vigils showed on his wife's face as she silently agonized over the decision she had just made. The head nurse and her husband's physician came into the room and, for a moment, stood close to her. Then the physician stepped to the bed and removed the respirator.

—The young man's father had spent hours venting rage and frustration. Finally, he collapsed on the floor in near hysteria. In about fifteen minutes the State would end his son's life with a lethal injection.

The common thread that links these cases is not only the overwhelming grief suffered by the spouse or parent. It is also the feeling each one experiences of being out of control. They perceive themselves, as much as the dying loved-one, as a victim. Whatever the cause of death, those who are left behind experience the loss of a part of themselves. Their agonized question, Why?, is not some philosophical inquiry as to the meaning of a life cut short. It's a cry from the heart that expresses hurt, sadness, and frustration over our total impotence in the face of "the last enemy."

Genesis lays responsibility for human mortality on Adam's rejection of God's commandment. The Wisdom of Solomon tells us death came into the world because of the devil's jealousy. The apostle Paul and later Christian tradition looked at the question from a double perspective. On the one hand, death is "the wages of sin," the inevitable consequence of human rebellion against divine righteousness. Yet on the other, death is seen as a welcome gift insofar as it sets a limit to the time of our alienation from God.

This means that death is both a blessing and a curse: a curse, because of the devastating rupture it causes in our relationships with loved ones; but a blessing, in that God is in total and complete "control," and therefore God can bring out of death ultimate good.

In First Corinthians, Paul reminds us that "The sting of death is sin . . . But thanks be to God, who gives us the victory through our Lord Jesus Christ" (15:56). In Romans, he declares: "For I am sure that neither death, nor life, nor angels, nor principalities . . . nor anything else in all creation, will be able to separate us from the love of God in Christ Jesus our Lord" (8:38,39). In the Son's agonizing crucifixion and wondrous resurrection, God has shown forth to humankind a love even stronger than death.

What does this mean for the grieving parents of an anencephalic child, or the wife obliged to make a decision that will end what remains of her husband's life, or the tormented father whose son is to be executed? What of these and multitudes of other deaths that seem so totally out of our control, to prevent, delay, or even understand?

A partial answer, at least, is provided by the Church's monastic tradition. Typically, the monk (man or woman) rises in the morning, makes the sign of the cross, and says quietly: "Remember that you are going to die."

There's nothing at all morbid about this way of starting the day. To the contrary, this is the ultimate gesture of surrender: not to fate or hopelessness, but into the loving hands of God. The monk lives to die: to make the final pilgrimage that leads to Pascha, the "Passover" from temporal death to eternal life.

How do we acquire some modicum of control in the face of impending death? As with the monk, the answer lies in the notion of "surrender": surrender of ourselves and of the dying person into the merciful embrace of the life-giving God.

By virtue of our baptism, each of us is a member of a "holy priesthood" (1 Pet 2:5,9). A priest's most fundamental gesture is to "offer": to receive the gifts of the people and offer them to God, and to receive God's gifts and distribute them to the people. This means first of all the Eucharist, but it includes every aspect of our life and being. Thus the petition so familiar in Orthodox litanies: "Let us commend ourselves and each other, and all our life to Christ our God!"

Those who cannot prevent the death of a loved one are nevertheless very much "in control." Their responsibility and their privilege is to make the priestly gesture that all of us want made for ourselves. It is to remember—to remind themselves day in and day out—that the purpose of life is to live and die to the glory of God, and, in the words of the old Reformed catechism, "to enjoy Him forever."

To "remember" our own death or the death of someone we love, and to do so in the most blessed and hope-filled way, is above all to remember the words of the apostle Paul as he faced his own death: "For to me to live is Christ, and to die is gain." And to take with utmost seriousness his insistence that what is "far better" in human experience is "to depart and to be with Christ" (Phil 1:21–23).

24
To Kill or Let Die (1)

O N AUGUST 8, 2000, Siamese twin girls were born to a deeply religious European Roman Catholic couple who preferred to remain anonymous. Because medical facilities in their own area (Malta) could not deal with the twins appropriately, the parents took them to England, hoping the girls could be successfully separated.

Although relatively little about it appeared in the American press (Roman Catholic ethics journals excepted), the case was reported around the world because of its profound moral implications. One of the girls, "Mary," was born with impaired heart and lungs that were incapable of oxygenating her blood and pumping it throughout her body. She remained alive only because she shared a common artery (the aorta) of her sister "Jodie." This artery supplied Mary with sufficient oxygen to sustain her life, at least temporarily. British medical specialists, aware that Mary was incapable of independent existence and was placing an ultimately fatal strain on Jodie's heart, wanted to separate the two immediately. This would have given Jodie a very good chance at survival and a relatively normal life. It would, of course, have led at once to Mary's death.

The parents refused to grant permission for the operation, and the medical specialists took the case to court. The High Court judge ruled in favor of separation and the matter went to appeal. Three Appellate Court judges called for a second medical opinion, and the decision went in favor of separating the infant girls.

Massive ethical issues were involved in this case. Those who wanted the twins separated immediately argued that Mary's inability to lead an independent existence meant that she was not "a person in being," and therefore she was not guaranteed protection as a person before the law. Others, also pressing for separation, held that it is better to sacrifice one life rather than to allow the natural course of events to lead to the death of both girls.

The parents disagreed. They stated they did not believe it was God's will that one child should die in order to save the other and that they preferred no active treatment at all to immediate separation, even though they would eventually lose both children. Who has the right to decide such an issue? The parents? The medical team (i.e., the "professionals")? The courts?

The matter carried on to the point that it became an international *cause célèbre*, because everyone concerned recognized what a heart-rending situation it represented, for the medical team and legal experts as well as for the parents. These parents took extraordinary steps to ensure the best possible treatment for their children. Then they had to face well-meaning people with a philosophy very different from their own. Had they been free to do so, they would simply have taken the children home and allowed them to die, convinced that they were placing them in God's hands. Who is right here? How indeed is such an issue to be judged and decided?

Roman Catholic discussion of the question has focused on two arguments that lead to opposite conclusions. Some argue that the separation could morally take place, on grounds of "the principle of double effect." Taking into account the negative conditions, they conclude that the evil incurred (Mary's death) was not intended, it did not as such produce the desired effect (Jodie's survival), and it was not disproportionate to the good attained. Taking into account the positive conditions, they deduce that the act itself was good (restoring organs to Jodie, thus offering the possibility of a normal life), the intention of the medical team was good, and the good effect was not the consequence of Mary's death. Most importantly, the two effects were proportionate: saving Jodie's life balanced the inevitable evil incurred with her sister's death.

To others, the principle of double effect could be read in a different way. They hold that the very act of separating the twins is immoral, since by clamping the artery the medical team knew that Mary's demise would be immediate and inevitable. Thus the first condition of the principle is violated, which holds that the act itself must be intrinsically good (or at least morally neutral).

Similar conflicting views have been based on the principle of self-defense, which holds that lethal force morally can be used to preserve one's own life or the life of another person. To some, Mary was Jodie's "aggressor," albeit unintentionally, and therefore Jodie could be spared even at the cost of Mary's death. Others read the principle to mean that Jodie's claim to life represented a lethal threat to Mary, and that medical intervention which would lead to Mary's death by that very fact would be immoral.

There is a further argument that can be made, one based on the principle of parental rights and responsibilities. However well-meaning the doctors and courts may have been, a Christian perspective must recognize that the responsibility for such a decision rests ultimately with the parents. There are at least four considerations that bear on the issue and support this conclusion.

First, the basic social unit is not the State, it is the family. There is an *a priori* right of parents to decide questions bearing on the welfare of their children that supersedes that of other interested parties, including the medical team, the courts, or "society."

Second, from a Christian perspective, there is a fundamental difference between "killing" and "letting die." The doctors knowingly acted in such a way as to kill one child, although their intention was to save the life of the other. (Clamping the artery sustaining Mary's life was a deliberate act they knew would result in her death.) The parents, in essence, argued that it is more in keeping with the gospel to allow both children to die, if that is the only alternative, than deliberately to put one of them to death in the hope that the other would survive.

Third, as the Author of life, God has ultimate authority over both life and death. Therefore life and death judgments should be based on His revealed will in Scripture and ecclesial tradition (experience). "Thou shalt not kill" thus takes precedence over the apparently more reasonable conclusion that one child should die in order that the other might live. (This is not to say that the medical team acted on utilitarian grounds. The decision to act in such a way that Mary would inevitably die did not flow from a "kill one to save the other" calculus, nor was it based on the presumed "quality" of Mary's life.)

Fourth and most importantly: human life finds its ultimate fulfillment only in the kingdom of God, in eternal life beyond the limits of biological existence. The parents seemed quite aware of this truth. Even if both girls had died as a result of no intervention other than palliative care, their life and death, like those of us all, are ultimately in God's hands; and God will bless and fulfill their existence as He intends.

Both children, Mary and Jodie, were from their conception bearers of God's image; therefore both are and always shall be fully "personal" beings. If Mary had been older and able to sacrifice herself knowingly and willingly for the sake of her sister, then that decision could have been accepted on the basis of Jesus' statement that the greatest sign of love is to lay down one's life for another person (Jn 15:13). She was not capable of making such a free decision, however, and no one had the right to make it for her.

The courts in this case usurped the most fundamental rights of parents to exercise their own judgment regarding the well-being of their children, including appropriate medical treatment. As a result, Mary was sacrificed in the interests of her sister. The parents' will was thwarted as one of their children was deliberately killed in the interest of saving the other. They were left no say in the matter.

What are the moral implications here? If these were your children, would you want the ability and the freedom to decide on their behalf?

25
To Kill or Let Die (2)

*T*HE CASE OF MARY AND JODIE raises an additional question that should be addressed. It concerns the limits to be placed on parental freedom to judge what is in their child's best interest. They may have a socially sanctioned "right" to make life and death decisions in the interests of their children. But what are the appropriate limits to that right, viewed from the perspective of the Gospel?

In this case, the parents of these Siamese twins refused to allow medical specialists to separate the children because it would inevitably have led to the death of Mary, the girl born with failing heart and lungs and dependent for life on her sister's circulatory system. We argued that the parents, rather than doctors or the courts, should have the right to decide in such a case, even if their decision leads finally to the death of both children.

Yet we are all aware—and generally accept the fact—that parents have been forced by the courts, against their religious beliefs, to allow other forms of intervention into their children's lives: for example, in the form of blood transfusions or routine tests for Phenylketonuria (PKU). If society can impose its will and interests in these cases, why should it not do so in the case of Mary and Jodie?

The moral issue concerns an obligatory preference for life. The parents of these girls opposed the operation to separate them not because they wanted both children to die. Rather, they opposed any intervention that would have deliberately caused the death of one child, even if it would have offered a good chance of survival to the other. In other words, they believed that deliberate killing is a moral evil, whereas letting die—when no other alternative is available—leaves the matter in God's hands. It also allows God, if He wills, to work what we recognize as a miracle.

Parents who refuse blood transfusions or tests that could ensure life for their children are operating from an entirely different perspective. To their minds it may be "religious." In reality, it is doctrinaire and morally unacceptable. Why? Because testing and blood transfusions do not jeopardize the child's life. To the contrary, they serve to sustain and improve that life. If a parent's philosophical view threatens the child's well-being, then a form of abuse is involved: the parent's philosophy takes precedence over the child's welfare.

In the case of the parents of Mary and Jodie, the primary motivating factor was the inevitable death of the weaker child if the two were separated. This is what the parents were objecting to, and it was the court-imposed decision to kill one twin to save the other that neither the parents nor their supporters (including England's Catholic Archbishop Murphy-O'Connor) could accept.

If the twins could have been separated by medical intervention in such a way as to give an equal chance of survival to each girl, then the parents could not have objected on moral grounds. In this case, their situation would have been analogous to that of parents who refuse tests and transfusions.

The issue, then, comes down to the distinction between "killing" and "letting die." Intentional killing, even with the aim of preserving the life of another person, is a morally unjustifiable act—except, most would argue, in cases of self-defense, national defense, and defense of innocent others. Although many ethicists argue that letting someone die is the moral equivalent of killing them, this view falters for at least two reasons. It ignores the crucial element of intention, and it dismisses the place and authority of God in matters of life and death. This is why the Orthodox Church opposes abortion and euthanasia (acts of intention), yet condones the withholding or withdrawing of life-support technology that merely prolongs the dying process (accepting the inevitable).

From a strictly human point of view, to take one life to save another—rather than lose both lives—seems logical and charitable. From the perspective of Christian faith, however, the only moral course is to "let die," even if it means the death of both children. This means that the aim of the medical team should have been the following: Work fervently and ceaselessly to save both children, providing the same level of care to each. If in the process Mary dies, then do all possible to provide life and health for Jodie. Equal care doesn't guarantee equal results. But it does respect the fact that each child is fully human, fully a person, fully a child of God.

Then, when the time comes, surrender one or the other, or both children, into God's eternal and loving care, with the firm conviction that by letting die rather than by actively killing, by allowing death but not imposing it, His will is done.

26
The "Right" to Kill

*I*N THE LAST TWO CHAPTERS I gave what I believe are the chief reasons why the separation of the Siamese twins, Mary and Jodie, should not have occurred. The primary reason concerned the inevitable consequence: Mary would die as a result of the operation. The hospital and the courts drew the conclusion that it would be better to kill one child and thereby offer a reasonable chance for the second to survive, than to refuse to separate them and run the very real risk that both would die. The courts in that case, in other words, have declared that the intentional killing of an innocent human being is justified in order to favor a particular result, namely the survival—or possible survival—of another person. This is a striking example of utilitarian consequentialism, involving the reshaping of ethical rules and moral principles to produce a desired outcome.

This legally sanctioned conclusion will go down in history and the law books as a classic violation of the most fundamental of human rights: the right to life. This means life protected by the State. It does not and should not mean life preserved by the State at the cost of another life. The "right" to life means that the State should never be able to claim as its own the right—the legal authority and power—to kill an innocent member of society, a member who is also a bearer of the image of God.

Ethics deals with intents, motives, and means: the what, why, and how of particular actions. It also deals with values: the attitudes and principles that lead us to decide in the first place what end is good, what motives leading toward that end are noble, and what means for attaining that end are just and appropriate. In the present case, the intent to separate the twins certainly can be construed as good, and the motive to maximize the chances that at least one child would survive is certainly noble. The means, however, involving the deliberate killing of one child, Mary, can be considered neither just nor appropriate. It denies the fundamental value of human life, expressed most succinctly and most eloquently in the commandment, "Thou shalt not kill."

There is another principle involved that is equally important. It concerns the question of just *who* has the right and the responsibility to make such life-and-death decisions for a person who is too young or otherwise unable to make autonomous decisions for himself or herself. By obliging the twins' parents to surrender that authority into the hands of the State, represented by the courts, society is undermining itself in an ominous way. It is denying that its most basic element is the nuclear family, in this case the mother and father of the twin infants. Implicitly it is affirming that institutions other than the family have ultimate authority over the life and welfare of our children.

In some instances a family can indeed forfeit that most fundamental right concerning their children (as, for example, when the parents refuse a blood transfusion needed to save the child's life). The case of Mary and Jodie, however, does not constitute one of those instances, since the operation itself inevitably would have caused the death of one of the twins. In their case, objection was raised by secular institutions to the belief—the deeply held Christian convictions—of the girls' parents. And those institutions, rather than the family, prevailed.

Here the image of the slippery slope is particularly relevant. If secular institutions can trump the desires of the family—even when those desires are based on broadly recognized religious principles such as the distinction between "killing" and "letting die"—then nothing stands in the way of government making other decisions for our children, particularly when they are born with disabilities that might impose an unwanted burden on the larger society. If we can kill one child in the interests of another, isn't it both logical and reasonable to kill many children in the interests of the greater number?

This sounds, I realize, as though I were some rock-ribbed Republican or Libertarian. I am neither. I'm simply pointing to what seems to be an increasingly slippery slide we are making toward undermining parental authority and establishing legalized infanticide. Public school sex-education courses and partial-birth abortions may already have taken us to a point of no return. If so, the tragic story of Mary and Jodie merely confirms the obvious and reinforces the inevitable.

I sometimes think of their parents, and of how deeply they must feel betrayed. It would be bad enough if all I could conclude were "There but for the grace of God go I." In fact, there go all of us. Whether we realize it or not, we share the parents' drama. This is because we are united to them and to their daughters in the universal Body of Christ. Their children, in a very real sense, are our children. And like Rachel lamenting her own (Jeremiah 31:15), we weep for them. For at least one of them "is no more."

The death of Mary is a tragic and unjust death, because it is a death taken out of the hands both of the parents and of God. Our intentions and our motives may be pure. But if our values are skewed, then we can adopt any means we please in order to achieve a desired end. And in the name of logic or expediency or even justice, we commit acts that destroy something vital within us, acts that make us something less than human.

27

"Love Is Strong as Death"

S OMEONE I HAVE KNOWN FOR many years was talking the other day about how much he loves God, and how tempted he is to commit suicide.

For decades he has had to deal with depression. A great deal of anger underlies it, caused in part by a legacy of childhood sexual abuse and abandonment by a father he loved and whose love he desperately wanted. This disposition toward what they call suicidal ideation might have some genetic etiology as well: messed up brain chemistry.

However that may be, he spends half his time thinking up ways to kill himself, ways that won't destroy his family as well, or give the insurance company a reason not to pay up. The rest of his time he spends trying to convince himself that he shouldn't do it after all.

Oddly, there's not the slightest doubt that this man loves God above everything else in life. When he comes to confession he has to unburden himself of a heap of anger—rage, really. He rants and rails at God, regularly takes the Lord's name in vain, scares his wife with his violent outbursts, and accuses himself of gross hypocrisy. Like Job, he rues the day he was born. And like Job's wife, he constantly is tempted to tell himself to curse God and die.

I don't pretend to understand the torment and confusion that have such a hold on him. Undoubtedly there's something demonic about it. None of the standard counsel seems in any way acceptable to him: therapy, medication, whatever. It's as though he felt called to wage some terrible battle on his own. Or, as he puts it, called to struggle against himself and God, by the grace of God.

I've come to know him pretty well over the years, and little has changed. In his times of inner torment there's nothing any of us can do but pray God's mercy upon him, that this friend of ours not succumb to the ultimate temptation and ultimate tragedy.

At times he may curse God, himself, and life in general. But at other times he is gifted with an extraordinary sense of lightness. The more skeptical of his friends pass this off as some form of manic depression, an affliction of bipolar highs and lows. Those of us who know him well see in these moments the person he really is, one gifted rather with insight, perception, the contemplative vision the Church Fathers called *theōria*. With the mystic's sensitivity he sees beauty, truth, and boundless grace in the little things around him. In the depths of his being he knows himself touched, protected, and blessed by God. When he is most fully and truly himself, he prays with anguished repentance and with the tears of a child.

In those rare, precious moments, the self-destructive rage dissipates. For a while, at least, the tears console and heal. Tomorrow, as he well knows, he may again want to kill himself. The depression may again take hold to the point where he says a final "to hell with it all."

If he does, those of us devoted to him will do our own weeping. And we'll have to remind ourselves of the blessed truth that in the end love is even stronger than death: God's love for him, but also his love for God.

28
The Thought of Death

*T*APED TO MY COMPUTER MONITOR, where I can't miss it, is a
quotation I found somewhere several months ago. Attributed to Saint Philotheos of Sinai (one of the writers listed in the
Greek *Philokalia*), it reads as follows:

> Chastise your soul with the thought of death, and through remem-
> brance of Jesus Christ concentrate your scattered intellect.

My first reason for taping it there was to remind myself to do battle with my increasingly scattered intellect. The term "intellect"
originally referred to the *nous*, that highest of all spiritual faculties
by which the saints can acquire direct knowledge of God. In my
more prosaic understanding, it refers simply to my mental disarray,
caused largely by my susceptibility to what the Fathers term
"thoughts": conceptual images, often of demonic origin, that draw
us away from God and focus our attention and our energy on idols,
gods of our own making.

As for chastising my soul with the thought of death, that was at
first only an abstraction or pious counsel, not to be taken too seriously. It was only after reading those lines day after day that I realized how intimately linked the two exhortations are: chastise the
soul / concentrate the intellect.

Without the second admonition, the first easily can lead to despair. A great many people actually do chastise their soul with the thought of death. They suffer acute anxiety at the thought that their life will come to an end, that they will die and be buried in the earth. They fear death because of the unknown. What lies beyond that threshold, behind that veil? Heaven? Hell? Nothing? The dread of death, which provokes questions like this, can, with tragic irony, push a person over the brink and into suicide.

The admonition to "remember Jesus Christ," on the other hand, is difficult to accept—the act itself is nearly impossible to sustain—if it is not grounded in the thought of death. This seems to be a universal intuition shared by all of the great spiritual elders of the Church. What explains this indissoluble link between faith and death?

Those who enter monastic life often follow a venerable tradition we recalled earlier, one that in fact could apply to all of us. The monk typically rises for the early morning office, makes the sign of the cross, then admonishes himself to "remember death." This is for two reasons. First, it affirms the willingness to live in order to die, as the Son of God accepted to be born in the flesh in order to die for the world's salvation. The monk is a martyr: a person whose purpose in life is to offer himself to the world as a living witness and to God as a living sacrifice.

Second, the monk in a very real sense already has made the transition from death to life. In John 5:24, Jesus makes the startling assertion that those who obey His commandment to love do not come into judgment, but already, in this earthly existence, have passed from death to life. The "gospel" or good news of Christian faith proclaims that by the death and resurrection of Christ, death has been defeated; its power has been decisively and permanently broken. Our physical death remains before us, certainly and inevitably. But it has been emptied of its *power*. For those who are "in Christ," true death occurs at baptism, when we go down into the baptismal waters, then rise up from them, in a *mimēsis,* or reactualization, of Christ's own death and resurrection. Baptism effects a "new birth," but only because it first signifies the death of the "old Adam," our former being.

In the perspective of St Paul (Romans 6), as much as for the evangelist John, eternal life begins *now*. We have died with Christ, in order that we might live forever in Him. In baptism, more surely than by any physical demise, we truly die. Through that sacramental death, Death itself is overthrown, and we are given Life.

From this perspective, to "chastise the soul with the thought of death" is less an act of penance than of celebration. To "remember death" is not, as our society assumes, a call to some morbid fixation on the dreaded inevitable. It is an invitation to open our heart and mind to a continual remembrance of the Paschal victory. It is to face death in a way that to many people seems incomprehensible: with peace and with joy.

So while I wait for those funny little icons to spread across the bottom of the screen or for that disembodied voice to tell me I've got mail, I look at that admonition-become-invitation of Saint Philotheos. And somehow, miraculously, the thought of death, coupled with remembrance of Jesus Christ, brings at least a modicum of order to this scattered intellect of mine.

29
Suicide around the Corner

A FRIEND JUST PHONED to tell me she hates God.

This is nothing new. She has MPD: Multiple Personality Disorder, what the *Diagnostic and Statistical Manual of Mental Disorders—Fourth Edition (D.S.M. IV)* likes to call today "DID," or Dissociative Identity Disorder. By any name, one of its major symptoms is despair. She's an incredibly courageous person who in fact loves God and longs for God beyond anything else in life. Sometimes she is in touch with that love and that longing. Most of the time she is fighting depression, isolation, abandonment, and deep-seated self-loathing. These are the hallmarks of despair, and they go with the MPD/DID territory.

As a child she was severely abused by older family members who belonged to a satanic cult. Ritual abuse became a staple of her experience, and the wounds it left still are gaping, full of infection. When the abuse got particularly bad, when she felt she literally was being destroyed, she split off from herself, creating now one, now another new identity or personality. It was an unconscious and, to some extent, successful strategy to survive. Like other victims of MPD, she is a walking horde of screaming, pain-ridden little kids, adolescents, and stunted adults, none of whom can successfully integrate into a whole and wholesome personality. During her good days, she can more or less hang on. On bad days she wants to kill herself.

Today she has to cope as well with the faddish diagnosis known as FMS, "false memory syndrome." It's true that the line between reality and fantasy is often blurred in cases of "multiplicity" or dissociative identity. Some therapists, though, conclude from this that persons with MPD are making it all up, that their memories of horrendous abuse are nothing more than figments of their imagination. Freud thought the symptoms of the disease were caused by female "hysteria." Nothing real there. No sir. It's all in the mind. But what's more real than the mind?

If only a psychiatrist could swap places with an MPD patient for a day. . . .

During our conversation, I asked her to fetch her Bible (from the trash can—she was *really* mad). When she did so, I asked her to read and reread the first five verses of Romans, chapter 5. At first she said things I can't repeat here, even in today's smutty atmosphere. Then, as she so often does, she began to giggle, then to laugh. The pain was no less, but the isolation had been broken. Finally she read those words as they should be read: as an unfailing promise of God's infinite, unqualified love, addressed specifically to her.

Someday she may very well commit suicide. Her brain chemistry is permanently affected by the abuse, she lives constantly in precarious material conditions, and her social isolation registers in her mind and nervous system as unending abandonment and torment. She is carrying an extremely heavy legacy, one few of us can even imagine. And it is not made up.

If she does take her own life in the end, I have no doubt that she will be welcomed and embraced by the God she loves and who loves her as His own. But if she does, it will also be an indictment of me and of all of us who know her and recognize how desperately she needs our love, support, and prayer.

In her day-to-day experience, suicide is just around the next corner. And I have to beg for divine mercy, to make me ready and willing to turn that and every corner with her, to journey with her, to protect her from her own worst self, and moment by moment to surrender her gently and peacefully into the the arms of the God she both hates and loves.

Losing It

MY GRAY MATTER IS DETERIORATING like a sand castle beneath a rising tide. Can't find my keys. Left my glasses on the counter in some store a few days ago and can't remember where I was. "Would you like a cup of coffee?," she asks. "No thanks," I reply, and focus again on the text I'm processing on the all too familiar little screen in front of my nose. "That coffee ready, yet?" I call out a few minutes later, a little irritated that it still hasn't appeared.

Am I losing it? I suspect she thinks so, but she just won't say it to my face. I'd likely forget anyway.

More and more I can't tell you what I preached on—not last week, but this morning. Did I ever answer that letter that's been staring at me for weeks from the corner of my cluttered desk? "WHO WENT OFF WITH MY ADDRESS BOOK?"

I walked into the drugstore the other day and couldn't remember "Ginko Biloba". . . .

So far, it's just symptomatic. Those symptoms, though, do include fear of losing it, fear of detaching from life, reality, friends, and family. Long ago I learned that God often leads us through trials and tribulations so we become more sensitive and more understanding of the similar trials borne by other people. Maybe this is what's happening. Maybe I have to take all this as both a call and a preparation to minister to those whose deteriorating minds leave them vulnerable, isolated, and desperately lonely. Sufferers of the pitiless

Alzheimer's disease, for example, or trauma victims, or just the average old folks whose short-term memory is as gone as my glasses.

Isolation, fear, anxiety, loneliness, confusion. These are some of
the things a dulling mind calls up within us. What if I reach the
point where I can't pray? What if I lose the sense of God, of His presence, and His love? Does that happen? Can God allow it to happen?
Is that the demonic outcome of Alzheimer's?

Or is there always, even there in the depths of senility, an aware-
ness of God's presence? Is that abyss maybe like the nether region
of Sheol, where God is nevertheless present, eager to convey His
care, understanding, and love? "If I make my bed in Sheol," the
psalmist declared, "Thou art there!" If my bed is made for me, can
I expect anything less?

Icons, or sacred images, of the Orthodox tradition suggest a com-
forting reply to that kind of question. In many of them, especially
those that depict events in the life of Jesus—His birth, baptism,
transfiguration and, finally, His resurrection—the scene is set in a
black hole, carved into the heart of creation. The Christ child, the
Light of the world, is born into the darkness of a cavern. The waters
of the Jordan in which He is baptized take on the form of a shad-
owy abyss. A dark hole appears at His feet as He is transfigured on
Mount Thabor. And before He rises into glory, He descends into the
somber depths of hell, to raise with Himself those who have lan-
guished in the shadow of death.

That hole means something. It means in part, at least, that
Christ also descends into the black hole of our forgetfulness when
it has intensified into a pathology. For those who have lost not just
car keys, but their conscious minds, He descends into their loneliness, their abandonment, and their lostness. He is, after all,
Emmanuel, "God with us."

For the time being, my "losing it" is all relative. In fact, I just lose
things, not "it." Not yet, anyway. As for those who have lost "it" or
are in the process of doing so, I can nonetheless identify to some
very small degree with their distress. In hospitals, retirement
homes, and in their own living rooms, I've encountered victims of

real "forgetfulness." The greatest tragedy in their life, and their greatest source of suffering, is not that they have forgotten things. It's the painful realization that others have forgotten them.

There are so many elderly people today who seem oblivious to the world around them, who appear to others to be simply "out of touch." We can visit them, hold their hand, and try to make conversation. But all too soon we get up to go, thinking to ourselves that there's something more important, more worthwhile to do elsewhere. Yet the look on their face pleads, "Keep in touch. . . ."

I'm not there yet, far from it. But maybe I will be, some day. Maybe then I'll realize you're visiting because you feel you have to, and you're holding my hand and making conversation because it's all you know to do. When you get up to leave, I'll look at you; and that look may say what I can no longer formulate in words: "Pray for me. And please, please, do keep in touch."

II

Bible and Liturgy

1

Take Up and Read!

O RTHODOX CHRISTIANS ALWAYS have known theirs to be a biblical Church. The Bible plays a key role in virtually every aspect of our life, from personal meditation to the public liturgy and mission outreach.

Yet it is true that we more often venerate the Bible than read it. We hear it in church, we encourage our children to peruse and even memorize select passages, and we bow before it and kiss it during liturgical processions. We would immediately miss its countless quotations if they were extracted from our services of worship, and we would be scandalized if someone casually tossed it onto the floor. Yet in many ways we treat it more as an icon than as a book, more as a sacred object than as a living Word.

St Augustine heard a child's voice summon him to "Take up and read!" He obeyed, took up Holy Scripture, and became a devoted disciple of Jesus Christ. That same voice speaks to each of us, calling us to take up the Word of God and to read.

Scripture is not like a newspaper or a novel that we scan for information or entertainment. It is an inexhaustible wellspring of wisdom and illumination that both reveals God to us and enables us to commune with Him. Therefore we need to ask just how we are to read His Word.

The Holy Fathers prescribe for us a certain approach to Scripture, one which is neither a method nor a technique. It is a vision (*theōria*), a perception of the presence and activity of God within history and in our personal life. That vision includes certain convictions about the nature of Scripture and its place within God's work of salvation. Here are perhaps the most important of those convictions.

First, the entire Bible is inspired by the Holy Spirit. Although it is written in human language, with human limitations, it is God's Word in the sense that the biblical authors were guided in their writing to convey all that is necessary for us to know God and to enter into eternal communion with Him.

Second, the Old Testament, as much as the New, is a Christian book. Its persons, events, and institutions are *types*, or prophetic images, that point forward to Christ and are fulfilled by Him. Whereas Moses is a figure of Christ as giver of the Law (*Torah*) to Israel, Christ is the "new Moses," the giver of the true Law of Righteousness that leads His followers to the kingdom of heaven (Mt 5–7). Under the Old Covenant (Ex 16), God provided manna— "bread from heaven"—to sustain His people during their journey through the wilderness toward the Promised Land. As the Bread of Life (John 6), Christ is the true Manna come down from heaven, who provides (eucharistic) nourishment to the children of God in their journey toward eternal life. Similarly, the temple of the Old Covenant is a type of the Church, as the burning bush of Exodus 3 is of the Virgin Mary (who bore divine fire within her womb, yet was not consumed). Old Testament types are related to their New Testament counterparts, or *antitypes*, as "promise" to "fulfillment": what God promises to His People of Israel He fulfills in the New Covenant of the Church, which embraces both Jew and Gentile.

Third, Holy Scripture contains both a literal meaning and a spiritual meaning. The former refers to the author's intended message, the revelation he understood and sought to convey. The spiritual sense, on the other hand, refers to the message God speaks to us today, *through the text of Scripture*. This is the higher sense that relates the biblical story to our own story, our own personal life, particularly in its moral and "spiritual" aspect—that is, as our life is lived out "in the Holy Spirit."

How do we move from the literal meaning of a biblical passage to its spiritual meaning? How do we discern within the text of Scripture the living Word that God addresses to us, to guide and nourish us in our quest for His kingdom? The answer can only be that God Himself creates this movement and this discernment within us, through the inspirational activity of the Holy Spirit. For the Spirit inspires not only the *writing* of biblical books. He also inspires their *interpretation* throughout the life of the Church.

To take up and read, in order to hear in Scripture God's Word for us today, is to open both heart and mind to God in prayer. We do not know how to pray as we ought, St Paul tells us. True prayer is the fruit of the Spirit within us (Rom 8). The same is true with our reading of Scripture. We hear God's Word in Scripture as the Spirit guides our reading and fills it with ever new meaning.

To come to know God and to commune with Him through the Scriptures, then, is to submit ourselves in prayer to the work of the indwelling Spirit. Taking up the Word of God, we truly *read* by the power and grace of God, who desires all of us to hear His voice and respond to it with faith and with love.

The Bible, then, is indeed an icon, or sacred image. This is true of the Gospels, and it is true as well of the entire canon. Yet it is more than an image, insofar as it is God's living Word addressed personally to each of us. To appreciate it as such, and to be sustained by it as we can be, we need to take it off the shelf or coffee table, dust it off, open it up, and read. Every time we do, we can experience God Himself speaking to us: in our own language but with His power, wisdom, and healing grace.

2
But What Shall I Read?

A VERY COMMITTED MEMBER of our parish came by the other day, and we talked for a while. As she left, she asked a familiar and awfully difficult question: "What translation of the Bible should I read?" In reply, I began as I usually do: "It's a shame there's not an Orthodox English translation. . . ."

Although several Orthodox scholars in this country have begun translations of Scripture, there has been little cooperation among those interested, and the project remains a distant hope. Although many of our faithful are qualified to undertake the task, it remains easier and more practical, at least for the moment, to rely on translations by professional teams that have been organized (and funded) especially by the mainline Protestant churches.

Here I'm sharing with you what I suggested to her: nothing definitive or even particularly helpful; just a few thoughts that might serve as guidelines in the selection of a translation that we feel comfortable with and can make our own.

Multitudes of translations exist, from the venerable *King James* or *Authorized Version* of the early seventeenth century to the *Good News Bible* of the twentieth century (which, as I've warned my students, is bad news for both Scripture and the English language). There are paraphrases such as the rendering by J.B. Phillips, and literary inventions like the *New King James Version* (both of which are useful but should be read with other translations). Also useful, but with certain limitations, are the *Jerusalem Bible* (overly dependent on the French original), together with the *New* (very) *English Bible,* and the highly popular and very Protestant *New International Version (NIV)*—cf. for example, 1 Timothy 3:1f and the atonement renderings of *hilastērion* in Romans 3:25 and *hilasmos* in 1 John 2:2.

Those who still appreciate the beauty (and linguistic challenge) of the 1611 *Authorized Version* may well appreciate the *Third Millennium Bible (TMB)*, although some of its renderings remain archaic rather than merely classical: the "thee/ye" and related personal pronouns referring to persons as well as to God (yet this at least has the merit of consistency, unlike our liturgical translations that use the archaic forms *only* for God), as well as phrases such as "to draw nigh," "the strait gate," "Holy Ghost," and so forth. Also, I find curious its disdain for the Sinaiticus Codex. But these reflect personal preferences that guide the choices most of us make in selecting biblical translations.

The Orthodox Church in America, to my knowledge, is the only jurisdiction in this country that has issued a formal statement forbidding use of the *New Revised Standard Version* in liturgical services. This was a difficult call to make, especially since the translation committee did all in its power to persuade some of us that it represents a significant improvement over the *Revised Standard Version*, or *RSV*, which most of us had been using since its initial publication half a century ago (2nd NT edition, 1972). I felt sympathy for the bishops' decision, particularly because of a number of unfortunate renderings in the *NRSV* that seem theologically motivated. The most egregious is perhaps John 1:14. The Greek can be rendered literally, "And the Word became flesh and dwelt among us, and we have seen his glory, glory as of the only Son of the Father . . ." (capitalizing to make the point that the context refers unambiguously to God, Father and Son). Use of the term *monogenēs*, as in Jn 3:16–17, makes it perfectly clear that the reference in 1:14 is to the *Logos*, the Son of God. The *NRSV*, however, translates the verse "we have seen his glory, the glory as of a father's only son. . . ." (with a note offering "the Father's only Son" as an alternative). This reading even appears in the Catholic version of the *NRSV*, leading one to wonder just what priorities guided the Catholic Biblical Commission that achieved an *imprimatur* for "their" version.

Let me conclude as I did with our curious parishioner: that is, by recommending the *Revised Standard Version* as the translation that is closest to the Greek yet expressed in good, reasonably literary English. This may be hard to find, since in some quarters attempts were made to suppress it in favor of the *NRSV*. If enough people ask for it, demand it, and otherwise insist on its availability, we might nonetheless succeed in getting it back on the shelves of our local bookstores.

Every Orthodox Christian is invited, indeed called, to peruse the Scriptures daily. (Look up the word "peruse"; it doesn't mean "skim"!) This obligation and this privilege is not restricted to tonsured Readers. The written Word of God can provide for all of us nourishment for our souls and light in the darkness of our daily lives, culminating in knowledge of God and communion with Him.

Despite problems of theology and biblical translation between ourselves and our Protestant brothers and sisters, we have much to learn from their respect for Scripture. I remember very well a dear friend, the late wife of a Swiss Reformed Church pastor, who pored over her Bible for an hour every morning, beginning at 6 a.m. Her life of service and devotion to others testified to its impact on her entire being. I remember as well a German Lutheran professor with whom I studied, telling me, with tears in his eyes, of his experience in a Soviet concentration camp during the Second World War. He and fellow Christian prisoners wrote out from memory long passages from the New Testament and Psalms, using bits of charcoal and scraps of toilet paper. Their very life and sanity depended on remembering, reproducing, and constantly rereading the Word of God.

From such examples, as from the Church Fathers, we can reacquire a love for Scripture and a thirst for the water of life that it offers. Again, we need merely to take up and read, with determination, constancy, and gratitude to the One who is Himself the very Word of God.

3

The Jesus Quest

M ODERN BIBLICAL SCHOLARSHIP has been taken by many people, including many Orthodox Christians, as both a blessing and a bane.

On the one hand, it has provided us with extraordinary insight
into the culture, language, and religious diversity of Jesus' day. It
has underscored the significance of His Jewish roots and placed the
"Jesus movement" in a social and historical framework that offers
readers of the Bible virtual participation in the story of Jesus and
the early Church.

On the other hand, it has focused so exclusively on the "historical Jesus" that the ultimate meaning of His person, life, and work
has largely disappeared in a fog of "facts." And facts by definition
are limited to what is historically verifiable, at least in principle.

If some occurrence of the past—a person or event, for example—
could have been tape-recorded, filmed, or otherwise media-cov-
ered, then we consider it to be factual. It actually happened, and we
can take it seriously. If not, then that occurrence is hardly worth
talking about. From this point of view, genuine knowledge is provided not by theology or metaphysics, but by the empirical sciences. This is a thumbnail description of what is known in
philosophical circles as "positivism."

To a great many readers of the Bible, modern scholarship
appears to be captive to a certain positivism in its approach to

scriptural interpretation. By restricting their inquiry to historical questions, including the process by which the Gospel narratives took shape, biblical critics generally seem unable to deal with events or realities that transcend history: the question of Christ's preexistence, for example, or the significance of His miracles, or the experience of the Holy Spirit within the Church and in Christian life.

This diagnosis of a positivist approach to Scripture seems generally accurate. More to the point, though, is the fact that the Church has always known another means, in addition to historical inquiry, for acquiring knowledge of God. This way doesn't at all deny the importance of historical study of the biblical period and personalities. Yet it does recognize that any quest for the "historical Jesus" is ultimately bound to fail if it does not lead to a living and life-giving communion with Him.

If Jesus truly rose from the dead, then any quest for the "Jesus of history" is useful only insofar as it serves to unite the believer to the resurrected Christ, who is alive and active within the Church and world of our day. It is the failure of so much modern biblical scholarship to achieve this lofty goal that leads many faithful to reject that scholarship as irrelevant, if not subversive, even demonic.

This is an unfair judgment, since the preaching and teaching of Scripture necessarily draw their insights from what biblical scholars—beginning with the ancient patristic authors—tell us about such things as the meaning of Jesus' parables and the significance of His crucifixion. The point is that responsible exegesis cannot and should not limit itself to what can be determined by empirical investigation. When it does, Jesus is inevitably reduced to little more than an itinerant wonder-worker or political revolutionary; and accounts of the Empty Tomb and His resurrection appearances are taken as pure metaphor or the product of a naïve, primitive worldview. To believers whose faith is grounded in an Orthodox Catholic tradition, responsible biblical interpretation takes seriously not only Jesus' person and activity during His earthly ministry. It also takes seriously His presence in the world and in human experience as the risen and glorified Lord.

We need to remember that the biblical authors themselves interpreted and transmitted the received tradition concerning events in Jesus' life, including His crucifixion and death, *in the light of the Resurrection*. That event shaped their interpretation of every other aspect of Jesus' life and teaching, from His conception and birth, through His public ministry, on to His glorification and the sending of the Spirit at Pentecost.

It is not only bad scholarship to dismiss the Resurrection *a priori* as myth, symbol or fantasy, as many do, and to focus only on what is empirically verifiable; it is disingenuous and self-deceptive. It assumes that scholars today, removed by two thousand years, are better able to discern "what actually happened," and the significance of those happenings, than were the disciples and others who lived with Jesus and formed the oral tradition that underlies the canonical writings. It is easy to conclude that we are scientifically and historically more sophisticated than they were; but again, that is an opinion that remains to be proved. And since we are dealing with matters that transcend empirical verification, such proof is unattainable. A positivist approach to discovering the reality of Jesus, therefore, is doomed to failure. It's like trying to investigate atomic particles with a magnifying glass, or to explain love by analyzing brain chemistry.

Equally disingenuous are entire "biblical" theologies built by isolating certain preferred scriptural themes and excluding others that seem incompatible with them. This results in the selection of a "canon within the canon," which attributes authority only, or at least principally, to particular teachings that conform to the interpreter's own theological preconceptions. An example is the way certain Lutherans expound the doctrine of "justification by faith (alone)." They tend to regard it as the sum total of the Gospel, whereas in fact it is based largely on a few passages from Paul's letters to the Romans and Galatians (a point well made by the influential Lutheran theologian, Krister Stendahl).

Protestants, however, are not alone in this practice. We need only recall former Roman Catholic attempts to ground teachings on purgatory and indulgences in biblical passages such as 1 Peter 3:19; or Orthodox tendencies to find a full-blown doctrine of *theōsis* ("deification" of the human person) in 2 Peter 1:4. Some of these teachings surely have more merit than others and can legitimately claim to be based on the witness of Scripture as a whole. To the degree that any teachings are derived and shaped only by reference to a narrow selection of biblical sources, however, they represent examples of mere "proof-texting." By ignoring or interpreting to oblivion other elements of the biblical witness with which they are incompatible, such teachings risk forfeiting any and all claim to authority in the realm of Christian life and faith.

Orthodox Christians especially are often accused of creating just such a divorce between Scripture and Holy Tradition, of placing more emphasis on doctrine and liturgy than on the Bible. This is not—and certainly should not be—the case, since Orthodoxy grounds its belief and its worship solidly in the biblical writings. It recognizes that the Bible is in the fullest sense "canon": the uniquely authoritative standard for belief, worship, and conduct. If creeds, hymns, and sacraments play such a major role in Orthodox worship, it is because they interpret for us and give expression to the essence of the *biblical* message. This is what gives them such a remarkable and vital capacity to create and nourish a living communion between Christ and His Body, the Church.

When Scripture is interpreted through good preaching, it becomes the source of a deep and intimate knowledge of God. The same is true when it is interpreted through liturgical hymns and confessions of faith, or when it is celebrated in the form of sacraments (all of which are grounded in the biblical witness). To someone who has never "lived the liturgy" or drawn grace from the sacraments, a statement like this will seem meaningless. To those who insist uncompromisingly on *sola scriptura*—the Reformed teaching which holds that the Bible alone is the final authority in matters of faith and morals—it will be dismissed as heresy.

But to those of all Christian traditions who have "tasted the heavenly gift, and have become partakers of the Holy Spirit, and have tasted the goodness of the Word of God and the powers of the age to come" (Heb 6:4–5), the truth is very different. They know, on the basis of personal experience, that God has placed within the depths of our inner being an insatiable longing for Himself. That longing—far more than intellectual curiosity, exegetical talent, or even a serious "religious concern"—is what drives their quest for knowledge of Christ and communion with Him.

In Orthodox worship, perhaps the best expression of that longing and its place in any true "Jesus Quest" is found in a prayer of thanksgiving which follows the taking of Holy Communion. It is a prayer that speaks of the awe and wonder we can feel in the presence of the living Lord, once the words of Scripture have been sacramentally transformed into a Word of Life:

"You are the true desire and the ineffable joy of those who love you, O Christ our God, and all creation sings your praise forever!"

4

The New and the Old in Typology

*T*HE FATHERS OF THE CHURCH often made use of *typology* in their efforts to interpret the Old Testament in the light of Jesus Christ. They found in the Hebrew Scriptures "types," or prophetic images, that point forward to and are fulfilled by persons and events of the New Testament (to recall examples given earlier: Moses and Melchizedek are *types* of Christ, the true Lawgiver and High Priest; the manna in the wilderness is a *type* of the Eucharist, and so forth). Typology as an exegetical method, however, is very much out of fashion today. Most scholars consider it to be a forced and arbitrary imposition of Christian beliefs on the Old Testament that does violence to both the Old Testament and the New.

Properly understood, however, typology is a valuable, even indispensable method for uncovering both the unity between the Testaments and their ultimate "spiritual" meaning, a meaning conveyed by the person and work of Jesus Christ.

The unity between the Old and the New Testaments is grounded in the Church's perception of both the historical and the symbolic links that exist between them. A distinction is usually made between two methods of deciphering those links: "allegory" and "typology." It is usually assumed that typology stresses the connections between actual persons, events, places and institutions of the Old Testament, and parallel realities in the New Testament that complete or fulfill them. These are related as (*proto*) *type* to *antitype* or Promise to Fulfillment. "Allegory," on the other hand, is usually defined as a quest for the "hidden" or symbolic meaning of a given Old Testament narrative, a meaning considered to be higher, fuller, or more spiritual than the meaning discerned by typology. The focus of allegorical exegesis is not on historical events as such, but on the underlying spiritual meaning concealed in the *words* that speak of that event. Like narrative criticism, it is primarily concerned with the message conveyed by the text itself, whether or not the biblical author grasped that message and intended to convey it.

Recent studies have nevertheless modified the traditional picture of typology and allegory in significant ways. They have demonstrated that typology is not primarily dependent on an historical extension through time, from past to future. Rather, the type contains a "representational" or "self-actualizing" quality that comes to expression through the biblical narrative, such that the antitype is already reflected by or "contained in" the type. (An excellent example of this is provided in St Paul's first letter to the Corinthians [10:4]. There he alludes to the Israelites' desert wandering following the Exodus from Egypt. To slake their thirst, God provided water from a rock [Ex 17; Num 20]; and this Rock, Paul declares to be Christ!) By anticipation, the Promise contains its own Fulfillment, since the type already contains and reflects the eternal truth to which it points.

This is not a new concept. In fact it goes back at least to Diodore of Tarsus, one of the greatest exegetes of the fourth-century catechetical school at Antioch. Ultimately, this perspective is rooted in St Paul's conviction that Christ is present and active in the Old Covenant, among the people Israel (1 Cor 10:4; 2 Cor 3:14). It perceives that the type possesses a symbolic, revelatory quality that comes to expression less through the historical event itself than through the narrative or story that recounts that event; that is, through the *text of Scripture*. Therefore it can be argued that typology, like allegory, finds ultimate meaning less in historical events as such than in the biblical witness to those events.

Nevertheless, it is essential that we not sever the historical roots of typology. Revelation necessarily occurs within the domain of what we call "history," and it does so through the medium of historical realities (events, persons, institutions, rituals). Those realities may not be objectively verifiable. They may even be essentially symbolic or parabolic (e.g., the etiological myths of Genesis 1–11 or the story of Jonah). They are not for that reason any less "real" than events of our immediate experience. Insofar as they exist in the *divinely inspired religious consciousness* of the people of God, they convey revealed truth and serve God's purposes for their salvation, even if the stories that convey them can properly be labeled myth, legend, or even metaphor.

The point is that behind the biblical narratives there is ultimate reality, ultimate truth, that at one point in time ("history") was revealed within the framework of objectively determinable human experience.

The Exodus, for example, as historical "event" and as symbolic "type," finds fulfillment in its antitype, the *historical events* of Christ's passion and His victory over death. Both must be rooted in history, that is, in experiential reality. Yet both find their ultimate meaning in and *beyond* history: the Exodus, in God's saving activity among His people *and* in their hope of the messianic kingdom; and the Resurrection, in Christ's victory over death *and* in the eternal life He offers to all believers. *Although rooted in history (the domain of fallen human existence), the type transcends history, insofar as it contains and reveals its own eschatological Fulfillment.*

The type, then, is "double." Necessarily grounded in historical reality—because that is where salvation must be worked out if it is to concern us as historical beings—the type bears and reveals eternal truth. Its uniqueness and significance lie in the fact that it serves as the intersection between life in this world and the reality of the kingdom beyond. This is why Diodore had to insist that the type contains a *double sense*, at once historical and transcendent, literal and spiritual.

The ritual gestures of the Church known as sacraments have been defined as visible (i.e., historical) realities that convey invisible (transcendent) grace. They, like Scripture, possess a "double sense," in that the physical reality (water, oil, bread, wine) contains and conveys spiritual power and meaning.

Typology reveals what we may call the sacramental value of Scripture. Its diachronic aspect (development through time) unites past to present and earth to heaven. Yet the type simultaneously (synchronically) reveals the future Fulfillment in and through the historical event itself. Transcendent reality becomes, as it were, "incarnate" within the type, whether that type is an Old Testament event fulfilled by a corresponding reality that takes place within the time of the New Covenant, or a New Testament reality that manifests and renders present in our life and experience some transcendent value and meaning that was revealed in Christ's person and work. It is by virtue of its revelatory yet *sacramental* character that Scripture unites us with the multitudes whom Jesus healed, grants us to share the disciples' communion with Him in the Upper Room, bestows upon us the blessing He pronounced on His followers just before His Ascension, and renews us through His perduring presence with us in the Person of the Holy Spirit.

It is through typology, in other words, that we can best grasp the sense of Jesus' assertion that the Kingdom of God is present in our midst, even within us (Lk 17:21). It is the dynamic of typology, by which God's Promise already contains and manifests its future eschatological Fulfillment, that reveals to us, in all its power and glory, the presence of the Kingdom which is to come.

5

Discerning Scripture's "Spiritual" Meaning

*P*RIOR TO THE TWO GREAT fasting periods that prepare respectively Christ's Nativity (Christmas) and His Resurrection (Pascha), the Sunday lectionary invites us to read the familiar parable of the Good Samaritan (Lk 10:25–37). This passage offers one of the best examples of the way the early Church Fathers moved from a literal to a spiritual reading of the text, from consideration of the biblical author's basic message to an allegorical interpretation that sought to draw out from the text a higher, or deeper, "hidden" meaning. They relied on allegory in an attempt to discern behind the words of the passage symbolic allusions to Christ, the Church, and Christian life in general.

Modern commentators, from Creed to Fitzmyer, stress what they consider to be the literal or historical sense of the passage: the meaning St Luke understood as he sought to transmit and interpret Jesus' message. Most find that meaning in the final words Jesus addresses to the Jewish lawyer, "Go and do likewise." He admonishes him to *be* a neighbor to others, regardless of their ethnic origin or other circumstances, and to do so by performing gratuitous acts of mercy.

The ancient Fathers, on the other hand, looked beyond the most apparent meaning of the passage, in order to discern what they took to be its hidden yet fuller spiritual sense. This *sensus plenior* they understood to have been incorporated into the passage by St Luke, under the inspiration of the Holy Spirit. And it is this same Spirit, they held, who inspires the reader or interpreter of the passage to *discern* that hidden, symbolic meaning.

This is not to say that they found two distinct and disassociated meanings in the text, one literal and one spiritual. Fundamental to their hermeneutic, or interpretive approach, is the conviction that the spiritual meaning of a passage is rooted in and flows forth from the literal meaning. There is total continuity between the two; the passage is essentially characterized by a "double meaning," at once literal and spiritual. Historical and allegorical exegesis, then, are not to be understood as two different and even conflicting ways of uncovering the meaning of a given passage, as many scholars today hold them to be. Rather, they are complementary and equally necessary for drawing out the message *God* seeks to convey, through the writing of the biblical author.

The great third-century biblical scholar, Origen of Alexandria, following St Irenaeus (*Adv. haer.* III:17:3), alludes to an ancient interpretation of the Good Samaritan parable which sees in the beaten Jew, Adam; in Jerusalem, an image of Paradise; in Jericho, the fallen world; in the robbers, demonic enemies; in the priest, the Hebrew Law; in the Levite, the prophets; and in the Samaritan, Christ. In typical fashion, Origen continues to draw symbolic (hyperbolic?) meaning from the text, seeing in the man's wounds an image of human disobedience; in the Samaritan's beast of burden, the Body of Christ (in what sense is not clear); and in the inn where the man was welcomed, the Church (*Hom. 34 on the Gospel of Luke*, PG 13:1886–1888). Pressing his interpretation to still further allegorical excess, he finds in the two denarii a symbol of the Father and the Son (why not of the "two natures"?); in the innkeeper, the episcopal authority of the Church; and in the Samaritan's promise to return, a prophetic figure of the Second Coming.

How are we to assess this kind of interpretation? Most exegetes today would dismiss it out of hand as a radical and fanciful departure from the "real" meaning of the passage. And in fact, Origen's brilliant interpretations of the Bible are often marked by an inflated use of allegory, and this homily is no exception.

If many of the ancient Fathers followed this approach, however, they did so for a theologically sound reason. Despite the distortions that an allegorical reading can inject into a biblical passage, that approach has the merit of underscoring a fundamental truth. If we are to take seriously the notion of "inspiration," this means that behind and beyond Scripture as a whole there is "transcendent meaning" to which those Scriptures point. While neither Jesus nor the evangelist Luke might have intended that others see in the person of the Samaritan an image of Christ Himself, a legitimate extrapolation can be made from the literal sense of the parable to a "fuller" or "higher" sense, by recognizing that many details of the story actually invite us to see in it allusions that can be properly termed allegorical.

Is it pure coincidence, for example, that the Samaritan, like Christ the true Priest, fulfills the moral obligations of the priest and Levite, who are, presumably, reluctant to do so out of an exaggerated concern for ritual purity (avoiding the wounded man's blood, refusing to touch a corpse)? Is it unreasonable to see in the Samaritan's gestures allusions to Jesus' own healing and saving activity (the Physician of the sick and suffering; the Shepherd of the lost sheep, which He takes on His shoulder and returns safely to the flock)? Or to see in the inn and innkeeper allusions to the Body of believers, called to continue Christ's healing, saving work within the world? Or even to perceive in the Samaritan's promise to return and repay the entire debt, an image of Him who will come again to fulfill His redemptive work for the world's salvation?

If such connections were not present to the mind of the evangelist as he composed his Gospel, using elements from oral and written tradition (his so-called "L" source), could they not have been present in Jesus' own mind, as He spoke the words of the parable both to the lawyer and to the multitudes, including those of later generations? Or could connections such as these not have been present to the Risen Christ, as He continued to speak His Word through the evangelist, by means of the inspirational activity of the Spirit?

Again, rhetorical questions of this kind will be dismissed by most commentators as exegetical heresy: allegorical fantasy imposed on an otherwise straightforward narrative that admits only a literal interpretation.

Yet the Church Fathers saw beyond the letter to the core meaning of the Gospel. Allegory for them was a tool that allowed them, despite frequent exaggerations, to perceive and convey a fundamental truth: Every passage, every word of the canonical Scriptures is filled with the Spirit of God, who speaks through those thoroughly human words, to reveal to us the presence and purpose of the Risen Christ within our life and within His world.

"These things are written," another evangelist declares, "that you may believe that Jesus is the Christ, the Son of God, and that believing you may have life in His name" (Jn 20:31).

6

Who Wrote the Books of the Bible?

*T*HE QUESTION ITSELF MIGHT BE considered inflammatory. To Evangelical Protestants and other conservative Christians, to suggest that traditional attributions of biblical writings may not always be historically accurate smacks of heresy. To Orthodox Christians, questioning the traditional authorship of a biblical book seems to be questioning biblical authority itself, throwing into question the judgment of Church Fathers and undermining Holy Tradition.

My purpose in raising the issue is not to provoke ire, nor is it to question the value and authority of tradition. It is simply to address a question that often arises in our parish communities, especially when they are visited by interested but suspicious inquirers who come from a conservative Protestant background.

It is important to recognize and acknowledge that the authorship of certain biblical books was a matter of dispute even in the early Church. Already in the second century, St Irenaeus had to defend the Johannine authorship of the Fourth Gospel against other Christians who rejected its apostolic authority. Origen (†254), after long meditating on the question, concluded that only God knows who wrote the Epistle to the Hebrews. The authenticity of the three small letters ascribed to the apostle John was widely doubted in certain areas of early Christendom. And if the book of Revelation was accepted in Syriac-speaking areas only toward the tenth century, it was also because of dubious apostolic authorship.

Jesus and the apostles, together with ancient Church Fathers, all presupposed "Mosaic authorship" of the first five books of the Old Testament (the "Pentateuch," the Hebrew *Torah* or Law; see for example Jn 1:45). Yet how would they respond if we could raise the question with them, "Did Moses actually write down all the material contained in those five books?"

Knowing how written texts were produced in their day, they would almost surely have replied that he did not. In the first place, authors frequently made use of a scribe, or amanuensis, who was often given a great deal of leeway in the final shape of the text. There is no more "Pauline" letter in the New Testament than the Epistle to the Romans, yet it was penned—and probably edited—by Paul's disciple Tertius (16:22). Then we should recall the Orthodox icons of St John the Theologian, shown dictating his Gospel to his disciple Prochorus.

The authorship of the Pentateuch, however, is a different matter. First, we should note that the book of Deuteronomy ends with Moses' death, an account which, of course, he did not write himself. This does not prove that he did not compose the remaining material, from Genesis 1 through Deuteronomy 33. To hold that he did, however, dismisses a great deal of convincing evidence to the contrary: evidence given in any standard introduction to the Old Testament, which demonstrates clearly that the Pentateuch was composed using a broad variety of traditions, both oral and written, and in stages spanning hundreds of years.

No serious scholar who has studied the question in depth doubts the composite character of the Pentateuch. Detailed studies have shown that it contains great varieties of literary style, vocabulary and syntax, together with "doublets," or repetitions, of discrete yet inconsistent traditions stemming from different periods, all of which argue powerfully against the hypothesis that it was produced by a single author. The differences between the ancient tradition recorded in Genesis chapters 2–3 and the much later creation account of Genesis 1, for example, are strikingly apparent, even to the casual reader. Oral traditions circulated in prophetic and cultic circles for many years before being gathered, edited, and by a process still unclear, incorporated into what became the Torah.

While some of the oral material behind those books may go back more or less directly to Moses, his association with Torah is important not from the point of view of *redaction*, but from the point of view of *authority*. To hold that those books are "Mosaic" is to affirm their canonical authority. Yet they are canonical not by virtue of the fact that Moses (or any other single figure) actually penned the words, but because they were received as canonical within Israel, under the guidance of the Holy Spirit. And tradition naturally associates such authoritative material with the revelation God accorded to Moses on Mt Sinai. Torah stands in direct continuity with that revelation and thus in its entirety is deemed to constitute "the Law of Moses."

The authority the Pentateuch possesses is greater than any human authority, that of Moses or anyone else. This is because both Jews and Christians recognize that God inspired the written witness—through a variety of authors and over a long span of time—and that God Himself invests those Scriptures with divine authority because they are truly revelatory. This, and not the redaction of a particular text by a particular author, is what makes the Scriptures uniquely authoritative, the vehicle of divine truth.

This approach to the question will be unacceptable to many Orthodox, just as it will be to many Evangelicals. Rather than undermine the faith, however, it confirms the essential truth that the true "author" of Scripture is God Himself, who conveys His revealing Word through a great number and variety of inspired human witnesses.

With this in mind, Readers in the Church often wonder if they should continue to announce during a liturgical service the traditional authorship of a book of the Bible whose authenticity is in doubt. Should we, for example, continue to refer to "the Epistle of the holy apostle Paul to the Hebrews"?

Certainly the answer should be "yes." These are traditional attributions, sanctioned by the Church, which have behind them a long and venerable tradition. And it should be noted that scholars very often disagree among themselves as to which books are "authentic" and which are pseudepigraphical. Traditional attributions, once again, usually arose out of a concern to recognize in a given writing its apostolic authority and revelatory value. It may be appropriate to discuss questions of authorship in a seminary classroom or even a parish Bible study. Nevertheless, we should let stand the traditional attributions when we celebrate the Divine Liturgy or other services, since those attributions are concerned less with historical accuracy than with the need to draw our attention to the canonical, and thus authoritative, Word of God.

Who, in the final analysis, wrote the books of the Bible? The faith and experience of the Church affirm that the true Author of Scripture is the Holy Spirit. It is He who inspires human authors to compose—in their own terms, in light of their received traditions, and with all the limits human authorship implies—the unique body of writings produced in and by the Church as its *regula veritatis*, its canon or rule of truth.

7
Are Jesus' Words "Authentic"?

*L*IKE THE TITLE OF THE preceding chapter, this one may be considered somewhat inflammatory. Again, our intent is not to be provocative. It is simply to speak to an often raised question regarding biblical authority. What gives the words attributed to Jesus their authority? Is it their *historicity*: that they might have been tape recorded to show their authenticity? Or is it their *canonicity*: that they constitute a major element of the divinely established "rule of truth"?

To the minds of many people, Jesus during His earthly ministry spoke each word attributed to Him in the Gospels (hence their preference for red-letter editions of the New Testament). Modern biblical scholarship, on the other hand, has shown that the tradition concerning Jesus' teachings contains variants and inconsistencies that lead most exegetes to attribute the form and, in many cases, the content of those sayings to the Gospel writers rather than to Jesus Himself. (Members of the radical "Jesus Seminar," taking this point to an extreme, argue that practically none of the words ascribed to Jesus in the New Testament are authentic in the sense of verifiably historical—except perhaps the counsel, "Render unto Caesar". . . .)

With only the most cursory reading, for example, the words attributed to Jesus in St John's Gospel "sound" very different from those he speaks in the Synoptics: the Gospels of Matthew, Mark, and Luke. ("Synoptic" means that "seen together" the first three Gospels exhibit striking similarities to one another in both tone and content.) In order to explain the unique voice of the "Johannine Jesus," we must first recall that the main purpose of the evangelists was to write *theology*, not biography or historiography. They were concerned to preach the Good News, not to offer a detailed account of specific events or reproduce verbatim specific sayings of Christ, except insofar as such specificity was needed to convey the message of salvation.

Each evangelist felt free to take the received tradition (what St Paul terms *paradosis*, 1 Cor 15:1–5) and reshape it according to his own experience, his own understanding of Jesus' person and work, and the particular needs of his own ecclesial community. This does not mean the evangelists willy-nilly changed Jesus' words. Nevertheless, we need to recall that those words appear in the biblical text in translation, from Aramaic (and occasionally Hebrew) to Greek. This in itself works a modification, if not of meaning then at least of tone.

Then again, a comparison between parallel Synoptic verses, like a comparison between John and the Synoptics, demonstrates clearly that many sayings of Jesus came down through oral tradition in several different versions. Similarly, the Gospels reflect different—and irreconcilable—traditions concerning even the most significant events in Jesus' life, such as the cleansing of the Temple (compare Mt 21:12–17 with Jn 2:13–22, in terms of date and content) or the day on which the Last Supper was celebrated (according to the Synoptic Gospels, it was a Passover meal; according to St John's Gospel, it was a pre-Passover meal served the preceding day, the "Day of Preparation" for the Passover).

What enables us, then, to affirm that the Gospels represent Jesus' words and teaching, rather than the literary invention of the apostolic authors? How can we honestly attribute those words to Jesus Himself rather than to the "post-Easter Church"?

The fundamental point is that *Jesus speaks His word—He reveals the person and will of the Father as well as the Truth about Himself—*

not only during His earthly ministry, but after His resurrection and ascension, in the time of the Church. How can we justify such a claim?

First, we need to point out that the real question is not whether all the words attributed to Jesus are "authentic" (meaning that they stem uniquely from Jesus' teaching during his earthly ministry) or that they are "historically accurate" in a way verifiable by a tape recording. The real question concerns the *canonicity* of those teachings, their divine origin and authority. If we indeed take the notion of "inspiration" seriously, it can only mean that the Holy Spirit both guides the composition of the apostolic writings and confers canonical authority on them. As in the case of the Pentateuch, this implies that "who" wrote those works is largely immaterial. What really matters is their God-given canonicity.

What does this mean about statements attributed to Jesus by the evangelist John? Can we call them "Jesus' own words" (*ipsissima verba Jesu*) if St John in fact modified the tradition he received, giving it a distinctively "Johannine" flavor? The answer is a robust "Yes!" How, then, is this so?

The answer is provided in John 14:26 and 16:13–15. The risen and glorified Lord, together with the Father, sends the Holy Spirit— the Paraclete and Spirit of Truth—upon the gathered Church, in order to guide Christ's followers into "all the truth." The Spirit receives what is Christ's and conveys it to the Christian community through the witness of the evangelist, beginning with his oral preaching.

Inspiration is the key to this point. It is the risen Lord Himself who speaks through the Holy Spirit, just as it is the Spirit who guides the composition of the Gospel. The words that St John attributes to Jesus, then, are definitely the *words of Jesus*. Perhaps they were not spoken during Jesus' earthly ministry in the precise way they appear in the Gospel. But the words the evangelist attributes to Jesus as he writes his Gospel are in fact the *words of the risen Lord*, communicated to him by the Holy Spirit, who dwells within the Church. (St Luke makes a similar point by showing the *risen* Lord "opening the minds" of His disciples to the true meaning of Scripture, Lk 24:27, 45–48!)

To defend the authenticity of Christ's words in the Gospels, therefore, it is not necessary to argue from the perspective of biblical literalism. Many people fear that if we admit that the evangelists felt themselves free to modify their received tradition, including the words attributed to Jesus, then the authority of those words collapses like a house of cards. If St John, for example, could "change" Jesus' words or put words into His mouth He did not actually speak, then this seems to mean that we cannot trust the Bible to be true.

In reply, we can only insist on the Orthodox understanding of the *synergy* that is at the heart of biblical composition. Synergy means "cooperation" between God and the biblical author. This does not mean a 50% division between God and man. God is the one who inspires; composition of the Scriptures depends on *divine initiative*, just as it depends on divine authority. But God uses his human creatures—with their unique historical, cultural, and linguistic particularities—to convey the eternal truths enshrined in *canonical* Scripture. We cannot deny the human element, any more than we can deny the advantages that a variety of approaches to the mystery of Christ provides for us.

We should remember that the Syriac Church tried to create a single Gospel from several that circulated in the Christian East. This produced the so-called "Diatessaron," compiled and edited by Tatian in the latter half of the second century. If the greater Church never accepted this reworking, it is because it always recognized the value in having *four* canonical Gospels, each of which complements the others. Certainly the earliest Christians were no less aware than we are that these writings present different perspectives and contain certain inconsistencies. Yet they recognized as well the unique vision and revelation offered by the four, both individually and taken together.

The mystery of Christ is greater than any human expression, even that of the Gospels. Language remains symbolic. It strives to grasp and express truth, but it can by no means exhaust truth. This is why some truths can only be expressed poetically. The Gospels have their own language, unlike that of any other writing. It is common human language, yes. But its uniqueness lies in the fact that it is uniquely *inspired* language, language shaped by the Spirit of the risen Lord, who works through the biblical author in such a way as to convey canonical authority to Scripture as *the* perfect and full expression of divine revelation.

Therefore the words of Jesus that appear in the Gospel of John—or elsewhere in the canonical Scriptures—are indeed "authentic." For whether they stem from the period prior to His crucifixion, or whether they represent the "words"—the ongoing revelation—of the risen Lord, conveyed through the apostolic writings by the Spirit of Truth, they originate with Jesus Himself and bear faithful witness to His continuing presence and purpose within the world, for the world's salvation.

"When the Spirit of Truth comes [following my resurrection and glorification], He will guide you into all the truth. For He will not speak on His own authority, but whatever He hears He will speak. . . . He will glorify me, for He will take what is mine and declare it to you" (Jn 16:13–14).

8

How Are We to Read the Scriptures?

L ITERARY CRITICISM OF THE BIBLE seems to be an area best left to the specialists. Yet virtually anyone can learn certain principles that governed the writing of biblical passages, and this insight can lead to a much greater appreciation of the meaning of Scripture. It can help us to read the Scriptures in a new and fresh way that corresponds to the way they were in fact written.

Ancient Hebrews and other peoples of antiquity tended to write in poetic fashion, setting two lines together which we can term "A" and "B." Thus Psalm 112:1,

> (A) Blessed is the man who fears the Lord, /
> (B) who greatly delights in His commandments. //

Note that the second line takes up the theme of the first line, "paralleling" it yet intensifying or fulfilling it by specifying just how one "fears the Lord": by taking great delight in obeying His Law. There is a movement from A to B, such that B completes, intensifies, or fulfills A.

Much of the Bible and other literary works as well were written according to a more complicated form of this pattern, called "chiasmus," or concentric parallelism. (The term "chiasmus" is derived from the Greek letter "chi," written like a capital X, implying a crossing or reversal of terms, as in "The *first* shall be *last* / the *last* shall be *first.*") The author of an individual biblical passage or entire book develops his thought, as we would expect, from beginning to end. Yet he conveys meaning as well by creating a concentric movement from the extremities of the passage toward its center. The movement, again, is one of intensification, completion or fulfillment, beginning with the first and last lines, then progressing toward the middle.

Occasionally that middle may contain more than one element. An example is the pattern A:B:B':A', in which the major "point" or center of meaning is expressed by B:B'. For example, Matthew 11:27–28 (the indentation facilitates a reading of the lines that parallel one another),

> A : *All things* have been *delivered* to me by my Father;
> > B : and no one knows the *Son* except the *Father,*
> > B': and no one knows the *Father* except the *Son,*
> A': and *all those* to whom the Son chooses to *reveal* Him.

In A', "all things" of A has been heightened and specified by "all those (people)," just as "delivered" has been heightened by "reveal." The main focus, however, is B:B', the reciprocal knowledge of Father and Son; and particular stress is upon B', the fact that only the Son knows God the Father. This "Johannine thunderbolt" in the Synoptic tradition serves to make the point repeatedly made in the Fourth Gospel: we can know God only through His Son, Jesus Christ.

Another good example is 1 John 1:6–7, a text that expresses antithesis between those who falsely claim to be in communion with God and those who, by virtue of their moral conduct, are truly in communion both with God and with each other.

> A : If we say we have *fellowship* with Him
> > B : and (yet) walk in the *darkness,*
> > > **C : we lie and do not do the truth.**
> > B': If we walk in the *light* as He is in the light,
> A': we have *fellowship* with one another. . . .

Here the last line (A') parallels and completes the first line (A) by distinguishing the truth from the lie. The same relation exists between B' and B. The primary message of the passage is expressed in C: those who claim they have fellowship with God, yet walk in the darkness (i.e., commit sin), are deceiving themselves: they "lie" and do not "do the truth."

The meaning of this passage, then, is revealed by the spiraling movement that complements the linear reading from beginning to end. This spiral leads the reader from line A to line A', then from B to B', and culminates at the center, C. Like a tornado, a whirlpool, or a spiral galaxy, the passage draws the reader into a vortex that leads, with increasing intensity, from the extremities (the opening and concluding lines) of the passage toward the middle or central point. This way of reading is usually unconscious on the reader's part. Yet the human brain seems to register the meaning of literary passages, and of much else in human experience such as classical musical works and landscape paintings, in two ways: from "beginning to end," and also from the extremities toward the center. A Bach fugue, for example, will reach a crescendo, followed by development and intensification of the original themes. A landscape artist will often paint a dark foreground, complemented by a shaded background, while the middle of the work is flooded with light.

One of the most interesting literary examples of this form appears at the opening of the Gospel of Mark (1:1–15). In a few deft strokes the evangelist describes the mission of John the Baptizer and the fulfillment of that mission in Jesus' own unique form of baptismal activity.

The passage can be set out as follows:

A (v. 1) : Beginning of the Gospel of Jesus Christ.
  B (2f): John the Baptist comes to prepare the "way" (= the Gospel).
    C (4): John appears in the wilderness.
      D (5): The people confess their sins.
        E (6): John clothed in camel's hair (like the prophet Elijah).
          F (7): One mightier than John is to come.
            G (8a): "I have baptized you with water,

> G' (8b): but He will baptize you with the Holy Spirit."
>> F' (9): Jesus comes and is baptized.
>>> E' (10): Jesus is "clothed" in the Spirit (as the eschatological prophet).
>>>> D' (11): The heavenly voice "confesses" the Son.
>>> C' (12f): Jesus is driven into the wilderness.
>> B' (14) Jesus comes to preach the Gospel (= "the Way"; see Mk 10:52).
> A' (15) "Repent and believe in the Gospel!"

We can read this passage spirally, from the outside toward the middle (that is, from A then A', to B then B', to C then C', etc.), finally arriving at the "point" or focus of meaning of the passage, expressed in G and G': John's baptism in water is merely preparation for the end-time baptism by Jesus. Jesus, and not John, is the true eschatological prophet, who will "baptize" His followers by bestowing on them the Holy Spirit.

Each line in the first half of this passage is paralleled by a complementary line in the second half. Those "prime" lines (marked by ') take up the same theme as the original line, yet they set it forward in a special way: they explain, amplify or otherwise "heighten" it, so that a centripetal movement draws the reader from the extremities toward the center, the focus of the author's message.

I would invite you to read this passage over several times, especially in the *Revised Standard Version* of the Bible (except for those who can read the Greek original). Gradually you will find yourself reading it in two complementary ways: from beginning to end, as we read any text; but also according to this concentric flow. Although this may seem to be a wholly new way of approaching a biblical work, you will nevertheless be reading it according to the same chiastic principles the author used to compose it in the first place.

9
Holy Spirit and Fire

*I*N THE LAST CHAPTER we pointed out that the evangelist Mark begins his Gospel (1:1–15) with a passage structured as a "chiasm," a form of concentric parallelism. Like any writer, Mark expresses his thought in linear fashion, from beginning to end. But he complements that linear flow with another movement created by a parallelism that progresses from the extremities of the passage (the "inclusion" and "conclusion" or beginning and end) toward the middle.

This produces a spiral movement, in which successive lines of the second half of the passage intensify or complete lines of the first half, leading the reader toward the center, which in this case is verse 8. This central verse represents the major theme Mark seeks to convey: John the Baptizer declares, "I have baptized you with water, / but He [the Christ or Messiah] will baptize you with the Holy Spirit." //

Scholars are in general agreement that the evangelist Matthew (like St Luke) used Mark's Gospel as one of his primary sources when he wrote his own Gospel. Often Matthew took chiastically structured themes of Mark's witness and expanded them, either slightly or more fully, to produce his own testimony to Jesus' life and the significance of His mission. One striking example is Matthew's reworking of the chiasm composed of Mark 1:1–15.

The passage in question is Matthew 3:1 to 4:17. The first and last elements consist of parallel statements that are in fact identical, the first uttered by John the Baptizer and the second by Jesus: "Repent, for the kingdom of heaven is at hand!" This summons frames the entire passage, just as Mark's double affirmation frames his: "Beginning of the *Gospel* of Jesus Christ // Repent and believe in the *Gospel*!" And just as Mark moves progressively, but in a mere 13 verses, from John's appearance, to the people's baptism, to John's proclamation concerning Jesus, to Jesus' baptism, and to Jesus' wilderness temptation (in fulfillment of Israel's forty year wandering in the desert), so Matthew follows a similar pattern. The outline of Matthew's much longer account takes the following concentric "shape":

A (3:1f): John: "Repent, for the kingdom of heaven is at hand."
  B (3:3): Isaiah's prophecy concerning John.
    C (3:4–6): John in the wilderness.
      D (3:7–10): Pharisees and Sadducees come to be baptized
        E (3:11ab): Jesus is mightier than John.
          F (3:11c): "He will baptize you with the Holy Spirit and with fire!"
        E' (3:12): Jesus will execute final judgment.
      D' (3:13–17): Jesus comes to be baptized.
    C' (4:1–11): Jesus in the wilderness.
  B' (4:12–16): Isaiah's prophecy concerning Jesus.
A' (4:17): Jesus: "Repent, for the kingdom of heaven is at hand."

The major themes developed by Matthew follow the order he found in the Gospel of Mark. Matthew has amplified the various segments with complementary material (the scene of Jesus in the wilderness, for example, where the long dialogue is added between Jesus and Satan). But essentially, Matthew follows Mark's outline.

In addition, St Matthew has preserved the concentric or chiastic flow that he discovered in Mark's Gospel. He has begun this extended passage with a command repeated at the end: John, then Jesus, summon the people to repent in view of the imminent arrival of the kingdom. Then Matthew moves to John's ministry in the desert and to his proclamation concerning Jesus. Each of these elements (B, C, D, E) is paralleled in the latter half of the passage by similar themes (E', D', C', B'). And, as with Mark, the "prime" parallels (marked with ') intensify, fulfill, explain, or otherwise "heighten" the original theme.

And, like the opening of Mark's Gospel, the whole passage in Matthew spirals from A–A' to B–B', to C–C', and so on, to arrive at the central affirmation F (the last line of 3:11): "He will baptize you with the Holy Spirit and with fire."

The focus is identical, with one significant exception. St Mark has centered his opening passage around Jesus' "baptismal" activity, which, although Mark does not say as much, will be fulfilled at Pentecost. St Matthew, on the other hand, has added an *apocalyptic* element. His concern is to demonstrate that the kingdom that comes in Jesus' person is the end-time manifestation of the Spirit (to fulfill the prophecy of Joel 2:28ff). Yet it also signals the coming of divine judgment. To the outpouring of the Holy Spirit, *fire* will be cast upon the earth: a powerful symbol of the judgment God was expected to execute once the Messiah had appeared.

Biblical authors (and many others as well) used this form of concentric parallelism to draw the reader step by step toward the central meaning or focus of their message. In this case, both evangelists proclaim that with the coming of Jesus, heaven itself has drawn near. And Matthew adds the ominous word that our true baptism consists not only of the gift of the Spirit. It also brings us into judgment before the holy and righteous God.

It is this focus on judgment that explains the urgency of the opening and closing of the passage according to Matthew's tradition. The kingdom of God—divine presence and power—has drawn near in the person of Jesus. "The people who sat in darkness have seen a great light, and for those who sat in the region and shadow of death light has dawned," Matthew declares in the words of the prophets. The way beyond darkness and death, he makes clear, lies in our acceptance of the call, uttered by both the Forerunner and the Messiah, "Repent!"

10
Liturgy: Here and Beyond

THE LITURGY OF THE CHURCH stands at the intersection between earth and heaven, time and eternity. Like an icon, liturgical worship allows us to perceive aspects of reality that go far beyond the limits of the scientifically observable; and like an icon, it allows transcendent light and truth to penetrate into the realm of our personal and ecclesial experience.

The liturgy is thus characterized by a double movement. By means of our celebration, we undertake a journey of the soul, whose end is communion with the eternal God. At the same time, God approaches us through our celebration, to give content and direction to our worship, and through it to unite us to Himself.

This double movement is especially evident in our celebration of the Eucharist or Lord's Supper. Orthodox Christians term the Eucharist the "Divine Liturgy," *theia liturgia,* since its source and ultimate end are in God Himself, in the communion of love shared by the three Persons of the Holy Trinity.

In Byzantine tradition, the heart of the Divine Liturgy is an offertory prayer situated just after the "Words of Institution" and the *Anamnesis,* or Memorial, and before the *Epiklesis,* or "Invocation of the Holy Spirit" upon the bread and wine, to transform them into the Body and Blood of Christ. That offertory prayer declares, "Thine own of Thine own, we offer unto Thee, on behalf of all and for all!"

These words affirm more clearly, perhaps, than any others just what the Liturgy means. It is a gesture on our part by which we offer ourselves and all of creation to the Lord. Yet it also acknowledges that everything we can offer to God is first granted to us as a gift of His loving grace and mercy.

"Thine own of Thine own, we offer. . . . " God provides the simple things of daily life, symbolized by the basic elements of bread and wine. When we transform wheat into bread and the juice of grapes into wine, we take what He has bestowed upon us and work the change according to our God-given abilities. We take what God offers, we do with it according to His will, and then we offer it back to Him as a gesture of thanksgiving and praise. And we do so for our own sake and for the sake of all of God's creation: "on behalf of all and for all!"

If it were not for the location of this simple prayer, between the Memorial and the Invocation, it would have little meaning. It would signify merely that we receive every earthly blessing from God and do so with gratitude.

But this Liturgy, once again, is the vital intersection between heaven and earth. In the Memorial, therefore, we "remember" not only things past ("the Cross, the Tomb, the Resurrection on the third day, the Ascension into heaven") but also things future ("and the Second and Glorious Coming!"). And in the Invocation, we ask God to work the miracle that transforms both ourselves and the elements of bread and wine into the Body and Blood of His Son. The limits of time, space and physical laws are overcome. A miracle occurs. We ourselves, together with the bread and wine, actually become the Body of Christ.

> Send down Thy Holy Spirit *upon us* and upon these Gifts here offered. . . . That they may be to those who partake for the purification of soul, for the remission of sins, for the communion of Thy Holy Spirit, for the fulfillment of the kingdom of heaven. . . .

In the Divine Liturgy, therefore, and especially as it culminates in eucharistic celebration, we have a foretaste of the world to come.

Transcending the limits of time and space, we enter into the presence of God. For a moment, we cross the threshold of eternity, to offer ourselves and our gifts to the Creator of all. In return we receive the Bread of Life that nourishes and sustains us, until the New Jerusalem descends into our midst, the radiant City of God, where eucharistic gifts of bread and wine are transformed into the Water of Life, and "death shall be no more" (Rev 21–22).

11

Annunciation: The Eternal Mystery

*I*N ORTHODOX LITURGICAL TRADITION, the rhythm of Great Lent is interrupted, and in an important sense fulfilled, by the Feast of the Annunciation. As we journey with Christ through the last days of His earthly ministry, our attention is focused on His impending crucifixion and resurrection. Yet this mystery is possible only because of another, equally central to His mission and to our faith: the mystery of His incarnation in the womb of the Virgin Mary.

We live in a time when serious theological works as well as the popular press depict Jesus of Nazareth as an itinerant prophet, a political zealot, or at best, an occasional worker of miracles. His "humanity" is stressed to the point that traditional language used to speak of the transcendent aspect of His person—"the God-man," "the eternal Son and Word of God," "One of the Holy Trinity"—is dismissed as myth or metaphor.

The bedrock of Orthodox faith, on the other hand, is the conviction that "the [eternal] Word," the preexistent Son of God, "became flesh and dwelt among us" (Jn 1:14). In the most literal, ontological sense of the term, He became "incarnate," taking human nature from the Virgin in whose womb He was conceived. As the apostle Paul so eloquently expresses it in the confessional hymn of Philippians 2, He who was equal with God (the Father) assumed human existence, "emptying Himself" to take on the form of a servant.

The *Monogenēs*, or hymn to the "Only Begotten Son and immortal Word of God" that completes the second antiphon of the Divine (eucharistic) Liturgy, qualifies this biblical affirmation by a single key word, *atreptōs*, "without change." *Without change* the eternal Son of God assumed human nature, thereby redeeming and deifying that nature, so that those who are baptized into Him and partake of His life-giving Body and Blood might share in His victory over death and ascend with Him into the glory that He shares with the Father from all eternity. *Without change* the Son of God became the Son of the Virgin; and therefore the Church honors and exalts Him as "the God-man."

In the language of the early Church Fathers, "He became what we are that we might become what He is," that we might share fully and eternally in His divine reality. The Son of God assumed fallen human nature in order to glorify that nature and to open before us the possibility to participate immediately, intimately, in His own divine life. Thereby human persons become "partakers of the divine nature" (2 Pet 1:4), virtually "deified" by sharing in the very attributes of God, the "divine energies" of righteousness, justice, holiness, beauty, and love.

This great mystery of our salvation and deification is grounded in a still greater mystery, the "eternal mystery" of the incarnation of the Son of God, the Second Person of the Holy Trinity. And the entire purpose of this greater mystery is precisely to create the indispensable conditions for our salvation.

> "Today is revealed the eternal mystery!
> The Son of God becomes the Son of Man!
> By accepting the lowest, He grants me the highest!
> Of old, Adam failed to become a god, as he wished,
> But now God becomes man, that He may make Adam god!"
>
> (Praises of the feast)

Without this eternal mystery of the Incarnation, Jesus of Nazareth would be nothing more than a prophet, a zealot, or a miracle-worker among many others. He might be a model of God-like behavior, a wise counselor, and a storyteller of extraordinary talent.

But He would be neither Redeemer nor Savior nor Author of Life. And you and I would be "dead in our sins," stripped of all meaning and devoid of hope.

But because of the Virgin's *fiat*, Christ is both Lord and Savior; and you and I share nothing less than "the hope of glory" (Colossians 1:27; 3:4).

> "The co-eternal Son of the Father
> Who shares His throne and like Him is without beginning,
> Has emptied Himself in His compassion and merciful love for
>   mankind.
> According to the good pleasure and counsel of the Father,
> He has gone to dwell in a Virgin's womb—a womb sanctified
>   by the Spirit!
> He who cannot be contained is contained in a womb;
> The timeless One enters time. . . ."
>
> (*Aposticha* of the feast)

This is why, on the feast of Annunciation, we proclaim: "*Today* is the beginning of our salvation, the revelation of the eternal mystery!"

12
Why the Incarnation?

T HE GOSPELS OF MATTHEW and Luke tell us that the Son of God was conceived in the womb of the Virgin Mary by the power of the Holy Spirit. This is a unique conception, a genuine *partheno-genesis*, since, as the liturgical texts declare, it occurred "without seed," that is, without the participation of a human father.

St John's Gospel begins with the startling assertion that the Word, or Son of God, who existed with the Father from all eternity, "became flesh"—that is, became "incarnate"—as Jesus of Nazareth.

Even as the Gospels were being written, the apostle Paul declared in his letters to various early Church communities that Jesus Christ, the Messiah of the Jews and Savior of the world, was "equal with God" (Phil 2:6), was "born of a woman at the [divinely] appointed time" (Gal 4:4), and that in Him "the whole fullness of deity dwells bodily" (Col 2:9).

The Nicene Creed, which is the most basic yet complete statement of Christian faith, proclaims that the eternal Son of God "came down from heaven, and was incarnate of the Holy Spirit and the Virgin Mary, and became man."

Every year Christians throughout the world proclaim the "birth of Christ in the flesh," the mystery of Christ's incarnation. Yet, as we are all aware, the tinsel and commercialism of our age have so obscured the "real meaning of Christmas" that we identify the feast more with Santa Claus (or St Nicholas) than with Christ, more with swapping presents than with celebrating the Gift of gifts which is new and eternal life made possible through the incarnation, the suffering, and the death of "Emmanuel: God with us."

This tragic reduction of the Christian mystery in the popular mind is both the cause and the result of efforts, even on the part of certain theologians, to redefine the person of Jesus until He is virtually unrecognizable. The one the Gospels and Epistles call Lord, Savior, and even God, is presented by the media and by many biblical scholars as an itinerant Jewish peasant or firebrand revolutionary. The only basis for these caricatures is personal skepticism. They certainly don't appear in the biblical texts or in any extra-biblical sources we can identify. In the final analysis, these caricatures amount to a rejection and denial of the very Gospel these scholars profess to proclaim.

Why the Incarnation? Why does traditional Christianity continue to insist that in Jesus of Nazareth God appeared "in the flesh"? Because, as a dying Protestant theologian of very Catholic leanings once reminded me, "We cannot save ourselves; only God can save us!"

How, then, does God work out our salvation? This raises the question of "atonement," the divinely initiated process by which we are reconciled with God.

According to Scripture, by means of His sacrifice on the Cross Christ fulfills and replaces the sacrificial ritual of ancient Israel and establishes a "New Covenant in His blood" between ourselves and God (Lk 22:20). As the Suffering Servant, He bears the sins of "many" (a Hebraism for all humankind; cf. Isa 53). In Johannine imagery, He is the Lamb of God who takes away the sin of the world. His sacrifice is the unique ground of our redemption, the source of our "atonement," or reconciliation with the Father. We enter into that new covenantal relationship by virtue of God's own free gift, the gift of His Son, slain on the cross and raised from the dead. Baptism unites us with Christ's death and resurrection (Rom 6). Yet that union presupposes on our part both repentance and faith.

Western Christianity (Roman Catholic and mainline Protestant) has offered numerous elaborations of Christ's saving work of atonement. One of the major developments occurred with St Anselm of Canterbury, in his treatise *Cur Deus Homo?* ("Why Did God Become Man?"). Anselm proposed a theory of "satisfaction," according to which human sin offends divine justice and brings condemnation upon us all. This requires a sacrifice offered to God in order to appease His wrath, which our sin stirs up against us. No human sacrifice is adequate to the task; no offering we can make can truly "satisfy" God's justice. The only sacrifice sufficient to assuage the wrath of God is the vicarious ("on our behalf") self-offering of God's Son, Jesus Christ. Christ, therefore, satisfies the debt which we ourselves owe to His Father.

Protestant Reformers, especially Martin Luther (†1546), rejected this satisfaction theory of atonement and placed primary emphasis on the substitutionary value of Christ's death. The Father accepted the voluntary sacrifice of His Son *pro nobis*, once again "on our behalf." We are "justified" before God, therefore, not because of our inherent goodness, nor because we are rendered free of sin. We are justified by *faith*, as the apostle Paul insisted, particularly in his letters to the Romans and Galatians. Luther, however, added a new element to the Pauline teaching. Justification, he insisted, is "by faith *alone*." This means, however, that atonement is achieved by something of a legal fiction. Although we are "justified" by Christ's voluntary sacrifice on our behalf, we remain sinners: *simul iustus et peccator*. Despite our sinfulness, God *imputes* justice to us; He behaves toward us *as though* we were innocent, free of sin.

This emphasis was intended to combat what Luther considered to be a heretical notion, stemming from medieval Roman scholastic theology, that placed primary emphasis on "works-righteousness," expressed as a doctrine of "merits": we are justified by performing good deeds, rather than by "faith alone."

This is an overly simplified version of the Western position. But it makes the point that Western theology, both Roman and Protestant, tended to consider the question of atonement from the point of view of human guilt and divine justice. In Roman Catholic thought, that justice requires on our part meritorious works; in Protestant thought, it requires faith. (These are primary emphases. In fact, faith plays a crucial role in Catholic teachings on redemption, just as works do in the Protestant, and especially Lutheran, doctrine of sanctification.)

More often than not, however, the term usually translated "justification" (in Greek: *dikaiosunē*) actually refers to the "righteousness" of God—the quality of righteousness proper to Him alone—which God *imparts*, that is, conveys or communicates, to those who receive it with faith and love.

This means that the "free gift of God's righteousness" is not merely imputed to us; it actually works out a transformation of our life and being: *we ourselves become righteous through the righteousness of God in Jesus Christ* (Rom 5:17–19, where *kathistēmi* means "made [righteous]"; Gal 5:4–6, where the "hope of righteousness" is grounded in "faith working through love"; and Phil 3:8–10, the righteousness from God, received by faith, gives knowledge of Christ and a share in His suffering and resurrection). It is this transforming, transfiguring gift of righteousness that enables us to increase in holiness, to "behold the Lord," and "be changed into His likeness, from glory to glory" (2 Cor 3:17; cf. 1 Jn 3:2).

Orthodox theology focuses surprisingly little on the question of justification. It understands Christ's redemptive work in a different way, one that takes with utter seriousness the New Testament proclamations concerning the Incarnation.

For the Orthodox, the great and last enemy is not sin (and guilt), but death. "The wages of sin is death," the apostle declares, "and the sting of death is sin. . . ." If we die, it is because sin has entered into the world. Sin is what separates us from God. But the wages of sin, the bitter fruit of our physical death, is not to be understood as punishment imposed by a wrathful God. Death, rather, results from our own willful rejection of the Author of Life (Acts 3:14–15).

Why the Incarnation? Precisely because we cannot save ourselves. For death to be overcome, destroyed, the Author of Life had to descend into the depths of death by His own death. He had to suffer death on a cross, descend into the realm of the dead, and there destroy the power of death. Only in this way could He give life to those who dwell in the grasp of death. Only by accepting death *as the God-man* could He raise the dead with Himself in His own resurrection, and grant them a full participation with Himself in the glory He shares with the Father from before the foundation of the world (Jn 17:5).

Why the Incarnation? Because in order for us to share in His life, He had to assume all the conditions of both our life and our death. He had to become what we are, in order to enable us to become what He is in the fullness of His eternal life and glory.

This is why Jesus is neither an itinerant peasant nor some violent revolutionary. He is the King of Peace, who "became flesh," died and rose out of death, in order to grant Life to the world.

O Christ our Defender, You have put to shame the adversary of man, using as a shield your ineffable Incarnation. Taking man's form, You have now bestowed upon him the joy of becoming God-like. . . ."

(Nativity Canon, Ode 7)

13

Nativity: A Sacrifice of Love

*T*HE MYSTERY OF CHRIST'S NATIVITY is above all a Paschal mystery. Pascha, in our Orthodox tradition, refers first of all to Easter, the feast of Christ's resurrection from the dead. Yet it refers as well to every image of sacrifice that was revealed during Jesus' earthly ministry, from His birth, through His baptism and transfiguration, to His crucifixion. Each stage of His pilgrimage, from the cavern and crèche in Bethlehem to His burial in the tomb of the noble Joseph, reveals the mystery of His vocation: to be a sacrifice of the Father's love, for our salvation and the salvation of God's world.

In the icon of the Nativity this mystery is revealed in a specially poignant way. The traditional image shows the Christ child in the center, surrounded by the walls of the cavern in which He was born. He is wrapped not in the swaddling clothes of a newborn infant, but in winding cloth: a burial shroud that foreshadows His repose in another cavern, another black hole, following His death upon the cross. He is laid not in a cradle, but on an altar of sacrifice: a place of ritual slaughter that points forward to the moment when He will stretch out His arms on the "tree," feel the nails pierce His flesh, and utter the final cry of a dying man: "Father, into Thy hands I commit my spirit!"

Mary, clothed in the red of death and resurrection, gazes past the child into eternity, pondering the mystery that has come upon her. She is in fact the central figure, since she is the Mother of God, the Holy Virgin in whom the eternal Son of God became man. Because of her "fiat," her acceptance of the awesome call laid upon her, God was able to assume "flesh," the fullness of our fallen humanity. "He became what we are," with the sole intent to open the way before us—the way of holiness, sanctity and love—so that we might "become what He is." So that we might share fully in the glory and joy of His resurrected life.

All of this is possible, because the Virgin replied, "Yes." Because she submitted herself to the most awesome and prodigious mystery of all, the mystery of "Incarnation."

Yet her expression reveals another side to her willing acceptance of the angel's call. Her destiny involves not only a miraculous conception under conditions that will expose her to ridicule and condemnation. It also involves tragedy. She senses from the beginning, the icon tells us, that her Son is born to die. She gives birth to a sacrificial lamb. She knows that this child, a gift to her, will also be a gift to the world. And she realizes that this gift will involve suffering for herself as well as for Him. She cannot yet see herself standing at the foot of His cross. Nevertheless, she already intuits what the Holy Elder Simeon will declare to her a few days hence: "A sword will pierce your soul also."

Despite the air of tragedy that hangs over the scene, the icon points well beyond darkness and death. Into the black hole of the nativity cavern there descends a brilliant ray of light and the image of a dove, symbolizing the presence of the Holy Spirit. Above is the hand of the Father, the source of all life, both human and divine. And on the altar, the Christ child. There, in the poverty and misery of a manger, appear the three Persons of the Holy Trinity. As in the scenes of Christ's baptism and transfiguration, God is present and makes Himself known.

Jesus of Nazareth, the eternal Son of God, is born in the most humble conditions imaginable, in a way that provokes skepticism and hostility on the part of his contemporaries and even members of His own family. He is born into the conditions of our daily life:

our routine, our stress, our anxiety, our mortality. Yet He comes as a sacrificial gift of the Father's love.

A little boy once asked me why God sent His Son Jesus to die and didn't come Himself. I showed him an icon of the Nativity and tried to explain what can hardly be put into words, but seems nevertheless more true than most things. I told him that any father would rather die himself than sacrifice his child.

When the Father offered His Son for the life of the world, He offered to us the ultimate gift of His love. With the death of Jesus, the Mother of our Lord knew infinite grief and sadness. And His Father did, no less.

14

The Meeting of Our Lord

*T*HE FEAST OF THE MEETING of our Lord in the Temple, celebrated on February 2, is one of the twelve Great Feasts of the
Orthodox liturgical year. Its theme is expressed with particular
poignancy in the icon we venerate on this day, as well as by the
feast's liturgical hymns.

The icon of the Meeting places the Theotokos and the Righteous
Simeon with the Christ child in the foreground, leaving Joseph and
the prophetess Anna standing apart as secondary figures. In obedience to Mosaic Law (Lev 12), Mary comes to the Temple on the day
of her purification to present her child as an offering of first-fruits
to the Lord (Num 18). Before the altar, the table of sacrifice, Simeon
stretches forth his hands to receive the fulfillment of the hope that
had so long burned within him and within the collective consciousness of the righteous Israelites whom he represents.

Simeon offers a prophetic canticle (Lk 2:29–32, the *Nunc Dimittis*
sung at every Vespers service) which proclaims that this child
shall be a "light to enlighten the Gentiles" as well as "the glory of
[God's] people Israel." Following the canticle, Simeon blesses the
parents of the child. Turning to Mary, he pronounces curious, ominous words, not of joy and gladness, but of coming conflict and suffering. In conclusion, he adds almost parenthetically, still
addressing the Virgin Mother: "and a sword will pierce through your

own soul also" (Lk 2:35). This represents the first prediction the evangelist makes concerning the Lord's coming passion.

"And a sword shall pierce your heart, O all-pure Virgin," Simeon foretold to the Theotokos, "when you shall see your Son upon the Cross, to whom we cry aloud: O God of our fathers, blessed are You!"

—Meeting Matins, Ode 7

The Holy Theotokos, Mother of God, presents her Son in fulfillment of the obligation to make an offering of her first-born male child. The deeper sense of her offering, intimated by Simeon's prophetic words, points to the Cross and to the victory to be achieved through sacrificial death. Thus the *megalynaria* (Ode 9) of the feast declare:

The pure Dove, the Ewe without blemish, brings the Lamb and Shepherd into the temple.

The lytia verses of Great Vespers proclaim the meaning of the sacrifice accomplished by the holy Mother and awaited by her Son:

Now the God of purity as a holy child has opened a pure womb, and as God He is brought as an offering to Himself, setting us free from the curse of the Law and granting light to our souls.

The light granted to the nations and to the soul of every believer is ultimately the divine, uncreated light of the triune God. As Isaiah received purification from a fiery coal taken from the altar by a seraph (Isa 6), so the Righteous Elder receives purification and the knowledge of salvation from the hands of the Virgin, as she entrusts to him the One called by the Matins Ode 5, the "Lord of light that knows no evening."

Touching the light, Simeon himself is filled with light. Like future generations of those who dwell in that light, he is nourished

by the very Body of the Lord, receiving Him as a prototype of the
bloodless sacrifice of the holy Eucharist.

As he takes his leave, the Elder is made to utter a final prophecy
that links this feast directly to the descent of Christ into hell.

"I depart," cried Simeon, "to declare the good tidings to Adam abiding in hell and to Eve. . . ."

To deliver our kind from dust, God will go down even into hell: He
will give freedom to all the captives and sight to the blind, and will
grant the dumb to cry aloud: O God of our fathers, blessed are You!

Matins, Ode 7

The Meeting between Simeon and the Christ child marks the
meeting of two Covenants, Old and New. It celebrates the fulfillment of God's promise to bring deliverance and salvation to what St
Paul calls "the Israel of God," the Church, and through the Church,
to the world. That deliverance and salvation, however, are achieved
only through the suffering and death of the crucified Lord. This little child, the eternal God, accomplishes His mission only by His
willingness to follow the way of the Cross.

Yet this is why we celebrate this meeting in the Temple as a great
feast of the Church. The Lamb and Shepherd, brought as an offering to Himself, comes in our liturgical worship to meet not only
Simeon but us as well. He meets us there where we are, in the midst
of our own suffering and our own longing to behold and to taste
God's victory on our behalf. Like Simeon, we can receive and
welcome Him. And like Simeon, we can hold Him in our hands
as eucharistic Bread, and consume Him as nourishment for eternal life.

Lord, now let your servants depart in peace, for by your infinite
grace and compassion our eyes have seen your salvation!

15
The Meeting of an Iconographer

L EONID OUSPENSKY was by any reckoning one of the greatest iconographers of the last century. He never sent a bill for his work and usually refused to suggest a fee. If his eyesight had not diminished beyond a certain point, he would have continued to produce miniature carvings of triptychs and single panels, gems of workmanship that rival his own painted icons—and most of the wood carvings found in museums. He was a blessed genius, a man whose humility hid an extraordinary, God-given talent.

One cold autumn day I visited the Ouspenskys in their apartment on the east side of Paris. I had met both Leonid and Lydia on several occasions, and I wanted to ask Leonid to paint an icon for me of the Meeting of our Lord. That feast is special to me because it marks the anniversary of my ordination to the priesthood. The most cherished gift I could imagine would be an icon of the feast, painted by this unquestioned master. [As an aside we might note that the widespread expression "to write and icon" is based on a misunderstanding. The Greek term *graphō* signifies not only "to write," but also "to sketch or paint." Books are written but icons are painted.]

I found the Ouspenskys' apartment building in a run-down neighborhood of the 11th arrondissement, climbed the dingy, winding stairway to the fourth floor, and knocked. The welcome into that tiny space, with its rough stone floor and straight-backed wooden chairs, was as warm as the atmosphere was ascetic. It was the home of poor folk, simple and good.

We talked most of the afternoon about the feast of the Meeting. I found the courage to ask if he would create an icon of the feast for me and explained why I wanted it—and why it would mean so much to me that he be the iconographer. Finally, he agreed.

During our conversation, I happened to mention that the image of the Meeting had always struck me as in some profound way eucharistic. We mulled that over for a while, and after another cup of tea, I left. I had the feeling my theological ramblings had left him quite unimpressed, and I wondered if I would ever hear from him again.

A couple of months later a package arrived, the rue Bréguet return address barely legible in the upper left hand corner. In the wrapping paper, with no special protection at all, was an icon.

Gone were the trappings of the Jerusalem temple. This icon revealed rather a New Testament altar, an altar of the Church. With Joseph in the background, Mary stands before Simeon, her hands upraised in a gesture of offering and supplication. Simeon holds the child in his arms, as though offering Him back to His holy Mother. The child's hand is outstretched in a blessing. And directly beneath that hand, resting on the altar, is a chalice.

The righteous Elder holds in his arms the Bread of Life. Beneath the infant's hand of blessing is the Cup of Salvation. This child, presented to the old man to receive his blessing, Himself blesses all those present. Simeon, for his part, performs the ultimate priestly gesture. Having received the child as a gift of Life, he offers Him both to God and to His Mother, for her salvation and for the life of the world.

With that icon, Leonid Ouspensky broke with tradition. Or, rather, this extraordinarily gifted artist, who preserved and reproduced the essence of traditional iconography with total faithfulness, expanded and deepened tradition. He sensed, better than most of us, that authentic tradition is truly "Living Tradition," which allows and even encourages freedom of expression and individual creativity. The only requirement is that whatever is new—in liturgy, in theological reflection, or in iconography—be created in faithful continuity with the past, with what has been "handed down" (*paradosis, traditio*) and accepted by the Church as canonical, authoritative, and normative.

Ouspensky's contributions in the area of iconography and other forms of graphic art are an encouragement to all of us to create, under the guidance of the Holy Spirit and in conformity with Holy Tradition, such things as new elements of liturgical worship, a new biblical lectionary (especially for the daily Epistles!), and new expressions of church architecture. The genius of Orthodoxy lies at least in part in its capacity to adapt: to express the truth of the Gospel of Christ in language and forms that speak to the contemporary culture. This includes expanding Holy Tradition as this man did, with faithfulness to the past and an eye toward the future.

Leonid is no longer with us in the flesh. I like to think, though, that he is still carving, still painting, still creating beautiful things—eucharistic things—in his own "Meeting with the Lord," whom he loved and so faithfully served.

16
Theophany: Divine Ecology

O NE OF THE GREAT THEMES of Orthodox theology is what we call the "transfiguration of the cosmos." It is a theme that underlies any truly Christian ecology. Ecology in the first instance concerns neither science nor politics. It describes the vocation that belongs to each of us as stewards of God's creation.

This theme has been a constant element of Christian life and faith since at least the end of the first century. Its fullest and most beautiful expression is given in the feast of Holy Theophany, which in Eastern Christianity is celebration of Jesus' baptism in the waters of the Jordan River.

Sometime between the years 107 and 117, St Ignatius, bishop of Antioch, was led in chains to Rome, where he met a martyr's death in the Colosseum. During his journey, Ignatius penned several letters to churches throughout the Mediterranean world. In one letter, to the Ephesians, he declares that Christ "was born and baptized, in order to purify the water by His passion" (18:2). The actual meaning of the statement has long been debated. What is clear is the fact that Ignatius affirms, for the first time, that Christ's baptism had the effect of renewing an element of creation, even creation itself.

Orthodoxy takes up this theme and develops it particularly during the Forefeast of Holy Theophany. The analogous celebration in Western Christianity is called "Epiphany," likewise celebrated on January 6. It focuses on the visit to the Christ child by the Magi or "three wise men." Both terms, "theophany" and "epiphany," signify "manifestation" or "revelation." Both forms of the feast, Western and Eastern, concern the revelation to the world of "God become man," of the "Word become flesh" (John 1:14).

Orthodox tradition celebrates the theophany, manifestation, or revelation of Christ as Son of God not at His birth, but at the time of His baptism in the Jordan River at the hands of His cousin "John the Baptizer." The Forefeast of Theophany captures the sense of this revelation in a striking vesperal hymn:

> Make ready, O river Jordan: for behold, Christ our God draws near to be baptized by John, that He may crush with His divinity the invisible heads of the dragons in your waters . . ."

Here the essential motifs of the feast express fundamental elements of the Orthodox faith. Jesus of Nazareth, who draws near to be baptized, is none other than "Christ our God," the Messiah of Israel and eternal Son of the Father. His descent into the waters of the Jordan is a prefiguration of His future descent into Hades, following the crucifixion. There He will liberate humankind through the power of His resurrection, His victory over the lesser powers of death and corruption. Here in the Jordan, His mission—the very effect of His presence—is to destroy the power of Satan and to free us from bondage to "the Evil One."

In a broader sense, the same motif appears in the compline service of the Forefeast:

> The earth has been sanctified, O Word, by Your holy birth, and the heavens with the stars declared Your glory. And now the nature of the waters is blessed by Your baptism in the flesh, and mankind has been restored once more to its former nobility.

The crowds who answered John's call came to be baptized with a "baptism of repentance." Jesus has no need of such a baptism. Yet He willingly enters into the waters of the Jordan and does so for two reasons. First, to demonstrate his loving solidarity with all those who seek God, who long through this purification to welcome the Lord's Messiah.

Equally important is the second reason. As St Ignatius and the festal hymns of Theophany make clear, Christ enters the waters to renew all of creation. By the power of His divinity, demonic influence is destroyed and the waters are purified. That purification, however, is a very real foretaste of the transfiguration and ultimate renewal of God's creation.

If there is indeed an "Orthodox ecology," it is one that must be grounded in this vision of St Ignatius and of the Church's liturgy: the vision of a new creation, of the New Jerusalem, of the restoration of all things to their primal purity and beauty.

The world we live in is tragically removed from this vision. Nevertheless, by keeping the feast of Holy Theophany, we reaffirm a fundamental hope: that little by little we may reassume our stewardship over God's handiwork, offer up the world to the Creator as an act of praise, and allow Him to bring about nothing less than the transfiguration of the entire created order.

> With mighty voice let us ascribe praise to the Master. He is come and is made manifest, He goes down into the waters. He who covers the heavens with clouds is stripped bare and baptized, cleansing us who sing: Let the whole creation bless the Lord and exalt Him above all for ever!
>
> (Feast of Theophany, matins of the Forefeast, canticle 8)

17

Tempted by Satan

*J*ESUS' BAPTISM IS THE ARCHETYPE and ground of our own baptism. By submitting to this sacramental ritual of the Church, we are enabled to participate in Christ's own death and resurrection. St Paul elaborates this theme in Romans 6. In Galatians 2, he spells out its consequences. Through baptism, the Christian can affirm: "I have been crucified with Christ; it is no longer I who live, but Christ who lives in me!"

The same may be said of Jesus' temptation in the wilderness and the reality of temptation in our own lives. Jesus' victory in the face of Satan is the archetype and ground of our own victory over demonic power.

Embedded in the opening passage of Mark's Gospel (1:1–15) is the brief account of Jesus' temptation (verses 12–13). This segment, like the entire passage, is structured in concentric parallelism. A literal translation gives us the following arrangement:

> A : And immediately the *Spirit cast* [Jesus] out into the desert.
> > B : And He was in the desert *forty days*
> > > **C : being tempted by Satan.**
> > B': And He was with the *wild beasts*,
> A': and the *angels* were *ministering* to Him.

Again, we can read the passage in two complementary ways: from beginning to end, and from the extremities toward the center.

169

The latter reading leads from the first line (A) to the last (A'), then from the second line (B) to the penultimate (B'), where in each case the prime element heightens or completes the first statement (the Holy Spirit sent Him / angels ministered to Him; forty days / wild beasts). The unit then concludes with the focus or center of meaning—the "point" of the entire passage—at C: Jesus is tempted by Satan.

The passage opens with the statement that Jesus was driven into the desert *by the Holy Spirit*. God the Father is "responsible" for the temptation experienced by His Son. This is paralleled by assurance that *angels* minister to Jesus during His time of trial. The intensity of the struggle Jesus had to assume is stressed by B:B'. He spent *forty days* in the wilderness (recalling the forty years Israel spent in its wilderness wanderings); and he was *with the wild beasts*. The central affirmation then focuses on the temptation itself: immediately after His baptism, Jesus is obliged to face the Tempter, whose domain is the desert and whose legions are symbolized by the wild beasts. Yet He is ministered to *by angels*!

Jesus' experience in the face of temptation thus prepares the way for the victory achieved by all those who struggle to live their life "in Christ." St Mark was acutely aware of this point. His entire Gospel focuses on Jesus' defeat of Satan, represented by a multitude of exorcisms and other healings. By virtue of His passion, death, and resurrection, Jesus faces and destroys the power of death. Similarly, at the beginning of His public ministry, the newly anointed Messiah is driven by the Spirit into the wastelands of human existence, there to do battle on our behalf with every demon we have ever welcomed as our own.

Temptation is not sin. Jesus was tempted as we are, yet He did not sin. His trials in this regard served to create a solidarity between Himself and every one of us. All that we suffer in the face of temptation He too has experienced. This testing which He assumed enables Him to accompany us through temptations that threaten to wreak spiritual havoc in our lives. And that accompaniment provides us with the power to withstand temptation, since our life "in

Christ" means that we participate in His victory over demonic might. "Because He Himself has suffered and been tempted, He is able to help those who are tempted" (Heb 4:15; 2:18).

Temptations can destroy us. Subtly, insidiously, they infect our mind, heart, soul, and body. The ancient Fathers and Mothers who voluntarily went out into the desert knew they would face terrible temptations. We create our own desert wastelands, and there we have to face our own demons. And they can certainly destroy us.

Jesus' own experience, though, can become ours, just as it became the experience of the desert dwellers. If we are driven into the wilderness of temptation, it is always with the presence and purpose of the Holy Spirit. In the midst of even the greatest temptations, God never abandons us. We may find ourselves facing Satan, surrounded by the "wild beasts" of passions, thoughts, doubts, and a multitude of other seductive desires or compulsive fixations. Yet the message of Jesus' own temptation is that He was there before us, and by His trials He defeated the Enemy once and for all.

In the course of our own life we are invited to make that same pilgrimage, from the baptismal waters through the wilderness of temptation. Yet all that is needed to withstand the Tempter has been provided. Through the worst of it there is the assurance that Jesus is present with us. Through the darkest night of the soul there remains the conviction—grounded in the personal experience of saints throughout the ages—that we are ministered to by angels.

18

Holy Saturday: "With Fear and Trembling"

MIRACULOUSLY, Orthodox Christianity has preserved the essence of "the faith once for all delivered to the saints" (Jude 3). By the sheer grace of God, it has maintained the apostolic faith in the face of extraordinary pressures, from persecution and martyrdom to Western secularism and pluralism. Without that grace, Orthodoxy would have disappeared before the end of the first millennium. And with it would have disappeared "true belief" and "true worship."

Because of its God-given survival and God-inspired expansion throughout what is called "the diaspora," Orthodoxy continues to preserve, proclaim, and celebrate the truth about God and about ourselves. More than any other expression of Christian faith, it enables us to know God, to celebrate His saving work, and to participate in His very life. To borrow the expression of St Innocent Veniaminov, Orthodoxy does nothing less than indicate to us and guide us along the Way that leads to the kingdom of heaven.

That Way, nevertheless, includes an aspect that is particularly difficult to preserve and cultivate in modern American society: an aspect expressed most eloquently in the Entrance Hymn of the Divine Liturgy of Holy Saturday, borrowed from the Liturgy of St James. On that day, we sing with solemn anticipation words that express *awe*—"fear and trembling"—before the ineffable mystery of the death and coming resurrection of God's eternal Son.

Let all mortal flesh keep silence, and in fear and trembling stand, pondering nothing earthly-minded. For the King of kings, and the Lord of lords, comes to be slain, to give Himself as food to the faithful!

In the usual celebrations of the Divine Liturgy, we exhort ourselves and one another to "lay aside all earthly cares," in order to receive "the King of all." On Holy Saturday, as we commemorate Christ's repose in the tomb and His descent into the realm of the dead, we recall the price paid for our own liberation from death and corruption. We declare that He, the preexistent divine Son of the Father, came into our world and into our life for one purpose: to die, that through His death we might have life, lived in eternal communion with the Holy Trinity.

There is nothing in human experience, nor even in the human imagination, that could offer greater promise and greater joy than this central message of the Christian gospel. Yet for most of us, the most familiar and painful aspect of our lenten journey is likely to be our inability to relate to that message—to that extraordinary promise—in a way that actually changes our life. Distraction, dispersion, and chaos, whether from outside or from deep within our own psyche, exercise their demonic influence in every phase of our daily life, while we are at work, with our friends or family, or in a liturgical service. And so we live our lives on the surface, feeling little and caring little for what is in fact the one thing in this world that really matters, the one thing that is truly needful.

Holy Saturday calls us back to what is essential. In the Entrance Hymn especially, it reminds us that our life is a battle ground, where a constant struggle pits us against the Enemy, against the worst inclinations of our fallen nature. Appropriately, it calls us to engage in that struggle with fear, with trembling, and in silence.

One of the great teachers of Orthodox tradition, the fifth-century mystic, Diodochos of Photiki, captured the vital link between inner silence and spiritual warfare with these words:

Spiritual knowledge comes through prayer, deep stillness and complete detachment . . . When the soul's incensive power [*thymikon*, spiritual wrath] is aroused against the passions, we should know it is time for silence, since the hour of battle is at hand.*

At the close of Holy Week, as we journey with our Lord toward His resurrection, we hear once again in the words of the Great Saturday Hymn of Entrance an invitation to enter into that silence: silence which is essential if we are to assume with real faithfulness the ascetic struggle that characterizes our entire "life in Christ."

In that silence we stand in holy awe before the King of kings and Lord of lords. For a few moments we move beyond the superficiality of our social and cultural existence: the noise, the distraction, and the pointlessness of our daily routine. By the grace of God we discover at least a minimum of "prayer, deep stillness, and detachment." In that stillness—in the silence granted to our mortal flesh— we contemplate the unfathomable depths of Jesus' sacrificial love, for ourselves and for all mankind. And "with fear and trembling" we receive Him as eucharistic food, the Bread of heaven, which nourishes us to eternal life.

---

*"On Spiritual Knowledge," *The Philokalia* Vol I (London, Faber & Faber, 1979) 255.

19

Pascha: Through the Cross, Joy!

T HE TWO MOST IMPORTANT antinomies or paradoxes of Christian faith are the incarnation of the Son of God and His resurrection from the dead. Both of these find their fulfillment in the celebration of Easter, known in Orthodox tradition as Holy Pascha: the Passover of our Lord from death to life.

A resurrectional hymn sung at each eucharistic celebration reminds us that every such celebration commemorates and actualizes for us Christ's victory over death. The theme of that hymn is the paradoxical affirmation, "Through the Cross, joy has come into all the world!"

This affirmation speaks simply and eloquently to the overriding concern of our generation: anxiety in the face of death. Our entire culture, it seems, from the distractions of creature comforts to the urge to clone ourselves, has been shaped—deformed—by the single-minded desire to deny, if not escape, the reality of death. For most people, death means the ultimate annihilation of their every achievement, their carefully cultivated self-image, their very existence. A voice whispers in their ear, "You are dust and to dust you shall return."

Yet the promise of Easter, and its miracle, is the promise of life beyond death. Through the Cross of Christ, by virtue of His death and resurrection, our life has become a spiritual pilgrimage that leads us beyond the crisis of physical death to life without end. This

175

pilgrimage is charted for us by the stages of Great Lent, with its ascetical practices and intensified prayer. Here, in this life, we engage in spiritual warfare so that one day we might enjoy everlasting peace in the kingdom of God. Here we dwell in exile, but with full knowledge that we are created and invited to partake forever of God's own divine life.

The true message of Easter is most eloquently expressed in the icon of the Descent of Christ into Hell, or Sheol, the abode of the departed. In Western traditions, the Resurrection of our Lord is depicted as a victorious rising from the tomb. In Orthodoxy, the Resurrection is proclaimed by the image of the glorified Christ descending into the abyss. "In the tomb with the body, in hell with the soul as God. . . ."

Without surrendering His divine nature, the eternal Son of God assumes all the conditions of human existence. In an act of total self-abnegation, in perfect obedience to the will of the Father, He accepts the "kenotic," or self-emptying, movement that leads from the Virgin's womb to the humiliating agony of the Cross.

Yet even on the cross His descent is not complete. The tormented cry, "My God, my God, why . . . ?" is not the final word, nor is the surrender of His spirit the final act of self-emptying. He must still descend into the far reaches of the Abyss, the realm of death, in order there to break the bonds of death. He, the Second Adam and perfect Man, must reach out to touch, renew, and raise into His glory the First Adam, humankind fallen from life, who dwells in the land of shadows.

This descent, this final and ultimate penetration into the realm of the dead, is accomplished once and for all. It frees patriarch, prophet, and king. But at the same time it frees us, liberating us from the consequences of death. The hand that reaches out to grasp the hands of Adam and Eve reaches out to embrace their descendants as well: every "Adam" who responds to His gesture with longing and with faith.

We, like Adam of the Paschal icon, are bound, held captive by the powers of sin, death and corruption. We too have "died" and have cast ourselves into a hell of our own making, far from the presence of the Giver of Life. Yet He comes to us as to lost sheep, descending in His compassionate love to seek us out in the darkness and to raise us up with Himself. Like Francis Thompson's Hound of Heaven, He pursues us "down the nights and down the days . . . down the arches of the years," that in the end He might summon us, "Rise, clasp My hand, and come!" Even if we make our bed in hell (Ps 138/139!), He is there, ever present, ever reaching out to lift us with Himself into the glory of resurrected life.

As the Scriptures so clearly attest, however, this life, this participation in the resurrection of our Lord, is not merely a future hope. It is, prophetically yet in truth, a present reality. Together with all of creation we sigh with longing, awaiting the revelation of the children of God. "Here indeed," St Paul reminds us, "we groan and long to put on our heavenly dwelling." Our true home, the fulfillment of our created existence, is in the heavens, beyond the pale of physical death. The true meaning of our life is only to be found in the transformation of this body of flesh into a body of spirit, through the full and perfect restoration within us of the image of God.

Yet this transformation begins in the here and now, in the present moment of our earthly life. For the victory of Christ is a victory over time, just as it is over sin and death. Dwelling within this earthly tent, struggling with the powers of darkness in the often tragic events of daily life, we can nevertheless walk here, today, in the eternal light of His glory. Reaching out to Him, often in lonely anguish, we find that He truly does wipe away every tear. And that experience allows us, even in the face of death—our own or that of a loved one—to live with a profound sense of hope. Through the Cross of Christ, death is no more, neither mourning nor sorrow, neither anguish nor pain. "For behold," the voice from the heavenly throne declares, "the former things have passed away; all has been made anew" (Rev 21).

Those who make the lenten pilgrimage, through the dark of night and on to the radiant brightness of the Paschal dawn, pass by the Way of the Cross to arrive at the splendor of resurrected life. To them, fear of the future—anxiety in the face of death—is transfigured into joy. For they know what each of us in the depths of our soul longs to know: that by enduring the Cross for us, Christ has truly destroyed death by death.

20

Emmaus: Image of the Liturgy

THE ENDING OF ST MARK'S Gospel includes several appearances of the Risen Lord to his disciples, beginning with Mary Magdalene. It also makes a brief reference to other witnesses: "He appeared in a different form to two of them, while they were walking to the country" (16:12).

This is almost certainly a summary account of the appearance to Cleopas and his companion—traditionally considered to be St Luke himself—which occurred as the two men journeyed from Jerusalem to the village of Emmaus (Lk 24:13–35). This "Emmaus story" is one of the most well-known and beloved narratives in the New Testament. As a report of an appearance of the resurrected Christ, it is a literary and theological masterpiece. Yet it is more than that. It also offers a striking description of the Church's eucharistic liturgies.

Those liturgies have come down to us, from both East and West, in very similar form. In Eastern Orthodox tradition, they begin with a Liturgy of the Word (also called Liturgy of the Catechumens), consisting of biblical hymns, followed by a reading of Scripture and a homily based on the selected text(s). The second major part of the eucharistic service is the Liturgy of the Faithful, during which bread and wine are consecrated and transformed into the Body and Blood of Christ, to be consumed in an act of "communion" in and with the living Lord. The service closes with a dismissal, which represents a sending forth of the worshipers to proclaim and live their faith through words and actions: proclamation of the gospel and works of love.

The foundation for this liturgical celebration is provided by the Passover meal Christ celebrated with His disciples on the night of His betrayal and arrest. In the Upper Room, He performed what is called the "institution" of the Lord's Supper or Eucharist, by adding to the Jewish Passover ritual the words, "This is my Body . . . This is my Blood . . . given for you." The bread and wine are images of His own body and blood, soon to be broken and shed on the cross. But they are more than images. They offer believers the possibility to share in His life and sacrifice by consuming what some have called "metaphysical food," the Body and Blood of the risen and glorified Lord.

Once the meal was finished, Jesus and His disciples sang the Passover hymn (Ps 117/118), went out to the Garden of Gethsemane, and awaited the tragic events that would lead to His death and resurrection. The appearances of the Risen Lord would then be followed by the disciples' extraordinary mission, proclaiming that Jesus is alive, that He has destroyed death itself by His victory over the power of death.

This is precisely the pattern of events experienced by the Emmaus disciples.

As they journeyed toward the village, the stranger who accompanied them explained, on the basis of the Law and the Prophets, that the events surrounding the mission of Jesus of Nazareth were ordained by God. "He explained to them [in fact] the things concerning Himself. . . ." Although their hearts "burned within them" at His teaching, they did not recognize Him. The meaning of Scripture became clear, but the One who taught them remained incognito.

As they approached the village, the disciples invited this stranger into the house where they were going and insisted that He preside at the evening meal. He took a loaf of bread and performed the same gestures He performed on the mountainside as He fed the five thousand and in the Upper Room as He "instituted" the Lord's

Supper. "He took bread, blessed (God), broke and gave it to them. And their eyes were opened and they recognized Him. And He vanished out of their sight!" Awe-struck and rejoicing, the two men left the house and returned to Jerusalem. There they proclaimed to the other disciples the good news that Jesus is risen, "and how He was recognized by them in the breaking of the bread."

On the roadway to Emmaus, the disciples participated with Jesus in the first post-resurrectional "Liturgy of the Word." In the house—an image of the Church—their eyes were opened, and they recognized Him once He took bread and performed gestures that would become the heart of every eucharistic celebration. Following this "Liturgy of the Faithful," they rose and went to proclaim the gospel, the good news that death has been overcome, and Christ has brought life to the world.

St Luke's message to his readers is this: through eucharistic celebration the gathered community shares in Christ's own death and resurrection. The faithful hear the gospel proclamation. Yet that proclamation must be complemented and fulfilled by the sacramental act of communion. Their eyes are only truly opened once they consume the Body and Blood of the risen Lord. Then they too must rise and go, to share their joy with others.

Their experience of the resurrected Lord becomes our experience through the celebration of "Word" and "Sacrament." And their Paschal joy becomes ours as well. For through our eucharistic communion we too come to know that Christ is risen, that death has lost its sting, and that we are given, through Christ and in Him, the gift of everlasting life.

21

Death's Demise

D YLAN THOMAS WROTE SOME eminently quotable lines on the
subject of death. The most familiar and powerful are also the
most troubling:

> Do not go gentle into that good night. Rage, rage against the dying
> of the light.

This ringing summons to courage (or revolt?) in the face of one's
approaching end betrays an all too common attitude toward death.
In this perspective, death is and remains the last enemy. However
much one may rage against it, death ultimately achieves its victory;
it inevitably makes felt its lethal sting.

More to the point is a line Thomas penned in 1942, while war
was ravaging Western Europe and North Africa. Each stanza of this
pained yet hope-filled piece begins and ends with the same word of
assurance:

> And death shall have no dominion.

These words come to mind at every Paschal season, and they
elicit a certain sadness. Behind the poem's call to courage and the
sense that in a mad and violent world something good will remain,
there lurks a persistent fatalism in the face of the inevitable. Sooner
or later, every personal existence will come to an end. The fierce

tears of rage are no defense against "that good night." One day dead men's bones will be picked clean, and lovers will indeed be lost, even if love is not. . . .

Prevailing pressures in Western societies for euthanasia and physician-assisted suicide are symptomatic. They reflect a culture obsessed with physical death: obsessed with it and in dread of it, because death signifies the frustration of individual ambitions and the demise of personal achievements. Its finality proves that life itself is devoid of meaning. Hence the frantic concern to "die with dignity," which means to die without suffering, without inconvenience, without noticing it.

It also means to die without the Cross. Jesus, on the other hand, did not die with dignity. He died with an anguished cry on His lips and a body wracked with pain. And by that death, stripped of every shred of "dignity," He gave every life and every death the possibility for infinite meaning.

Where do we locate that possibility, and how do we actualize it in the course of our everyday life? In his letter to the Romans the apostle Paul provides us with the only reasonable answer to that question. There, in chapter six, he makes the point that our real death occurs at baptism.

> We were buried with [Christ] by baptism into death, so that as Christ was raised from the dead by the glory of the Father, we too might walk in newness of life. For if we have been united with him in a death like his, we shall certainly be united with him in a resurrection like his.

Prior to baptism the life we lead is strictly biological. We are born in the "old Adam" and continue in him until we die. That death, for the great majority of people, is itself biological: it comes as the result of an irreversible cessation of brain and cardio-respiratory function.

For those who are baptized into Christ, though, the matter is very different. Their actual death occurs at the moment they are plunged into the baptismal waters. Co-crucified with Christ, they are "co-buried" with Him (Col 2:12)—and raised up into a "newness of life." From this point on, they lead what can be called "eschatological existence." Dwelling on earth in the dimensions of time and space, they share at the same time in eternal life: a radically new, transcendent mode of being. United to Christ as members of His Body, they commune already, here and now, in the peace, the righteousness, and the glory of the kingdom of God.

For such people, physical death is no longer a source of dread. It no longer signifies the end of personal existence, and with it the frustration of hopes and ambitions. It no longer means that life is devoid of meaning, that we await nothing more than the return to dust of our mortal bones.

For those among us who have died in baptism and risen to newness of life, the imminence of death no longer portends the dying of the light. Through the victory of Pascha, our physical death translates us precisely from darkness into light, into the radiant splendor of the everlasting Light that illumines all things. So rather than dread death, we embrace it. Rather than flee, deny and curse it, we welcome it as the final stage of our earthly pilgrimage, our life in Christ, that gives ultimate meaning and value to even the smallest tasks we accomplish with faithfulness, the most personal relationships we assume with love.

For those who die with Christ in baptism and rise with Him in newness of life, that life has value and meaning beyond all they can hope and imagine. Their flesh may well return to dust, and their bones, picked clean, may one day disappear. Their earthly ambitions may remain unfulfilled, and their suffering in this present age may go unexplained. Their approaching end may still provoke anxiety, and their infirmity bring with it dependency, pain, and doubt.

But one thing above all preserves them from despair and the temptation of suicide. It is the absolute certainty, grounded in their experience of the inexhaustible love of the Crucified Lord, that for them, just as for Him, death indeed has no dominion.

22
During the Fifty Days

*T*HE GREAT FEAST OF PENTECOST occurs fifty days after Easter, known in Orthodox tradition as Holy Pascha. Between Pascha and Pentecost we celebrate our liturgical services using the book called the *Pentecostarion*. Like all liturgical books, the *Pentecostarion* is filled with hymns that offer praise and glorification to God for His saving work. That work reached its culmination with Christ's resurrection and ascension, together with the sending of the Holy Spirit upon the Church, the gathered community of the faithful.

The *Pentecostarion* focuses to a large degree on the theme of water. Reference is made repeatedly to images of "flowing streams," "well-springs," and "living water." In ancient Jewish liturgical practice, priests processed to the Jerusalem Temple at this season, bearing water from the fountain of Siloam. This occurred on the first day of Sukkoth, the feast of Tabernacles, or Booths, which originally celebrated the harvest but came to signify God's deliverance of the Israelites from the land of Egypt (Lev 23:42f).

In Christian practice, this festival is replaced by an ongoing celebration of Christ's resurrection, with a particular focus on the theme of water. During this fifty-day period the Sunday Gospel readings include Jesus' healing of the paralytic by the sheep-pool of Bethzatha, His encounter with the Samaritan woman at the well of Jacob, and His healing of the blind man in the waters of Siloam

(Jn 5, 4, and 9). In each case, the water symbolizes Christ, the "Living Water," who quenches every thirst and sustains His people in their pilgrimage toward eternal life. It also symbolizes His *replacement* of both the Old Covenant feasts and their symbolic water sources: Christ replaces the sheep-pool, Jacob's well, and the Siloam fountain by providing "spiritual water." As He declares to the woman of Samaria, "Whoever drinks of the water I shall give will never thirst again. The water I shall give will become a spring of water welling up to eternal life!"

The great but often neglected feast of Mid-Pentecost (Wednesday of the fourth week after Pascha) brings together with magnificent hymnody the major themes of Pascha, Ascension, and Pentecost: the Resurrection and Christ's glorification, together with the outpouring of the Holy Spirit. On the eve of the feast we read a passage from the prophecy of Isaiah 55, which again focuses on the image of water: "Thus says the Lord, 'Everyone who thirsts, come to the waters . . . Incline your ear, and come to me; hear that your soul may live; and I will make with you an everlasting covenant'." As the day of Pentecost draws near, the Holy Spirit Himself is depicted as Living Water, poured out upon believers to fulfill God's promise made through the prophet Joel: "I will pour out my Spirit upon all flesh."

Yet the feast of Pentecost—and the entire *Pentecostarion*—can only be understood if we perceive it "eschatologically," that is, in light of God's promise finally, "at the last day," to bring light out of darkness and life out of death. Just as the feast of Tabernacles became transformed into a living commemoration of Israel's liberation from Egypt—itself a symbolic image of coming salvation—so Pentecost and all that precedes it commemorates both past and future.

On the one hand, we remember the former outpouring of the Holy Spirit upon the Church, recounted in Acts 2, and we celebrate His life among us and within us as we journey toward the kingdom of heaven. At the same time, we celebrate what has not yet occurred, but exists in our collective "memory" in the form of hope.

Just as we "remember" during the eucharistic prayer "the second and glorious Coming" of Christ—which has not yet occurred—so we commemorate the final outpouring of Living Water that will bring God's saving work to its completion.

With the Church of all ages, the living and the departed, we celebrate the great feast of Pentecost with the fervent hope expressed by the prophet John at the close of the Book of Revelation: "The Spirit and the Bride [the Church] say, 'Come.' And let him who is thirsty come, let him who desires take the Water of Life without price."

During those fifty days, we are invited to come to that Living Source, the Fountain of Living Water, who is Christ the Lord. We remember and celebrate His resurrection from the dead, His ascension into glory, and the outpouring of His Spirit. Yet we remember and celebrate as well the hope that is ours, in anticipation of full and perfect sharing in Christ's life: that hope which the apostle Paul calls "the hope of glory" (Col 1:27).

23

Ascended in Glory

*T*HE FEAST OF CHRIST'S Ascension is seldom given its due in the cycle of liturgical services, even within the Orthodox tradition. This is in part because it falls awkwardly on a Thursday, when most of our parishioners are at work. More significant is the fact that the theology, the deeply spiritual meaning of the feast, is not well understood.

The Ascension is difficult for us to grasp because the image it evokes seems so improbable. St Luke gives us two accounts of the event, at the close of his Gospel and at the beginning of the book of Acts. In the Gospel account, the risen Lord leads His disciples to the village of Bethany, beyond Jerusalem. Then, "while He blessed them, He parted from them, and was carried up into heaven" (Lk 24:51). In Acts Christ's Ascension occurs forty days after the Resurrection. He promises to send upon the disciples the gift of the Holy Spirit, then He gives them the charge to be His witnesses to the ends of the earth. "And when He had said this," St Luke continues, "as they were looking on, He was lifted up, and a cloud took Him out of their sight." At this point, a pair of angelic beings informs the disciples that Jesus has been taken up into heaven and will return to them in the same manner as He ascended, "on the clouds."

It would be easy to dismiss these accounts. First, they reflect what many consider today to be a naive and untenable cosmology, the vision of a universe in which Jesus was literally "taken up" to heaven, understood as "up there," geographically locatable some-where in outer space (or beyond). Second, the accounts seem to contradict each other. Did Jesus ascend on the Sunday of the Res-urrection, or on a Thursday, the fortieth day?

In attempting to grasp the real meaning of this celebration, we need to remind ourselves once again that the Gospel writers were concerned less with history than with theology. They sought, through multiple images expressed by divergent traditions, to con-vey the inner meaning of Christ's life, even if that led occasionally to inconsistencies (John and Luke offer two differing accounts of Pentecost as well, in John 20 and Acts 2, just as Matthew and Acts differ in their description of Judas' death). What, then, is the theo-logical significance of Christ's Ascension?

The Ascension is in fact the fulfillment of the Incarnation. The eternal Son of God "took flesh" in the womb of the Virgin Mary. That is, He assumed human nature and "became man"—a particu-lar man, Jesus of Nazareth—without giving up His divinity. As we sing in the troparion "Only Begotten Son of God," He became man "without change." In the language of the Eastern Fathers, He became truly the God-man, "fully God and fully man." And He did so in order to restore our humanity from its fallen, sinful state to its state of original perfection, as God created it to be.

God intended His human creatures to share forever in the joy and gladness of Paradise, that is, in the deepest possible commun-ion with Himself. But God also created us as free beings, in order that we might love Him in perfect freedom, without constraint. Sin, though, put an end to that intended relationship. We rebelled against God, and continue to do so. The result is our alienation from the only real source of life, love, and salvation. Finally, that rebel-lion leads to our death.

Most of us memorized John 3:16 in church school. Those famil-iar words contain the whole of the mystery of God's ineffable love for us: "God so loved the world that He gave His only Son," that through His sacrifice death might be conquered, and we might receive the gift of eternal life.

The great feast of Christ's Resurrection, Holy Pascha, enables us to recall and to relive His victory over death. That victory becomes our own, however, only through the Ascension. For Christ's Ascension marks the final step in God's movement toward His fallen creatures. "No one has ascended into heaven," Jesus tells His disciples, "except He who descended from heaven, the Son of Man" (Jn 3:13). If the Son of Man and Son of God "descended" from heaven, it was to become "incarnate": to assume our fallen human nature, and as a human being to suffer, to die, and to rise from the dead, in order to vanquish death and restore our nature to its intended perfection.

Yet in order for that work to be fulfilled, He must "ascend" to His place of origin, bearing our human nature in Himself, in order to glorify it with Himself. This is the meaning of the kontakion of the Ascension in the Orthodox liturgy:

> When Thou didst fulfill the dispensation for our sake, and unite earth to heaven, Thou didst ascend in glory, O Christ our God, not being parted from those who love Thee, but remaining with them and crying, "I am with you and no one will be against you."

By virtue of His Ascension, Jesus the "Forerunner" has entered the heavenly sanctuary, the Holy of Holies, and has done so on our behalf (Heb 6:20). There as the great High Priest He serves an eternal Eucharist, a celebration of His triumphant victory over death and the restoration of the created order to its "original," that is, its intended beauty and harmony (the meaning of "cosmos"). There as the heavenly Paraclete He makes perpetual intercession on our behalf before the Father (1 Jn 2:1–2). From there He reaches out, in communion with all the saints and the heavenly host, to bless, guide, and preserve us in this present age, in the time and space of our daily life. And thereby, through His presence in our own ceaseless eucharistic celebration, He fulfills His promise to remain with us until the end of the age.

However much we may have lost touch with the significance of the feast of the Ascension, it remains a central and indispensable celebration in the life of the Church. By ascending into the heavenly sanctuary, Christ fulfills the movement toward exaltation begun with His Resurrection, and prepares the Church for a continual pentecostal effusion of the Holy Spirit.

By that Ascension, as the kontakion declares, "Christ unites earth to heaven." He completes the work of incarnation by uniting our fallen nature to His perfect divine nature. Thereby, exalting us with Himself, He fulfills our deepest hope and our deepest longing, by granting us a share in His eternal glory.

24

Pentecost: The "Person" of the Holy Spirit

THE SEASON AFTER PENTECOST seems to be another of those lost periods of the liturgical year. The joyous celebration of Holy Pascha is over, and with the feast of Pentecost we revert to the "ordinary" time of the Church's calendar.

This feast, nevertheless, like that of the Ascension, reveals and fulfills the work of the Son of God for the salvation of the world. Rather than mark a simple transition from Easter joy to summer doldrums, it opens the way for us to share, directly and personally, in Christ's victory over the powers of sin and death.

In Orthodox tradition, Pentecost Sunday is actually dedicated to celebration of the Holy Trinity. To understand the deeper meaning of Pentecost and to grasp something of the ineffable mystery of the Holy Spirit, we need to proclaim and celebrate what Scripture reveals and ecclesial experience confirms: that the One God in His innermost reality (*ad intra*) is a communion of three Persons, united by a common divine nature, a common will, and an inexhaustible mutual love.

On the Monday of Pentecost, we celebrate the momentous event recounted in Acts 2: the descent of the Holy Spirit upon the gathered disciples, to constitute the apostolic Church. We remember, through Scripture readings and liturgical hymns, that following His Ascension into heaven, Christ prayed to the Father, asking that He send the Spirit upon the nascent community, to make of its members "fishers of men": apostles sent into the world to call women and men everywhere to repentance and to a living participation in the life of the Risen Lord.

This celebration proclaims as well the presence and power of the Spirit within the Church and within the world of today, within our own immediate experience. It is this living experience of the Spirit within and among us that obliges us to ask in what sense the Spirit is a "Person," an *hypostasis,* or substantial reality characterized by personal qualities of reason, will, and love.

By dedicating Pentecost Sunday to celebration of the Holy Trinity, the Church affirms that the Spirit, as fully as the Father and the Son, is God. The Nicene Creed states unambiguously: the Holy Spirit is "Lord and Giver of Life." He "proceeds from the Father" from all eternity (Jn 15:26), and together with the Father and the Son He is "worshiped and glorified." These are qualities that can only pertain to a personal being. Therefore we proclaim, as Orthodox Christians, that the Spirit, as fully as the Father and the Son, is indeed a divine Person. Such is the faith, the bedrock conviction, of the Church.

But is this conviction biblical? The question arises because in the Old Testament we read that the Spirit of the Lord, the *ruach Yahweh,* descends on prophets, judges, and kings as some impersonal force, a virtual fluid, sent by God and originating with Him, but not necessarily of divine nature, and certainly not a "personal" being. Rather, the Spirit of the Lord is likened to God's "breath," an aspect of His own being and indistinguishable from Him.

The same seems to be the case in certain key passages of the New Testament. In John 20, the risen Christ appears to His disciples on the evening of the Resurrection, breathes on them and says, "Receive the Holy Spirit!" Is this any other than the "spirit" Christ gave up at His death on the Cross? Then again, during His earthly ministry Jesus declared to Nicodemus, "the Spirit (*pneuma*: breath, wind, spirit) blows where it wills. . . ." Finally we may note the way the apostle Paul speaks in a single verse of "the Spirit," "the Spirit of God," and "the Spirit of Christ" (Rom 8:9). References like these might well lead us to conclude that the Spirit is merely a manifestation of divine "breath," divine power that operates within the world as an impersonal force, to accomplish God's will. On what grounds can the Church claim that the Holy Spirit is a truly "personal" reality?

While a great many passages from both Testaments could be cited to support the Church's traditional view, the most important are to be found in the Gospel of John. These are passages that speak of the "Spirit of Truth," or "Paraclete" (Advocate, Counselor, or Helper). In His final teaching to His disciples shortly before His arrest and crucifixion, Jesus depicts the Spirit as a divine being like Himself, originating with the Father and destined to appear within human history, to fulfill the work of salvation and sanctification that Jesus Himself had begun. As Spirit of Truth, He dwells within the faithful. He receives the words of the risen Lord, in order to convey and interpret them to the Church and the world, and thereby He glorifies Jesus and fulfills Jesus' own ministry as Teacher and Prophet (Jn 14:16–17, 26; 15:26; 16:13–15). As Paraclete, the Spirit defends the faithful against persecution by a hostile and unbelieving world, while He pronounces judgment on the world and on its *archon*, its "Ruler," the devil (16:7–11). While Christ serves as our heavenly Paraclete or Advocate before the Father (1 Jn 2:1–2), the Spirit acts as our earthly Paraclete or Defender (hence the common translation of *parakletos* as "Comforter"). In all of His presence and operation, the Spirit is as "personal" a being as Christ Himself.

Then too, the second chapter of the Acts of the Apostles attests unequivocally that the earliest Christians knew the Spirit not merely as an occasional, charismatic power, but as the very presence of God in their midst. Although St Paul might qualify this presence as "of Christ" or "of God," he also knew the Spirit to be essentially "personal." The Spirit, he declares, prays within us and on our behalf (Rom 8:26); He works out our sanctification (Rom 15:16; 1 Cor 6:11; 2 Thess 2:13; cf. Gal 5:16–18); He pours out God's love into the hearts of believers, enabling them to address the Father by the familiar and intimate name, "Abba" (Rom 5:5; 8:15–16;

Gal 4:6); He confirms our status as "children of God" through His indwelling presence and power (Rom 8:16; Gal 4:6); He guides and preserves the faithful in their ascetic struggle against the passions (Gal 5:16); and He serves as the source and guarantor of our "freedom" from the constraints of the Law, a freedom which enables us to behold the glory of the Lord (2 Cor 3:17–18).

Through His activity within the world and within our life, the Spirit reveals Himself to be an essentially personal being, whose mission complements the saving work of the Father and the Son. Why is it so easy for us to conceive of the Father and the Son as persons, yet we find it so difficult to perceive the personal quality of the Spirit? The reason has been well articulated both by the ancient Fathers and by contemporary theologians who have prayerfully contemplated the mystery of divine life *ad extra*, within our life and experience.

The Spirit, they remind us, is the only divine Person who has no other Person to make Him known. The "face" or personal identity of the Father is revealed by the Person of the Son, the Father's eternal Word. The face of the Son is made known within the Christian community by the indwelling presence and inspirational activity of the Spirit. Yet the Spirit has no other Person to reveal His own face, His own personal identity, to us.

Nevertheless, the real significance of Pentecost lies precisely in its ability to reveal that identity, to make it known through the gospel proclamation and liturgical celebration. Through these ecclesial acts, the Church fulfills its primary mission: to lead us into the kingdom of God, where the face of the Spirit will finally be made known in all of its beauty and splendor. There, His face, His very Person, will be revealed in the radiant faces of the multitudes of human persons we know as "saints," holy people of the kind you and I are invited to become.

25
Bible and Liturgy

A DEFINING CHARACTERISTIC of Orthodox Christianity is the intimate and inseparable relationship it preserves between Bible and liturgy, between divine revelation as the canonical or normative source of our faith, and celebration of that faith in the worship of the Church. Faith, grounded in Scripture, determines the content of our worship; worship gives expression to our faith.

This principle, once again, is expressed most succinctly in the Latin phrase *lex orandi lex est credendi*, our rule of worship is nothing other than our rule of belief. Our prayer is shaped by and expresses our theology, just as our theology is illumined and deepened by our prayer.

In our liturgical services we praise, bless, and adore the God from whom we receive saving grace and the gift of eternal life. Accordingly, our eucharistic Divine Liturgy concludes with a "Prayer before the ambon"—in the midst of the people—which begins,

> O Lord, who blessest those who bless Thee, and sanctifiest those who place their trust in Thee: Save Thy people and bless Thine inheritance. Preserve the fullness of Thy Church. . . .

The deeper meaning of "faith" (*pistis*) is "trust," total and unwavering confidence in God's utter faithfulness towards us. In response to our trust, expressed through the worship by which we "bless" Him, God bestows upon us still further blessings. Our relationship with Him involves a reciprocal movement. Through worship we offer ourselves to Him, yet through that same worship He offers Himself to us. We "bless" Him by our thanksgiving, our adoration, and our praise; and we are blessed by Him through the continual outpouring of His divine grace.

This mutual gesture of self-giving reaches its apex in the Divine Liturgy when we offer to God the fruit of the earth that He has already bestowed upon us, "Thine own of Thine own. . . ." In return we receive nourishment from His hand in the form of "communion," which enables us actually to participate in His life through partaking of the Body and Blood of His risen and glorified Son. In the eucharistic service, we experience the reality and fullness of the gospel. There above all, we are made aware of the vital link, the virtual unity, that exists between Bible and liturgy, between the written, canonical source of our faith and the actualization of that faith in the prayer of the Church.

This intimate relationship between Bible and liturgy is evident in the Holy Scriptures themselves. The Hebrew Bible, our Old Testament, is filled with liturgical hymns, the most familiar of which are the Psalms. The intertestamental period gave rise to an abundant hymnography, incorporated into canonical and non-canonical writings, including the Song of Azariah and the three young men (Dan 3 in the Septuagint version), the Prayer of Manasseh, the *Hodayot*, or Hymn Scroll, and the Songs of the Sabbath Sacrifice from Qumran, and the first century Psalms of Solomon.

In the New Testament we find fragments or portions of text that were adapted from early Christian hymns, such as the songs of Mary, Zachariah and Simeon in St Luke's narratives of Jesus' birth and infancy (Lk 1–2). St Paul refers to "psalms, hymns and spiritual songs," difficult to identify but which clearly denote liturgical elements familiar to early Christians. Hymnic compositions may well lie behind passages such as 1 Corinthians 15:54–55, Ephesians 5:14, Hebrews 1:1–4, 1 Timothy 3:16, 1 Peter 2:22–24, and throughout the book of Revelation.

Confessional or creedal hymns very likely appear in the well-known passages Philippians 2:5–11 and Colossians 2:15–19(20). And some reputable biblical scholars hold that the Prologue to St John's Gospel (1:1–18) was adapted from an early (quasi-Gnostic?) Christian hymn. However, since these are structured according to the literary pattern known as "chiasmus," which we discussed earlier, it is difficult to say whether their rhythm is actually "hymnic," meaning that their original form was sung in liturgical services (many scholars hold that Philippians 2, for example, was sung antiphonally in the worship of certain Pauline communities), or whether that rhythm derives from the poetic balance resulting from concentric parallelism. In either case, lying behind these biblical passages are almost certainly elements of the early Church's communal worship: some sung, others recited as confessions of faith.

It is essential for us to recognize and preserve this close relationship that exists between the Church's canon and its liturgical tradition. What we confess with our lips in the form of creedal statements, what we sing in the form of *antiphons* and *prokeimena* (derived from the Psalter), *stichera* (e.g., verses from the *Otoechos* on the *Lucernarium* ["Lord I Call"] and *aposticha* of vespers), and similar liturgical elements, all express the deepest convictions of the heart. And those convictions derive directly from God's self-revelation in Holy Scripture.

If other Christian confessions today often find themselves in a state of crisis, it is largely due to the fact that in their historical tradition this vital link between Bible and liturgy has been severed. When this occurs, the inevitable result is to produce biblical studies that are little more than exercises in text criticism or literary analysis, and worship services that are practically devoid of authentic spiritual content. Logical outcomes of this break between the Church's Scriptures and its worship are phenomena such as the Jesus Seminar on the one hand and the jazz mass on the other. A hermeneutic that is not grounded in worship will inevitably limit its field of interest to the "literal sense" of biblical passages; just as worship that does not proclaim the gospel will inevitably degenerate into pious noise void of serious content, or simply aim to provide a psychological "uplift" equally devoid of spiritual depth and transcendent purpose.

It would be easy to fault Protestant and Catholic Christians for allowing this separation to develop over the years within their respective traditions. That would be to overlook the fact, however, that the intimate and reciprocal relationship between Bible and liturgy, faith and worship, has been preserved in Orthodoxy not by our own doing but as a gift of sheer grace—without which the Orthodox Church itself would have long ago disappeared under pressures of persecution and martyrdom. If "Orthodoxy" is truly "right worship" and "right belief," it is because it has been sustained as such through the ages by the Holy Spirit.

Our task as Orthodox Christians is not to criticize and condemn those who have lost a sense of the vital unity that should exist between the gospel and worship. It is rather to celebrate, with joy and humble gratitude, the gift of the God who blesses and sanctifies those who place their trust in Him. It is to acknowledge in the words of the apostle James, also taken up in the "Prayer before the Ambon," that "every good and perfect gift is from above, coming down from the Father of Lights," including faith born of the gospel.

Our task, then, is to express this biblical faith through the liturgy of the Church, and to do so with unfailing faithfulness. Thereby we can fulfill the ultimate purpose of our life and calling, which is to "ascribe glory, thanksgiving, and worship to the Father, and to the Son, and to the Holy Spirit, now and ever and unto ages of ages."

III

Of God and Ourselves

1

September 11, 2001

*T*HIS IS A DATE we shall never forget.

And these are images we shall never forget: images of planes hurtling into the twin towers; the collapse of the buildings; the faces of the police, firefighters, and other rescue workers who lost so many friends and coworkers; the anguished cries of family members who refused to accept the obvious. Images, too, of the Pentagon in flames, followed by the rerouting of Air Force One and the cautionary hiding out of the Vice President. War had come to American soil.

The World Trade Center and the Pentagon are the most powerful symbols of our nation's economic, political, and military might. And with the continuing threat of biological and chemical assaults, we well know that the terror, and our sense of helplessness, are not over.

In times like these there is a great temptation to fall into despair, to lapse into a kind of fatalism because it all seems so cruel and meaningless. "Why do bad things happen to good people?" is the age-old question victims of barbaric acts have been asking themselves throughout history, in the wake of the sack of Rome or Constantinople, in the aftermath of the Holocaust, in the face of the heartbreaking grief and agony brought on by ethnic cleansing. It was a question raised by the parents whose infants were slaughtered by Herod's soldiers. It was surely on the lips of the Mother of

God as she watched her beloved son endure the agony of crucifixion. Why must the innocent suffer?

The only reasonable, the only acceptable, answer to the question is the one God Himself offers us in the gospel of His Son.

God has created us as free human beings, capable of goodness and love, but also capable of wanton sinfulness. Our freedom is necessary for us to love God and one another. Without it, there is only compulsion; and love cannot be compelled. Therefore, God runs the risk of granting us freedom, so that we might love Him and each other.

That freedom, as we know from personal experience, can be tragically misused. In some cases, as on September 11, it can lead people to perpetrate horrendous acts, believing all the while they are faithfully obeying the will of God. Without the message of the New Testament—the good news revealed in Christ: that God is Love and that He loves us from the depths of His heart—our natural human inclinations or passions lead us inevitably to sin, even to justify acts of murder and mayhem. Without God, Dostoevsky declared, anything is permissible. He was speaking of the one true God, the God and Father of our Lord Jesus Christ. Seen through any lens other than the gospel, the image of God is distorted. As a consequence, our understanding of His will and purpose are distorted as well. Today this is nowhere more evident than in the twisted version of Islam represented by militant Muslim fundamentalists. Yet so often even we who claim allegiance to the gospel read into it our own will, our own desires and prejudices. The result is that we, too, distort the image of God, both in Scripture and in ourselves.

It would be easy to conclude from this that suffering is God's punishment meted out to the guilty. That, we know, is simply not true. In the first place, God is not vengeful. If He allows us to experience His "wrath," it is for our spiritual growth and edification. But He does allow us to bear the consequences of our own actions. Much of the suffering we endure results from our rejection of God, our rebellion against His will and refusal of His guidance, which always serve our well-being and salvation.

On the other hand, we are also painfully aware that a great deal of suffering is borne by those who are basically innocent. In the case of these recent events, the tragedy so outweighs whatever sinful acts any of the victims might have committed, that the "punishment," if it were such, would be wholly disproportionate and unjust. Yet God is a God of justice, righteousness and mercy.

What, then, can we say about the reason God allows events such as those of the September 11? The Church Fathers made a crucial distinction between God's intentional will and His permissive will. God certainly did not intend the WTC attack and other tragedies of that day, yet He did permit them to occur. *Why* He did so is a question we simply cannot answer. Its answer lies hidden in the impenetrable mystery of the divine will. In fact, it is this unanswerability of the question "Why?" that distinguishes suffering from mere pain. Pain becomes suffering to the degree that it remains inexplicable.

There is one thing, though, that God reveals to us that speaks directly to the problem of suffering. It is the fact of His presence and His participation in our anguish, our pain, our sense of overwhelming loss. He drinks the cup of our suffering to the bitter dregs. He shares our pain, our grief, our agony to the full measure.

When I think about these things, there are three passages that always come to mind, two from Scripture and one from the French Catholic philosopher Pascal. "If I make my bed in Sheol," the Psalmist declares, "Thou art there!" (Ps 138/139:8). As the angel greets the myrrhbearers in the empty tomb, he speaks of the Risen Lord as "the Crucified One" (the actual meaning of the Greek in Mark and Matthew): the resurrected Christ will forever remain "the Crucified One," bearing in Himself the suffering of us all. Finally, this truth, was well expressed in a familiar phrase of Pascal: "Christ is in agony until the end of the world."

These three statements don't answer the question as to why in this tragic and sinful world persons acting in the name of God could perpetrate horrific acts that killed thousands and brought unspeakable grief to so many more. But they do say what each of us needs to hear in these days.

They remind us that in our doubt, our fear and our pain, the Risen Lord is present in our midst. He is and remains "Emmanuel, God with us." As the Crucified One, He journeys with us, He bears us up, He consoles us, He shares to the full our pain and anguish. In return, He asks merely that in the darkness of our incomprehension, we place our firm hope and our unwavering trust in Him, the Vanquisher of death and the Author of eternal life.

2

The Mystery of Innocent Suffering

T HERE IS A QUESTION to which we all want a reasonable and satisfying answer: Why indeed do bad things happen to good people (meaning ourselves)? Why is the world filled with suffering, particularly innocent suffering? Why September 11, or suicide bombings; why kidnappings or child abuse; why identity theft or massive job layoffs? The answer in any particular case may lie on the shoulders of others, but that doesn't explain why so many of us suffer as innocent victims from their violence, greed, or exploitation.

In addition to the tragic reality of our common fallenness, we are aware that much of the pain and anguish of our lives has no evident cause for which we are directly responsible. In so many ways we find ourselves out of control, victims of events and circumstances that threaten to do us in. Whether they have an impact upon us directly, or concern those whom we love and care about, images of pain surround us relentlessly. The media furnish them every day: images of adults and their children, wasting away throughout Africa because of the horrendous AIDS crisis; random violence in the streets of Los Angeles that takes dozens of lives in a two-week period; whole villages in southeast Asia lost under mud slides or devastated by cyclones; parents lying in a burn unit, grieving the loss of their children while they struggle to survive their own domestic holocaust. . . . And all this, post-September 11.

The greatest temptation in the face of such suffering is to question, Why? Why should I, or someone I love, bear this kind of affliction? So often this leads immediately to other questions: Why is God punishing us? What have I or they done, that we should have to endure such pain?

Search as we may, if we understand the suffering to be truly "innocent," then there is no answer that ultimately satisfies. We can proffer any number of theological responses that have been suggested over the years. We can speak, for example, of the freedom God bestows upon us in order to give us the capacity to love; a freedom we have abused to the point that we have alienated ourselves from the Source of life and plunged ourselves and creation as a whole into an abyss of evil, suffering, and death. Or we can suggest, as many have done, that God uses even innocent suffering to help us mature spiritually; or to demonstrate our utter helplessness, to the point that in our desperation we are forced to throw ourselves upon the divine mercy.

There is truth in each of these responses. But when the suffering we know strikes close to home—when it's *our* child who is born with severe deformities; when it's *we* who are victims of another's wanton violence; or when *our* loved one is killed on the highway—then the theological reasonings ring hollow. Their abstract truth simply does not touch us at the level of our pain.

The point is that we can never, in this life, find a reasonable and acceptable explanation for the mystery of innocent suffering. Indeed, our very inability to explain that suffering is what makes it so difficult to endure and tends to drive us from anguish to despair. Suffering remains a "mystery," in the popular sense of the term, precisely because we cannot explain—or explain away—its ultimate origin or meaning. This is why it is *suffering*, and not simply pain, hurt, or grief.

Yet there is another way of considering the mystery of suffering. That is by taking the term "mystery" in its more basic sense of "sacrament." Few of us who are grieving the loss of a beloved family member, or going through the stress of chemotherapy, or struggling with clinical depression can appreciate the etymology of the term *mysterion*. But it does signify "sacramental reality." And therefore it casts on the problem of suffering a new, radiant, and healing light.

We are members of the Body of Christ. This is our most basic identity, and it defines our most basic calling (Rom 12; 1 Cor 12). "If one member suffers," St Paul affirms, "all suffer together" (1 Cor 12:26). Yet the Head of the Body suffers as well. This means that whatever we experience is never experienced in isolation. We never suffer alone. Although other members of the Body may be oblivious to our suffering, Christ bears it to the full. We know that He even longs to assume our suffering, to assimilate it to His own, in order to transfigure it and ourselves into the image of His wholeness and His ineffable peace. This is the great truth of the Cross: that Jesus freely and lovingly unites Himself with us, not only to redeem us from sin and guilt, but to share our suffering and to bear it to the very end.

God allows our suffering, but He never imposes it. Human suffering is not punishment for sin, except (as a former seminary professor of mine once put it) to the extent that God "allows us to stew in our own juice." "Who sinned," the disciples ask Jesus, "that this man was born blind?" And the answer: "Neither he nor his parents, but that the works of God might be made manifest in him" (Jn 9:3).

In the best of times suffering can educate and fortify us. It can purify our heart, curb our ambitions, and lead us to focus on "the one thing needful." At other times, suffering can overwhelm us, leading us to the brink of despair. This occurs especially when it remains a "mystery" in the usual sense: a crushing, perplexing, unexplainable, and apparently, unjust weight of anguish, loss and pain.

One thing, and perhaps only one thing, transforms such suffering into a genuine mystery, an experience permeated by sacramental grace. That is to *surrender* our suffering, whatever its cause or form, into the loving hands of the Crucified One. It is to offer that suffering—through gritted teeth, if need be—to the One who is "in agony until the end of the world." By this simple, sacramental gesture, accomplished through fervent prayer (our own and that of others who accompany us), we can offer every shred of pain, anguish, and despair to Him who is the source of all genuine healing, peace, and joy. This, it seems, is the only thing that allows us, as the apostle Paul declared, to "rejoice in our sufferings," knowing that through it all God ceaselessly pours into our hearts His inexhaustible love (Rom 5:3–5).

3

The Suffering of the Innocent One

W E CAN'T BEGIN TO EXHAUST the mystery of innocent suffering. One further thing needs to be said, however, and it leads us to the close of Holy Week and the remembrance of Jesus' crucifixion. The great truth of the Cross, we affirmed in the last chapter, is that Jesus freely and lovingly unites Himself with us, not only to redeem us from sin and guilt, but to share our suffering and to bear it, with us and for us, to the very end.

If that were the end of the story—if Holy Week ended with the death and burial of the wholly innocent Son of God—even then we would have reason to rejoice. For the great promise of the Nativity and Theophany feasts would be fulfilled with the sacrificial death of Emmanuel, and through that death we would know indeed that "God is with us." By His voluntary death on the cross, Jesus would affirm the love that the Father has for each of us, the boundless love that reveals itself in the solidarity of mutual suffering. By accepting death and burial, He would declare His utter faithfulness to us, in our own mortality and corruption. He would be with us, to accompany us from life, through death, and into the grave. And because of His vicarious death *pro nobis*, we would know that even in the grave, our own grave, God is present.

The death of Jesus, however, is not the end of the story, for the mystery of the Cross contains within it the assurance of ultimate victory, a victory that offers a powerful and definitive answer to the question of innocent suffering.

"Why do you look for the living among the dead?," the angel asks the Myrrhbearing Women; "He is risen, He is not here. Go, and tell His disciples!" (Lk 24:5; Mk 16:7). He who was crucified and buried has vanquished death; He is alive! From Galilee to Jerusalem, and to the ends of the earth, He appears to His own people, to bless, to guide, and to save. Through the anguish of the Cross, hell has been overthrown, death has been transformed into life, and joy has come into all the world. What was scandalous to the Jews and folly to the Gentiles has become, for those who know and who love Him, the Tree of life, the Fountain of immortality, the ever-flowing Source of God's saving power.

To know "nothing but Jesus Christ and Him crucified" (1 Cor 2:2), is to know the mystery that reveals the ultimate meaning of every human life and every form of human suffering. It is to know the infinite depths of the love of Christ, who in perfect freedom and boundless devotion lays down His life for us, His friends. And He does so with the single purpose of raising us up with Himself, to share fully in His eternal life.

At the close of the vesperal service on Holy Friday, we the faithful come to venerate and lament the wasted body of our crucified Lord. Our sadness, as it is in the face of all innocent suffering, is deep and real. Yet in the light of the lenten Spring, it is transformed into a truly "bright sadness" because of what is yet to come. As we draw near to the image of Christ's burial shroud, we take up the plaintive cry of the holy Mother of God, conveyed to us by the liturgy of this tragic yet glorious day: "My beloved Son and my God, I cannot bear to see Thee unjustly crucified! Hasten, then, and arise, that I may also behold Thy resurrection from the dead on the third day!"

Hasten, O Lord, and arise! Transform our suffering and our lamentation into unending gladness and exultation! Unite us with the Holy Church throughout the ages, with the angels and archangels, with the living and the dead in the fullness of the communion of saints, that we with them might behold—before our eyes and in the depths of our hearts, in our joy and in our anguish—the victory, the power, and the radiant glory of Thy holy resurrection!

4

Questions about God

T HERE ARE QUESTIONS little children ask that never seem to receive a satisfying answer. The toughest and most urgent tend to be religious, such as "Who is God?" or "Where is God?" In the wake of recent tragic events that have so shaken our country and the world as a whole, a great many grown-ups are asking the same things.

As adults we may formulate the questions in a more sophisticated way, but basically we still want to know just who God is and where He is to be found. This is especially true when we have to deal with acute suffering and loss. The spiritual tradition of the Church tells us that God Himself inspires us to raise questions of this kind, since they serve as stepping stones along the pathway that leads us from knowledge about God to eternal communion with Him.

On the one hand, we affirm on the basis of scriptural revelation and the Church's tradition that God both creates and sustains everything that exists. He "brings all things from non-existence into being," the liturgical text declares. In technical terms, God creates *ex nihilo*. He is the source and origin not only of existing reality, but of the primal matter out of which, "in the beginning," everything came to be.

God not only creates all things. He also sustains the existence of all things through time. God is the unfathomably great power behind the birth of galaxies (the Eagle Nebula, for example, that spawns countless solar systems, is estimated to be a light year, or some six trillion miles high; and it's just a minor implement in the cosmic tool box). God is also the source of energy behind the force of gravity, the vastly stronger electromagnetic force, the weak nuclear force responsible for radioactivity, and the strong nuclear force that holds together the elementary particles in the nuclei of atoms, of which all matter is constituted. He is the answer to the basic question, How do things endure through time? What preserves the physical universe from moment to moment? And ultimately He is the answer to the quest for a unified field theory of physics.

God is the answer to other questions as well. He is the source and power behind the various life-forms whose being is radically different from inanimate matter. A slug may not be much to look at when it's compared to a rose, but it's still a marvel when it's compared to a stone. That difference is due to God's power, but also to His design. And the ultimate expression of that design is ourselves, humankind created in God's own image and called to grow toward His likeness.

With regard to God's creative, sustaining power, there seems to be no significant conflict between Genesis 1 and the findings of quantum mechanics or astrophysics. To eyes of faith, an electron microscope or the Hubble telescope simply confirms what biblical authors intuited nearly three thousand years ago, namely that God is the creating, sustaining power in and behind everything that exists. Or put another way, the unique and unified power that brings all things into being and preserves their existence through time is what we term "God." If we were to stop there, not even the most skeptical scientists could reasonably maintain that "God" does not exist. At least not those scientists who argue for some form of intelligent design.

But of course we cannot and do not stop there. The real mystery and wonder of it all is that this same ineffable power that creates and sustains everything from the macro cosmos to the micro cosmos, is also, by its very nature, "personal." In the words of the Church's theology, God is a Trinity of Persons—Father, Son, and Spirit—united in an eternal communion of love. And this one God, experience tells us, is closer to us than our own heart.

Who is God, and where is God? Christian faith answers that God is both the creator and sustainer of all things, and the one who gives all things meaning and purpose. He governs the universe, from the birth of stars to the movement of atoms. He shapes historical events and personal destinies. Nothing is beyond his purview and nothing is devoid of his loving care. He is "everywhere present and filling all things," investing all of creation with value, purpose, and direction. He is Lord over the cosmos and Lord over our lives, infinitely powerful and infinitely loving.

This God of limitless power and boundless love is and remains Emmanuel, "God with us." And this is why, despite September 11 and despite our own personal tragedies, the world is still a good place to be.

5

"Where Is God When You Need Him?"

*T*HAT QUESTION HAS A blasphemous ring to it. But it's one we ask so often, openly or not, that it's worth giving it serious consideration. The Gospels, in fact, give the only answer that matters, and that's where we have to begin.

Of the many passages we could quote, one stands out, especially in the wake of the terrible tragedy that not too long ago sent more than a hundred Russian submariners to their death.

Matthew 14 recounts the extraordinary episode of Jesus' encounter with the disciples on the Sea of Galilee. At the end of a day of teaching and healing the crowds, Jesus sends his disciples off in a boat while He goes up into the hills to pray. In the middle of the night the disciples are rowing frantically against strong winds and high waves. Suddenly they see a figure draw near to the boat. Thinking it's a phantom, they cry out in dread. Jesus speaks to them a phrase that reveals both His presence and the significance of His appearance: "It is I, do not fear."

The meaning of that phrase is lost in translation. "It is I" is in fact the divine Name, revealed by God to Moses on Mount Sinai (Ex 3). It should be translated, "I AM!" God proclaims Himself to be the One Who IS, the "Existing One," the only true God. Jesus took up this name for Himself in order to disclose His true identity to His disciples: "I AM the Lord." Thereby He made Himself known as the eternal Son of God, God Himself, whom the later Church would worship as "One of the Holy Trinity."

The second element of that phrase also reveals Jesus as God and Lord. "Be not afraid," the angel Gabriel tells the Virgin Mary at the Annunciation. "Be not afraid," the radiant Christ urges the astonished disciples on the mountain of Transfiguration. On that mountain, St Matthew (17) tells us, Jesus spoke these consoling words, then he performed a striking and profoundly significant gesture: He lifted up the disciples with the command, "Arise!" This is the language of the Resurrection. Once Christ reveals Himself as the glorified Lord, foreshadowing His own resurrection from the dead, he declares by word and gesture that He will raise them with Himself and grant them a share in His own glory. This is the real meaning of the Transfiguration account.

The same is true with the episode of Jesus walking on the water, at least as St Matthew relates it. In obedience to Jesus' command "Come!," Peter steps out of the boat and begins to walk across the water toward his Lord. The moment he takes his eyes off of Jesus and becomes aware of the impossibility of his actions, he begins to founder. Sinking into the turbulent waters, he cries out a prayer that will become the foundation of all prayer: "Lord, save me!" And, as He did on the mount of Transfiguration, Jesus lifts him up; He raises him out of the watery depths and sets him safely in the barque.

In ancient Israel, water was symbolic of both good and evil. Water is essential for life in that desert region. But for those who earn their livelihood on the sea, water is also a potential tomb. Jesus raises Peter from that tomb, but in doing so He conveys a deeper message, one that speaks eloquently to the situation of those young submariners who so tragically lost their lives. That message is addressed as well to everyone who faces the crisis of sudden death, including those who, in moments of terror and panic, cry out to God, "Lord, save me!"

The meaning of that message is more than simple rescue or the saving of biological life. Like all those Jesus raises from death—the son of the widow of Nain, his friend Lazarus, Jairus' daughter— restoration to life is symbolic of a greater restoration to be accomplished at the General Resurrection.

Yet, we can object, God did not save those young men in the submarine. And so often when we cry to Him, the response is a deafening silence. Where indeed is God, when you need Him?

There is only one answer to that agonizing question, one that God Himself gives. It is the truth that ultimate salvation is not of this world but is fulfilled only after our biological death. Jesus came not to heal every malady or save everyone from physical death. Lazarus, after all, would one day die a natural death; and Peter would follow his Lord to martyrdom. Similarly, you and I will die our own death, even if in the meantime God works in our lives miracles of healing.

What does this mean for the submariners and all those who face death, who cry out to God from the depths of hell, beseeching Him to save them? It means that Christ is there, present in their midst. He is there to suffer with them, to share their anguish and agony, and to lead them through the valley of the shadow of death. They, like Peter and Lazarus, can hold in their hearts and minds the absolute conviction—the absolute truth—that insofar as they seek their salvation in Christ, He will grant it in full. Accompanying them in their dread and their hopelessness, He will guide them—as He guides each of us— toward the ultimate salvation, the ultimate source of life.

Peter's rescue from the waters, then, is a prophetic image of a greater rescue, a greater salvation to come. He, like Lazarus, like ourselves, and like those young Russian sailors, is bound one day to die. That is inevitable. What provides hope, however, is the certainty that Christ journeys with us through that final agony, through the anguish of death. And as the icon of the Resurrection announces so poignantly, He reaches out to embrace each of us. He commands each of us, "Arise!" Then He lifts us up out of death, and grants us to share fully in His own resurrected Life.

Where is God when you need Him? As the "One Who Is," He is present with us, wherever we may find ourselves, in life and in death. "Everywhere present and filling all things," He was in that submarine as well, just as He will be with us at the moment of our own death, and with us in the darkness of our own tomb.

6

Threefold Splendor

O RTHODOX CHRISTIANITY—the faith of the One, Holy, Catholic, and Apostolic Church—has always known and proclaimed God to be both One and Three: a single divine essence, or nature, shared fully and equally by three divine Persons, who reveal themselves to us in Scripture as Father, Son, and Holy Spirit. Everything else we know about God—from the incarnation of the Son as Jesus of Nazareth, to the continual outpouring of God's love through the Holy Spirit into creation and into our life—is based on and derived from that most fundamental teaching: the God of the Scriptures, the God of the Church's life and faith, is One God in three Persons.

If we were to hand a New Testament to people who had never read it, the God they discovered in its pages would not appear as some abstract monolith. Like Christian people from the time of Christ, they would encounter a threefold God whose inner life and outward activity in our world are the expression of a "communion in love."

This communion, and the profoundly personal quality of God's inner life and presence in the world, are expressed with special poignancy in the icons of three major feasts of the Orthodox church year: Nativity, Theophany, and Transfiguration.

Originally, the Nativity of Christ (December 25) and His Baptism in the Jordan River (January 6) were celebrated as a single feast, whose purpose was to commemorate God's "epiphany," "theophany," or manifestation in the person of Jesus.

The icon of the Nativity depicts the Christ child, born in a cavern, illumined by a radiant beam of light, on the outskirts of Bethlehem. In the upper corner a hand sends forth that light into the darkness surrounding the manger. That hand is an iconic symbol for the presence of God the Father, the source of all divine life. Utterly transcendent, inaccessible, and unknowable in His inner essence, the Father makes Himself known in the person of the Son, who shares fully of that same divine essence. In the beam of light there appears the image of a dove—another symbol, this time representing the Holy Spirit. In the Person of the Spirit, God is also fully present, since the Spirit likewise shares fully in the divine nature and being.

At Christ's baptism in the Jordan, the three Persons appear again. Jesus, the incarnate Son, enters the waters to be baptized at the hand of John; the voice of the Father reveals the true origin of this man from Nazareth; and the Spirit, in the form of a dove, hovers over the river, then rests upon the Son (Jn 1:32). Just as the Spirit "moved over the face of the waters" at the first creation to bring order, harmony, and life to all things (Gen 1:2), here He moves over the baptismal waters, prefiguring the "initiation" that will transform the lives of all those who are baptized into Christ and thereby "put on Christ" (Gal 3:27). Together with the Son, the Spirit brings about a New Creation: transfiguration of the cosmic order and baptismal "illumination" for those who, like the Lord Himself, submit themselves to the ritual by which God reveals Himself as Trinity, and they are reborn as children of God.

Finally, the same threefold divine presence manifests itself on the Mount of Transfiguration. The voice of the Father declares, in words identical to those spoken at the Baptism, that this, His beloved Son, possesses authority to speak and to reveal the Father and His purpose for the salvation of the created order. Patristic tradition is divided over the manifestation of the Spirit at the Transfiguration. Some Fathers see the Spirit in the overshadowing cloud that envelopes Jesus and the disciples. Others see the Spirit in the uncreated light that shines forth from the Son, announcing the coming glory of His resurrection. In either case, the biblical narrative reveals once more the threefold, personal reality of the one God.

In a remarkable homily on the mystery of Baptism, St Gregory Nazianzus (†389) expressed his own experience of God and the paradoxical reality of Trinity in the following words (Oration 40):

> No sooner do I conceive of the One than I am illumined by the splendor of the Three; no sooner do I distinguish them than I am carried back to the One. . . . When I contemplate the Three together, I see but one living flame, and I cannot divide or measure out the Undivided Light!

This kind of language has little meaning to many people. The other day I was speaking with a non-Orthodox friend who voiced the strongest objections to the understanding of God as Trinity. To his mind, God is beyond any formulation we can possibly devise. He is the "wholly other" in the most literal sense: a God beyond all creation and all imagination. I had the feeling he could have added, a God beyond His own self-revelation.

His problem, as he describes it, is with the Church's traditional doctrines—which he referred to with a slight edge of hostility as "dogmas"—that appear to "put God in a box." Formulas such as "One in Three," or "three Persons united in a single divine essence," strike him as artificial and woefully inadequate. He reads them as nothing more than human constructs designed to impose on believers a uniform orthodoxy.

This is especially true of formulas concerning the Holy Spirit. Why, he wanted to know, do we Orthodox make such an issue of the *filioque*, the clause added to the Nicene Creed that affirms "[I believe] in the Holy Spirit . . . who proceeds from the Father *and the Son*"? Who, he added, can presume to say anything at all about this most unfathomable aspect of the Godhead?

When I got home, I took out St Basil the Great's marvelous fourth-century treatise "On the Holy Spirit." Opening it at random brought me to where I wish I had been during our conversation.

In chapter 16, St Basil speaks about the absolute unity of nature, purpose, and work shared by the three Persons of the Trinity. "In everything the Holy Spirit is indivisibly and inseparably joined to the Father and the Son." This is revealed most fully in creation itself. "When you consider creation, I advise you to think of Him who is the first cause of everything that exists: namely, the Father; and then of the Son, who is the creator; and then of the Holy Spirit, the perfecter." The Author of creation, the creative Agent, and the Perfecter, or Sanctifier of all things. "The Originator of all things is One," Basil insists. "He creates through the Son and perfects through the Spirit."

Then Basil quotes from Psalm 32, "By the Word of the Lord the heavens were made, and all their host by the Spirit [*ruach, pneuma*] of His mouth." The specific work of the Spirit, he continues, is to perfect and strengthen: to produce "perfection in holiness, which expresses itself in an unyielding, unchangeable commitment to goodness." That goodness characterizes God in His innermost being. "No one is good but God alone," Jesus declares. And readers of the Gospels recognize that by that very fact Jesus Himself is essentially good, essentially God.

It is this goodness, expressed as sacrificial love, that motivates the three Persons of the Holy Trinity to work out the world's redemption. "When we speak of the plan of salvation," St Basil declares, "accomplished in God's goodness by our great God and Savior Jesus Christ, who would deny that it was all made possible through the grace of the Spirit?"

The Scriptures affirm that God is good, God is light, God is love, God is Spirit. And that Spirit, who is God, fills all of creation, including every human life, in order to lead it to perfection, to sanctify and render it holy. Thereby He offers to creation, as to us, the possibility of sharing forever in that goodness, that light, and that love.

This is why Trinitarian theology is so important: because it expresses God as He actually is—as He reveals, manifests, and confirms Himself to be—in the experience of those who love Him and know they are loved by Him.

This emphasis on the tri-unity of God is such a central and indispensable tenet of Orthodox Christianity that we must reject the popular, well-meaning notion that Jews, Muslims, and Christians all worship "the same God." God is One, and He is the God of all monotheistic believers. He is, in fact, the God of all mankind, whether they acknowledge Him or not. But if God is, as we affirm, three divine Persons [*hypostaseis*] united in a single divine essence, or nature, then those who worship a monolithic God—including Christian unitarians of whatever denomination—in fact worship someone or something other than the God who is known only by His self-revelation in the person of His incarnate Son, Jesus Christ. The God of the Bible reveals Himself in the Old Testament as *Father* (Ps 67/68:5; Isa 9:6; 63:16!), God's creative (Gen 1; Ps 33:6; Isa 55:11) and prophetic (Am 3:8; Jer 1:4, and so forth) *Word,* and *Spirit* (Gen 1; Num 24:2 and *passim*); and in the New Testament as *Father* (Jn 1:18; 5:19f; Rom 8:15, and *passim*), *Son/Word* (Mk 1:1; Jn 1:14; 3:16 and *passim*; Rom 5:10; Rev 19:13, and so forth) and *Spirit* (Lk 1:35; Jn 15:26; Rom 8:9ff, and so forth). He is to be worshiped accordingly. He is to be worshiped "in Spirit and in Truth" (Jn 4:24), that is, in the Holy Spirit and in the eternal Son of God who embodies and discloses ultimate Truth (Jn 14:6; 1 Jn 5:20).

God is indeed the "wholly Other," infinitely beyond created reality. Yet this same God shares fully in every aspect of that reality, filling it with His goodness, His light, His love, His Spirit. As a trinity or threefold unity of divine Persons, the Father, the Son, and the Spirit dwell in an inexhaustible communion of mutual love. That love is so abundant that it overflows the boundaries of divine life to embrace and transfigure the entire creation. Nothing lies outside the warmth of that embrace: not sin, not death, not even my friend's well-intentioned agnosticism.

If I could leave this friend with anything at all, it would be this: that in the depths of his being he should come to know and experience trinitarian dogma, not as abstract formulas, but as liturgical poetry which speaks ineffable truth; that he see God and come to know His Spirit, not as totally and infinitely beyond this universe, but as "everywhere present and filling all things." Above all, I would want him to come to the point where he could have his own mystical experience, akin to that of St Gregory:

"When I contemplate the Three together, I see but one living flame. And by the radiance of that Undivided Light, I am bathed in the threefold splendor of the one Godhead."

7

Antinomies

O RTHODOX CHRISTIAN LIFE is filled with paradoxes, what the Holy Fathers referred to as antinomies: conflicts between two principles, laws, or truths that seem equally valid. An example would be "bondage to sin" and "freedom in the Spirit," both of which accurately describe the Christian person (Luther's *simul iustus et peccator**). Another would be the affirmation, "Through the Cross, joy has come into the world!" Or the fact that at the *anamnesis* of the Divine Liturgy we "remember" Christ's second and glorious Coming.

Each of these pairs, read through the lens of ordinary logic, seems irreconcilable. We cannot be both slave and free; joy cannot be the emotion accompanying a hideous execution; and we can hardly remember what has not yet happened. In the light of the Gospel, however, these make perfect sense.

One of the most familiar antinomies involves our own life in the most direct way. We are bound by sin, unable to free ourselves from the corrupting influence of our passions. Yet we are freed from the consequences of sin through the forgiving, reconciling work of Christ which becomes accessible to us in the Holy Spirit. In this life we continue in sin, bound by its power that leads only to death. Yet in Christ, that power is broken. Even though sin remains a reality in our everyday experience, Christ has set us free to walk in "newness of life," sustained, guided, and preserved by His Spirit. "For

---

*The Christian is simultaneously justified and sinful.

freedom Christ has set us free" (Gal 5:1). "Where the Spirit of the Lord is, there is freedom" (2 Cor 3:17).

Because of Christ's crucifixion, voluntarily accepted for our sake, we have been released from ourselves and from demonic oppression. Through Christ's sacrifice, death has been overcome and we are given life, such that all people now have access in the Holy Spirit to God the Father (Eph 2:18). Through the Cross "death is swallowed up in victory" and we are given Life. This is Life beyond life, eternal communion in the boundless love that unites the three Persons of the Holy Trinity. And it is the source of the only real and lasting joy we ever can know. Authentic joy requires sacrifice; it comes most fully with tears. And therein lies another antinomy.

Finally, "to remember" in the Biblical sense is basically to reactualize a past event, to bring it from the past to the present, so that we experience it as an immediate reality. This is why we can proclaim at Pascha, "Yesterday I was buried with Thee, O Christ. Today I arise with Thee in Thy resurrection!" The act of remembering has the effect of telescoping both past and future into a present moment. Time and space are transcended in liturgical celebration, such that events of the (eschatological) future become "real," "actual," "present" for us today. Thus we *remember* not only the Cross, the Tomb, the Resurrection and Ascension, but also the "second and glorious Coming" of our Lord.

"Life is full of contradictions," they tell us. Most of these we dismiss as annoyances or take on as problems to be solved. Some of them, though—like the God-Man, the Virgin Mother, and the Trinity of God—are mysteries of life and faith before which we smile, open our hearts, and give thanks.

8

On Preaching Judgment

*I*N A WORLD MARKED BY such things as childhood trauma, terror-
ist attacks, and a collapsing economy, the anxiety level is
understandably high.

We have structured our lives in such a way as to shield ourselves
as much as possible from the violence, corruption, sickness, and
death that provoke that anxiety. Yet most of us still live with uncom-
fortable amounts of stress, worry, and assorted "problems." It
doesn't help to remind ourselves that millions are starving in
Africa, that thousands of women are sold every year into sexual
slavery, that diseases such as the Ebola and HIV viruses are deci-
mating entire populations, or that Christians are facing increasingly
severe persecution in Muslim countries, including those we consider to be our allies. We Americans are tired, overworked, and
stressed out. And most of us are not happy about it.

Priests and pastors who are charged with preaching the gospel
tend to respond to this situation in a predictable way. With the best
of motives, they try to relieve the tensions and stresses of their
parishioners by preaching a "good word," an uplifting message of
assurance and consolation. Their very genuine concern is to convey the promise of God's love, forgiveness, and tender mercy. Yet
all too often their sermons, and the church service itself, take on
the aspect of a therapy session. The pastor is driven by an unconscious need to make the people feel better about themselves and

their lives. As a result, the message he proclaims expresses emotion more than truth, "pop" psychology more than the gospel.

Whether it comes from the lips of an Orthodox priest or a Baptist preacher, that word is no longer God's Word. This is because it has lost the vital element in all of Christian, and especially Orthodox Christian, life: the element of balance.

It is said that Sergius Verhovskoy, the late professor of dogmatic theology at St Vladimir's Seminary, defined Orthodoxy as "the lack of one-sidedness." This is a marvelous definition. It makes clear that heresy of every sort results less from conscious attempts to deny the faith, than from often noble attempts to stress one or more truths of the faith that, taken in isolation, create distortion or imbalance. (This is reflected most clearly in the unending christological debates of the first Christian millennium.)

Pastoral concerns in recent years have tended to focus in a one-sided way on all that is "positive" in the gospel. Whether in sermons or in confession, priests very often emphasize the love, forgiveness, and mercy of God while neglecting to stress the less acceptable and less consoling message of divine *judgment*.

Of all the New Testament passages in which judgment is a basic theme—from the Sermon on the Mount (Mt 5:13) to the Book of Revelation (22:12)—one in particular comes to mind. It is no more condemnatory, no more "judgmental" than many others. Its force lies in the way it unmasks our every attempt to demonstrate self-righteousness or to create the conditions by which we may guarantee our salvation.

> Not every one who says to me, "Lord, Lord," shall enter the kingdom of heaven, but he who does the will of my Father who is in heaven. On that day, many will say to me, "Lord, Lord, did we not prophesy in your name, and cast out demons in your name, and do many mighty works in your name?" And then I will declare to them, "I never knew you; depart from me, you evildoers!" (Mt 7:21–23)

As much as the parable of the Last Judgment (Mt 25), these words make clear the depths of our blindness with regard to our actions and intentions. With the proper words ("Lord, Lord!") and the proper deeds (prophecy, exorcism, miracles!), there comes the subtle temptation of "entitlement." We imagine that if we conform in word and deed to what we understand God expects of us, then He is duty-bound to grant us our reward.

Yet God judges not words and actions, but the motivations of the heart.

This is why an Orthodox Christian can never claim to "be saved," as though that were a once-for-all, established fact, an obligation on God's part to make sure that *our* will be done. We can long and pray for salvation; but it is never guaranteed. There is no such thing as "once saved, always saved." There can only be ongoing repentance and hope—with the firm conviction that God is faithful, not capricious, and that He desires from the depths of His heart that *everyone* be saved and come to full knowledge of His truth and His glory.

In the Gospel of John, Jesus declares, "He who hears my word and believes Him who sent me has eternal life; he does not come into judgment, but has passed from death to life" (5:24). That hearing and believing, however, are ongoing, continuous. At every moment we stand before judgment because at every moment we can refuse to hear and refuse to believe. We may utter prophetic words and work astonishing miracles. And at the same time we can bring judgment and condemnation down upon ourselves, simply because what moves the heart is something other than the single-minded concern and desire to hear the Word of God and to do it.

All of us desperately need to hear the message of God's love, mercy, and saving grace. It is the only word that offers hope and the prospect of genuine peace to a world torn by violence, persecution, exploitation, and death. It is the only word that really offers a solution to the stress, fatigue, and anxiety that so many people bear today.

That message needs to be proclaimed everywhere and to everyone, since it remains the heart of the gospel. Equally a part of the Gospel, though, is the word of judgment. And that word, too, needs to be preached and needs to be heard.

If we grant the need to give full consideration to the many New Testament passages that speak of divine judgment, however, then we need to ask just *how* that judgment should be preached or otherwise conveyed. One of the greatest imbalances in Christian preaching, and consequently in Christian experience, occurs when judgment is confused with condemnation or when the judgment proclaimed is our own rather than God's.

As our preeminent Judge, Jesus never condemns. If goats are separated from sheep, if the unrighteous are cast into outer darkness, and if those who are angry at their brother are "liable to judgment" (Mt 5:22), in each case that judgment is self-inflicted. We bring judgment upon ourselves. The "wrath of God" St Paul warns us about (Rom 2–3) does not at all describe God's attitude or emotional state, as though God were vindictive. He does not punish us with His righteous judgment, as though it were some weapon to be wielded against those who offend His dignity and authority. God respects our freedom to rebel against Him. His judgment, His divine "wrath," consists in allowing us to suffer the consequences of that rebellion.

Judgment is indeed self-inflicted. God offers us life, and we choose death. He opens before us the way into the kingdom of Heaven, and we continue down our own pathway, which leads to destruction. Yet like the father of the prodigal son, God pursues us along that pathway, desiring only that we repent and return home. It is our decision to do so or not.

This means that judgment can only be preached in the light of the Cross, as an expression of divine mercy. St Paul expresses the ineffable paradox of God's love fulfilled through the sacrificial death of His Son: "For our sake [God] made Him to be sin who knew no sin, so that in Him we might become the righteousness of God" (2 Cor 5:21). Christ is our Judge; yet it is He who took upon

Himself the consequences of our sin by submitting to crucifixion. The judgment we merit has fallen on Him, and He bears it for the sake of our life and our salvation.

Whenever the theme of judgment appears in Jesus' parables or other teachings, it is always to summon people to repent, to return home. The motivation behind divine judgment, then, is neither vengeance nor self-righteousness. It is love. Jesus' word of judgment is intended neither as a threat nor as condemnation. It is an appeal, a call, an invitation. As such, it is an integral part of the gospel of love.

We are to preach and teach the message of divine judgment, then, not as an expression of God's vindictive wrath, but as an expression of His saving love. Too often we *pass* judgment rather than *proclaim* it. Then the word of judgment degenerates into a word of condemnation. And more often than not, that condemnation expresses our own feelings, attitudes, anger, and righteous indignation, rather than the true "wrath of God."

To proclaim the gospel faithfully requires us to preserve the delicate balance between mercy and judgment, between God's tender compassion and His righteous wrath, which is "revealed from heaven against all ungodliness and wickedness" (Rom 1:18). The crucial point is that we preach God's wrath with love.

As paradoxical as that may seem, it becomes possible when we center our proclamation about a truth transmitted to us by James the Just, the brother of our Lord. "Judgment is without mercy to one who has shown no mercy," he warns; "yet mercy triumphs over judgment!" (Jas 2:13).

9
"Radical Orthodoxy"?

*T*HERE'S AS MUCH PERPLEXITY as there is excitement these days over a new movement in Protestant theological circles, referred to as "radical orthodoxy." Many people consider it to be a trendy, unfocused yet hyper-intellectualized version of theological positions that died with the "neo-orthodoxy" of the 1950s and 60s. Others see it as a breath of fresh air, a wafting of the Spirit, that promises to reintroduce transcendence into theological inquiry and reestablish theology itself as the indispensable foundation of secular academic disciplines.

A basic premise of the movement is that ultimate truth can only be grasped by means of ritual, symbol, and allegory. Reason has its place but also its limits. A purely conceptual, rational approach to the world and human relationships has proven to be inadequate— hence the bankruptcy of so much that passes for "theology" today— and needs to be complemented by more traditional approaches to reality in general and the secular sciences in particular.

Neo-Orthodoxy? Radical Orthodoxy? Where have we been all this time?

How has it happened that persons and movements reacting against secularism, nihilism, and general spiritual decay over the past century have had to reinvent "orthodoxy"?

We Orthodox Christians know ourselves to be baptized members of the One, Holy, Catholic, and Apostolic Church, with a theological and liturgical tradition firmly rooted in the teaching of the apostles and the Fathers of the great Ecumenical Councils. It's this tradition that provides the only serious and solid insight into "reality," whether we label it "religious," "scientific," or "political."

We experience "transcendence" in the most powerful way at virtually every liturgical service. At every eucharistic celebration we commune in the Body and Blood of the risen and glorified Lord, consuming Life itself. We constantly perceive the world around us as "symbol," both a prophetic image and a real foretaste of the kingdom to come. "Eschatology" for us is not some catchy concept; it is our most basic experience in the little things of daily life.

Through eyes of faith—Orthodox faith—we behold the presence and glory of God in human persons and in the beauty of creation, as well as in mundane events and tragic suffering. The whole of our life is lived in an exquisite tension between heaven and earth, time and eternity. Our prayer lifts us beyond the world—or rather, lifts the world with us—and unites all of created reality with the Author of Life in the eternal communion of saints.

Consequently, we interpret revelation given in the Holy Scriptures with the aid of allegory as well as by means of the critical sciences. Thereby we constantly reach beyond the "literal" sense of God's Word to perceive its deeper meaning, its meaning *for us* in the "today" in which God calls us to live, to work, and to love.

Yet where have we been all this time? How is it that we have kept this treasure under a basket, hidden in a musty closet, more concerned to bicker among ourselves over liturgical details or jurisdictional prerogatives than to share, proclaim, and live *Orthodoxy* as a witness to a world that so desperately needs it?

As a result, our Protestant and Catholic brothers and sisters have to reinvent something rather like Orthodoxy, at least in certain aspects. Inevitably it is one-sided and ultimately inadequate, because it is "neo-orthodoxy" or "radical orthodoxy," and not Orthodoxy.

But that's not their fault. It's ours. And the burden of judgment will not be theirs either. Sadly, tragically—because it didn't have to be this way—that burden will be ours as well.

10

Cultural Wars and Orthodox Christianity

*T*HERE IS A TROUBLING AND fascinating debate going on right now with which we should all be at least somewhat familiar. It concerns our most fundamental vision of God, the world, and ourselves. And it has divided Christian against Christian, and Christians against the secular, "post-modern" culture in which we live.

The debate has been expressed in clear and sharp terms in the periodical *Christian Bioethics*, edited by H. Tristram Engelhardt, a well-known Orthodox physician and bioethicist who teaches at Rice University in Houston, Texas. In an issue published last year (vol. 8, no. 1, April 2002) the debate heated up. What are its main issues? In overly simplified terms, they are the following.

Orthodox authors of several articles that have recently appeared in the journal argue that many Roman Catholic ethicists and philosophers have unwittingly succumbed to the secular, post-modern mentality they seek to combat. This is because their chief emphasis, following the lead of Pope John Paul II, is upon the shaping of a philosophical—rather than a traditionally Orthodox spiritual and therapeutic—approach to issues such as abortion, end-of-life care, and single-payer health care (meaning the government).

Orthodox critics perceive that Roman Catholic calls for such noble causes as "social justice" and "a consistent life ethic" can lead to policies that in fact do more harm than good. An example is the tragedy of abortion. If the good end of universal health care is bought at the price of a government-imposed, single-payer policy, then the government—under secularist pressure—inevitably would require as well that physicians and other health-care personnel accept the moral perspective of the secular society, a perspective "free of religious constraints." Thus, under conditions of universal health-care funded by tax monies, physicians would be required either to perform abortions themselves, or to refer patients to other professionals who would.

The same holds true for issues such as physician-assisted suicide, euthanasia, and, we may presume, the procurement of vital organs from those not yet dead, including the poor, the marginalized, the mentally ill, and the cloned. Moral norms would no longer be determined by traditional religious values and perspectives. They would be determined by a perspective that is purely immanent, devoid of transcendent perspectives and values. Moral discourse, like today's public education, would be shaped by a vision of reality that is totally foreign to the gospel.

What distinguishes the Orthodox position from that of the secular world around us? In a word, it is its ascetic, spiritual, liturgical quest for *holiness*. God is holy, meaning "set apart," manifesting from His very being qualities, attributes, or virtues such as goodness, justice, righteousness, beauty, and love. It is by virtue of the work of the indwelling Holy Spirit, whom we receive at baptism and through the sacramental life of the Church, that these divine attributes actually may become our own. These attributes are forms of power. They radiate from God as "divine energies," communicated by the Spirit with the purpose of leading each of us along the pathway of holiness that comes to its fulfillment in the kingdom of God, in a true and eternal participation in God's very life.

Why should we be concerned with this debate? Because Orthodox values and Christian tradition in general are threatened today, more severely than ever, by the secularizing pressures of contemporary American society and Western culture. These pressures stem from a mentality that exalts hedonistic forms of consumerism, pleasure, self-fulfillment, and autonomy while it denigrates traditional Christian values of self-sacrifice, ascetic struggle, and worship of God.

Father Alexander Schmemann often pointed out that secularism is not a matter of unbelief, since many Christians, as well as many Jews, Muslims, and others of faith, are profoundly secularized. Secularism is marked primarily by a *rejection of worship*, a refusal to acknowledge that God has created us not primarily as *homo sapiens*, but as *homo adorans*, persons whose ultimate purpose in life is to worship God: to offer praise, adoration, thanksgiving and supplication to the three Persons of the Holy Trinity. It is only through worship—liturgical surrendering of our life and the world into the hands of God—that we can establish a firm basis for social justice, appropriate health-care, and other issues, including the question of national defense in an age of terrorism.

If I call attention to this debate, it is because each of us is called to live in the "real world" around us, however great its pressures and however distorted its perspectives. We are called to be witnesses to God's presence and purpose at home, at the office, in the shopping mall or in the hospital. It is there, in the little things and inconspicuous places of everyday life, that we live out our primary vocation to *pray* for the world, to live and die for the world's salvation.

We are called to be holy. This does not mean that we isolate ourselves from the ambient culture, making ourselves "separate" in some physical or psychological sense. It means that we seek holiness in the midst of an unholy world, in the hope that through our faithfulness to God and our witness to Him who alone is holy, we might touch the lives of others around us and help restore the world to the One who is both its Creator and its Lord.

11

The Faith of Our Fathers

N OT LONG AGO I READ an article by a well-known Anglican theologian that pointed up the radical difference in world-view
that separates him, and people who think as he does, from the
Orthodoxy that I treasure.

Well crafted and articulate, the article lays out reasons why the
author cannot accept traditional dogmatic statements that speak of
God, including the doctrines of the Trinity and the incarnation of
the Son of God. His point is that Christians in the post-apostolic
period projected Jesus onto the metaphysical plane, making him
virtually equal to God the Father. Whereas the New Testament, he
argues, presents Jesus as the man in whom God's love comes most
fully to expression, later Christianity transmogrified Jesus' very
being into the "God-Man," in response to the conviction that only
God can save us.

Although he is a New Testament scholar, this Professor of Divinity completely overlooks or ignores the canonical witness to
Christ's preexistence (Jn 1:1–14; 3:13; 17:5; 2 Cor 8:9; Eph 1:4; Phil
2:6; Col 1:15ff; 2 Tm 1:9–10; Heb 1:2–3; cf. Rev 22:13); his essential
union with God the Father (Jn 10:30; 17:5, 21; Col 1:15–20; 2:9; Tit
2:13; 1 Jn 5:20); his role as the agent of creation (Jn 1:3, Col 1:16,
Heb 1:2); his literal incarnation (Mt 1–2, Lk 2; Jn 1:14; Phil 2:7); and
his resurrection from the dead (*passim*). Nor does he give any consideration to the multitude of tripartite formulas throughout the

New Testament that speak of the essential unity of being, purpose and act shared by the Father, the Son, and the Holy Spirit (Mt 28:19; Lk 1:35, 9:28ff, 24:49; Jn 1:14, 5:23, 14:16f, 26, 15:26, 16:7–15; Rom 1:1–4, 5:1–5, 8:2–17, 15:15–21; 1 Cor 2:10, 6:11; 2 Cor 13:13; 2 Thess 2:13f; 1 Pet 3:18ff; and so forth).

There's no need to belabor the point. It is an old story, and a depressing one, because it is based on the assumption that we can always select our own canon within the canon, taking (and believing) those elements of the biblical witness that appeal to us and discarding the rest as myth, misunderstanding, or wishful thinking.

Orthodox Christianity is grounded in a single basic conviction that constitutes the core of the faith of our Fathers. It is borne out by the witness of countless martyrs and other saints, as well as by our personal and communal experience. This is the conviction that Jesus of Nazareth *is* the eternal Son of God and one of the Holy Trinity who appeared within human history to reveal the person and purpose of God the Father, and to work out that purpose through his teaching, death, resurrection, and glorification.

In the language of the Church's creeds, Jesus is one with and inseparable from the eternal Son of God, Author of creation and of our salvation. Born of the Father through eternal filiation, the divine Son appeared on earth, having taken on human existence in the womb of the Virgin Mary, thereby restoring and perfecting fallen human nature. He taught and worked prophetic miracles, he suffered and was crucified. His dead body was buried, then raised from death by the power of God the Father, working in the Holy Spirit (1 Tim 3:16, the probable meaning of "vindicated in the Spirit"). He ascended into heaven and assumed Lordship over all creation (Acts 1:9; Phil 2:9–11). We await his coming in glory, as the Father fulfills the divine "economy," or plan for the salvation and deification, of those who—through baptism, eucharistic communion, and prayer—unite themselves to Christ in faith and in love.

Orthodox Christians also share the conviction that these affirmations, given lapidary formulation in our creeds, faithfully reflect the witness of Holy Scripture. Although many of the creeds took shape in an atmosphere of controversy to combat various heretical views of Christ and the human person, those creedal statements accurately reflect the reality of God and his purpose in and for the world. As such, they are faithful summaries of scriptural teaching, as are the *anaphoras* of our eucharistic liturgies. (The finest creedal formulation or expression of authentic Christian belief, apart from the Nicene Creed itself, may be the anaphora or eucharistic prayer of the Divine Liturgy of St Basil.)

Over the last few decades, many Christian bodies have drifted ever farther from anything that resembles the biblical faith each of them claims to represent. This is a tragic state of affairs; yet I'm still convinced that God calls us to pursue ecumenical dialogue, even with those whose perspective on reality and way of reading Scripture are radically different from our own.

Whenever I get involved with that dialogue, though, I keep coming back to words from the dismissal of many of our liturgical services, words we repeat so often that we easily forget how vital they are for the world's salvation. They are the words of a simple but urgent prayer:

"Preserve, O God, the holy Orthodox faith and Orthodox Christians, unto ages of ages!"

12

Do Icons Really Weep?

*I*N A GREEK ORTHODOX CHURCH on Long Island there is an image of the Virgin Mary, the "Theotokos" or "Mother of God." This sacred image or "icon" has stains from the eyes to the cheeks. Those stains, according to countless witnesses, were produced many years ago when the icon wept.

In April of 1994, another icon of the Theotokos began weeping in an Antiochian Orthodox church in Cicero, Illinois. Again, literally thousands of worshipers witnessed the phenomenon and proclaimed it to be a miracle. Father Douglas Wyper, who first saw the tears and has subsequently written of his experience, declares to skeptics: "There were no tubes, there is no plumbing, no reason for condensation to form on that one icon and none of the others. The tears were coming directly out of the Virgin's eyes. You could see them welling up deep within her pupils. Since then, the tears have regularly renewed themselves." (*Again* 18/1, 1995, 21).

More recently, an Orthodox family in Michigan has been blessed with half a dozen weeping icons, five of the Theotokos and one of the glorified Christ.

In traditional Orthodox countries such as Russia, Romania, and Greece, the faithful take such phenomena for granted. Whether they have experienced a weeping icon or not, there is no question in their mind that these sacred images—most often depictions of the Virgin Mary—really do weep. Throughout the United States great numbers of Orthodox and other Christians have been deeply moved by similar experiences. To them as well, the tears are real.

I had long heard of weeping icons and, as I look back on it, I believed the reports to be true. The whole matter, though, had no real significance for me on any personal level. That changed, however, when my wife and I received a phone call from a young priest who invited us to visit his parish one winter evening a few years ago. He claimed that a weeping icon had been brought to his church a day or two before. He also asked us not to mention it to anyone else, chiefly because he wanted to avoid invasion by the media. More out of curiosity than conviction I accepted the invitation, and we drove over to his parish.

The church was lit only by candlelight. A dozen or so parishioners were sitting around the sides or standing, offering up their silent prayer. An extraordinary odor—a perfume like rose water, only vastly more beautiful, more heavenly—filled the entire building. In the center of the nave, in a glass-covered wooden case, lay the icon. I lifted the lid and looked at the image, which was clearly illumined by dozens of surrounding candles. In the corners of the Virgin's eyes, oil welled up in the shape of tears, then slowly ran down the cheeks. Cotton laid at the base of the image was drenched with the liquid. Those tears exuded the heavenly aroma.

We watched for nearly twenty minutes as dozens of tears gradually formed in those lovely, tragic eyes. The priest joined us and invited us to lift up the icon and examine the back. The entire board was saturated with the oil. Then, to my astonishment—and with a slight sense of disappointment—I realized that the icon was a copy: a piece of paper glued to the board. This was no "original," no "authentic" icon. It was a copy. Can copies weep?

Mindless questions like that went through my head for a few minutes. Then things fell into perspective. It is not the paint—not even "sacrosanct" egg tempera—that makes an icon. An authentic icon is made by God. Original or a copy, its truth and its value lie in what it depicts. Ultimately they lie in the person of Christ Himself, since every genuine icon is "Christ-centered," whether it be of Jesus, of His Mother, or of the saints.

Like every true icon, this one of the Mother of God depicted transfigured humanity. In the face of the Virgin we beheld our own true face, the image in which we were created and to which we are ceaselessly called. And this image had the added grace of tears.

On our way home, we wondered aloud about the reason for those tears. Why, in fact, do icons weep? Is it because of our sins? Or because of the threat of some impending tragedy? Or because we have forgotten the grief of Jesus' Mother, as she helped take down His tortured body from the cross, washed and anointed it, then laid it in a tomb?

I still can't answer the question, Why do icons weep? But weep they do. "There are no tubes, no plumbing, no reason for condensation to form". . . . The tears in those eyes are real. And they express the full reality of heavenly beauty and heavenly grief.

Some of the tears we saw that winter evening I mixed with olive oil and keep in a little flask. They are used to anoint the sick, and, at times of great feasts within the Church, all the faithful who take part in worship.

Thinking about it, I doubt I'll ever know just why icons weep. But I have no doubt that they do. On the other hand, I do know that those tears are a gift to all of us. I know beyond question that they bless and they heal. And that, really, is enough.

13

The Gift of Wonder

S CHOOL STARTS IN TEN DAYS and the local kids are moaning already. To ease the pain, I just took two of them, a nine-year-old girl and her eleven-year-old brother, to the aquarium It was the first time they had ever been.

Andrew moved quickly through the crowds, pressing against the walls of the massive tanks, looking above all for turtles. He was impressed by big fish (a fresh-water sturgeon elicited a long, low whistle), practically ignored the snakes and alligators, and kept hunting for turtles. He was a boy—maybe from Mars?—full of curiosity and fun. And very much on the go.

Tania, on the other hand, ambled behind us, taking in now one exhibit, now another, staring at swarms of yellow, striped fish, timidly advancing toward the huge, green, moray eel, and gulping hard when a shark passed right in front of her nose. She hardly spoke a word. At first I thought she was bored. Then it struck me that she was absorbing it all with a quiet sense of wonder.

I watched her for a while, fascinated with her fascination, impressed with the way she absorbed impressions. She took it all in, not so much because it was new but because it was beautiful. Her eyes, already lovely at her tender age, reflected the loveliness of movement, flow, color, harmony, even sound. Above the chatter of the crowd we could hear the piped in music of frogs, cicadas, and forest birds. Steam rose from the cypress swamp with a hiss. A small 'gator slid off a rotting log and splashed into the dark water.

Tania watched and listened, oblivious to other people, fixed on natural things that brought a gentle thrill. In that place she lived a moment of quiet ecstasy, dancing inwardly with the graceful, rhythmic choreography of life.

Watching her brought a trace of sadness. Life without wonder is empty, dull, humdrum, suffocating. Little children who have been allowed to see and hear and feel good and lovely things, who have felt beach sand between the toes and seen calves being born and touched a snake—they know what life is in its depths. This is because they bring to it a sense of wonder.

We have lost wonder, we adults. All these "Something Generations" we're surrounded with these days, young people and old, seem jaded. People are seeking thrills, looking for kicks, yearning for distraction. It affects our lives at every level, corrupting our relations with one another and with the world we live in. We have become so "functional," so absorbed with doing things, that we not only can't take time to smell the roses, but also sneer at the very idea.

By losing a sensitivity toward wonder, we have lost life itself, life as God intended it to be. Our plasticized and polluted virtual world is a poor substitute for the Eden God held out to us and which we rejected. And so we live in the world as in Pilgrim's "slough of despond," a world devoid of value, meaning and beauty, because it's devoid of wonder. Eden seems irretrievably lost.

Little kids, on the other hand, know that Eden still exists. They find it all about them—if we allow them.

Looking at Tania as she looked at fish and other creatures was a wonderful way to spend an August morning. There was something Socratic in the experience. Unbeknownst to her, she taught me to watch rather than just look, and to listen rather than just hear. Her wonder was a catalyst that brought back to me the gift of wonder.

It also brought to mind some lines from a poem by Sara Teasdale, words I had thought rather corny when I first read them in my own jaded youth. After the aquarium, I don't feel that way any more.

Life has loveliness to sell,
    All beautiful and splendid things,
Blue waves whitened on a cliff,
    Soaring fire that sways and sings,
And children's faces looking up
    Holding wonder like a cup.

There in the aquarium, this little child's face held wonder like a cup. And I suspect that, for a moment at least, mine did too.

14

Physical Fitness Program

V ICE PRESIDENT CHENEY and I have something in common. I haven't had his spate of heart attacks. But we both suffer from a lack of physical exercise. He has the Secret Service to pace him around the block. I have our son's husky. Neither of us, though, seems likely to take advantage of these assets any time soon.

Why is it so hard for some of us to get off our duff and flex a little? Why is our most nimble move to flick to a new channel when surfing lands us on a sweaty fitness program? Why does the Nordic Track gather dust like no other object in the house? Or the cheery, "Want to join me for a walk?" elicit a cold sweat and a grumbled, "Thanks . . . not right now . . ."?

Maybe this doesn't apply in your house, but it does in mine. Or rather, it does to me. My wife is out striding a country mile to the mail box, while I sit immobile, staring at a computer screen and flexing nothing more than my fingers.

Every once in awhile I make a stab at getting back in shape. Yet I have to admit that the motivation is more to relieve a mild sense of guilt than to achieve washboard abs. At one point I even developed what could be called a physical fitness program. Both the aim and the result lacked something, as the following diary entry indicates.

I jogged a mile or two today
But retold in my fantasy
My exploit gains in magnitude
and quickly mounts to three
Or more.

Although my weight stays much the same,
My self-deception's worth it if
My gnawing conscience is assuaged
Yet I am neither stiff
Nor sore.

It's easy enough to kid about this: to take it so lightly we don't have to do anything but laugh about it. Yet every once in a while the realization strikes home that there is a profound spiritual problem involved here.

Lack of proper exercise, whatever the reason, leads to a spiritual malaise that envelops our entire being. That malaise is caused not merely by laziness, or boredom with exercise routines, or disdain for the obsessive fitness-culture that drives so many overfed and underflexed Americans to the local gym. It is caused by a major failure in the realm of stewardship. I am as responsible for the welfare and well-being of this body that is mine as I am for the welfare and well-being of members of my family.

This point is made clear by the apostle Paul, when he addresses the abuses of the body inflicted by the lifestyle of certain Christians in Corinth. There sexual abuses were a prime concern, as First Corinthians 5–7 makes abundantly clear. What he says about the spiritual aspect of the body in those chapters, though, pertains as well to those of us whose major corporal sin involves sedentariness (that's not in the dictionary, but it should be).

In First Corinthians 6, St Paul reminds us: "Do you not know that your body is a temple of the Holy Spirit within you, which you have from God? You are not your own! You were bought with a price (meaning the blood of Jesus Christ). Therefore, glorify God in your body!"

To face the rest of his mandate, Mr Cheney needs much better advice than I can give him. But I would like to urge him to do what I need to do for myself: honor our Creator by honoring our physical being. Indeed, glorify God by maintaining the health, strength, and general fitness of the muscles, bones, and tissues that constitute our "outer nature." Although that outer nature may well be wasting away, as St Paul also tells us (2 Cor 4:16), the renewal of our inner, spiritual nature depends directly on preserving the integrity and well-being of its external counterpart. For the "body," in the profoundly biblical sense of the term, includes both aspects of our being; and both exist with the primary purpose of glorifying God.

My wife just came home. "Would you please turn up the heat?" I asked. "No," she replied. "You need to get up and move around!" And she hadn't even seen what was on the computer screen.

15
Local Developments

W E LIVE IN AN AREA of the country that until the early 1980s had hardly changed from pre-Civil War days. This is the lowcountry of South Carolina, a mystical land of charm and weathered elegance, slightly run down at the heels but essentially beautiful. Much of its charm, as well as its importance culturally and historically, lie in the generations of rural African-Americans who have lived here since slavery and emancipation, and who call this land home. Home under the live oaks and Spanish moss; home in the oyster beds and pluff mud; home among myriad song and sea birds, cultivated azaleas grown wild, magnolia trees with their ivory blossoms; home in the heat and the damp, among no-see-ums that pass right through the screens and cicadas that sing you to sleep every night. Home, too, among varying degrees of rural poverty, with rusted auto carcasses in the front yard next to the tire-swing, and chickens running all over the place. Home in a land of peace and occasional violence, of hammocks and slamming screen doors, of dirty, barefoot kids and dogs galore. To these people, families black and white who have lived here forever, as to relative newcomers who have been here for only a generation or two, this is home.

In the past couple of decades, it has also become a developer's dream.

Everybody, it seems, wants to live on the water—especially if that water is lazy, tidal, and close to the ocean. So land prices around here have soared and development has boomed. Myrtle Beach, a haven of dunes and saw grass when I was a kid, has been turned into the Atlantic City of the South. From the Grand Strand on down below Savannah, the lowcountry is threatened with annihilation. This rarest of beautiful things is doomed, as is the way of life of rural blacks and laid-back local white folk. Many of them can't afford the rising land taxes. Others are being bought out: offered what seems a fortune for land that a developer knows he's getting for a song, as he plans for the next multimillion dollar condo project, marina, or conference center.

I should probably feel guilty about complaining. If my family, my neighbors, and I can live here, why shouldn't anybody? Two reasons are obvious: limited resources and exploitation by the wealthy of the relatively poor.

The lowcountry is a magnificent example of our national heritage, one every bit as significant as Yellowstone or Niagara or Muir Woods It's not just beautiful. It's home to a culture: to Gullah culture with its marvelous language and gestures; to Charlestonian culture with its eminently "southern" way of life that shapes both language and thought; to Savannah culture, now hopelessly threatened in the wake of *Midnight in the Garden. . . .*

What makes it especially sad and hard to deal with is the fact that so many of the developers are from out of town or out of state. The local ones, to be sure, have constructed housing, office buildings, and other necessities of urban and suburban living that have provided jobs and homes for a large number of grateful people. And many of these native entrepreneurs have practiced land management with skill and a sincere concern to preserve the area's natural beauty.

My quarrel is with those from outside who see a good thing, then swoop in for the kill. And the local people—especially the African Americans of Gullah extraction, with their unique language, culture, manners, and outlook—become victims. Now on the endangered list, they are moving inexorably toward extinction.

What is happening here can and will happen across the nation, if something more powerful than money isn't brought to bear. No ecological pressure group or organized letter-writing campaign is going to hold back the tide. The matter is ultimately a profoundly spiritual one. It concerns people and creation: bearers of God's image and the particular Garden in which God has set each of us, so that we might serve as faithful stewards of the beauty and wealth of lands that are His. Genuine 'ecology' is a matter of the soul. It means we receive and care for what has been given us, with diligence and love; then we offer it back to the Creator, to whom it belongs. Otherwise we betray our calling and God's very purpose for the world.

At the end of its series of exhibits the Charleston Aquarium displays the statement, "In the end, we shall save only what we love." Where, in our hierarchy of values—of things we love—belong such things as memory, custom, and culture? Where do we place a salt marsh or a massive live oak or the sound of wind in the pines? Where do we locate, in that hierarchy, the old black woman who has lived all her life next door, who now has to move inland because she can no longer afford the taxes? Where do we put people and creation?

If balance there is, I can't indulge in self-righteous, wholesale condemnation of developers. I can't forget that. But I can't forget either a little bit of verse I jotted down many years ago when our rural area of northern New Jersey became Suburbia once I-80 was put through, and many local farmers had to give up their way of life. It's dedicated simply to

The Developer

> To beauty, life and growth he is a bane
> Whose only passion is financial gain
> That leads him to exploit for all it's worth
> The holy order to subdue the earth
> And make of field and forest a terrain
> Where nothing green will ever grow again.
>
> Mammon's blessed this builder from his birth
> Who longs to leave upon the earth his stain.

16

Symbiosis

I N THE LOWCOUNTRY WINTER, some twenty miles south of the Holy City (as Charlestonians like to call their home town), the temperature at mid-morning was just under 70 degrees. By late afternoon it was 38 and dropping. The fog had lifted and the rain had stopped. Brilliant, almost blinding light sparkled across the surface of the tidal river next to the house.

A school of dolphins—more than I had seen since early fall—was playing and feeding just off the near bank. Usually they move up or down stream in a steady undulation. This time they were cavorting in circles and enjoying themselves, while surging now and then after some unseen prey. There must have been eight or ten in all.

Occasionally one would stick its bottle-nosed snout well out of the water, mouth agape. It was strange behavior, inexplicable until I made the connection. A flock of terns circled overhead. Every once in a while, one tern found the courage to swoop down toward a dolphin's open mouth and snatch a morsel of fish from those teeth. The dolphin, in fact, was offering food to the bird. I had never seen this before, and the sight was mesmerizing.

In summer especially, small pods of "po-pusses," as the local folk call them, will circle a school of fish, and using their powerful tails, sweep water and fish up onto the mud bank. Then they surge toward shore, sometimes lunging completely out of the water. They grab a fish, then slither down the incline of wet mud back into the river. It's a sight to watch: chaotic and noisy, since hovering above are terns and gulls, and standing on the bank, ready to stab at a stray fish, are blue herons and egrets. Everybody's squawking yet everybody gets something.

Today, though, was the first time I have seen dolphins actually feed the birds. Like the little old lady in *Mary Poppins,* sitting in front of St Paul's Cathedral and selling crumbs for tuppence a bag, these creatures of God were serving the hungry. And they were not even of the same species. . . .

Somehow there came to mind George W. Bush's inaugural speech, in which he called us all to assume genuine "citizenship." Watching those dolphins, I wondered what shape that citizenship could take that might bring it into line with the simple but extraordinary gesture made by those highly intelligent and socially adapted creatures. The President challenged us to feed our own poor and to provide for the less fortunate among us. Since the loudest applause accompanied his promise of major tax cuts, though, there had to be an element of wishful thinking in his call to benevolence.

Then I thought, too, of the lingering racism in this country, of ethnic strife in our ghettos, not to mention in our churches, that drive a wedge between us and "them," whoever the "them" might be. Then again there's the matter of competition raised to the level of a national virtue, coupled with a passion for individual "rights" and privileges that not only trump civic responsibility but make of us an increasingly litigious society. There's a reason why the prince of demons is called the Devil. The word *diabolos* means the one who slanders and separates.

Still watching those dolphins, I also wondered if there's the time and the will in this country to hear the gospel call for cooperation, love, self-sacrifice, and devoted service out of concern for others. Maybe those lost virtues are gone forever.

Nevertheless, when Americans put their minds to it, they can accomplish just about anything. We are really blessed that way. But we are also cursed with a knack for getting in our own way and shooting ourselves in the foot, especially when concern moves from the private realm to the public, when we try to take on the challenges and obligations of genuine citizenship.

Those dolphins aren't "just fish." They're mammals, like us, with a remarkable degree of intelligence and social organization. Although the mechanism remains a mystery, they can communicate effectively with each other. And they can be both playful and charitable, or so it seemed this afternoon. In any case, they demonstrated a remarkable symbiosis with those terns—which were not even of their own species.

Playful and charitable, even with people who are "not of our own species." Highly intelligent and socially conscious. We can become like that, if we really want to. It's not too great a challenge, and it's not too much to ask. Especially since the future of the country likely depends on it.

17

Wasting Whose Time?

"**N**O NEED TO RUSH**," my wife assured me as we bumped over ruts and small branches strewn along the dirt roadway that leads through the woods to the main road nearly a mile from our house. "We've got plenty of time." It was early morning and we were headed for church. A wind storm the night before had brought down all sorts of debris, the roadway was passable but barely, and we were running late. "Plenty of time," I mumbled. "I don't think so. . . ."

"How did it go today," she asked with a bright smile as I came in the kitchen door. "Fine," I replied. "Only I wasted nearly half an hour waiting for the bridge to open, then more time standing in line at the DMV." It seemed like a petty complaint, but I really don't like to waste time. It makes me feel guilty.

Not enough time. Don't want to waste time. In this workaholic society we live in, time seems more valuable than money. We never have enough of it, yet when we do, we tend—in our own minds, at any rate—to waste it. Whose time is it, anyway? Why do I so often feel pressured by a lack of it, or annoyed at myself when I feel I've squandered, abused, or otherwise misused it?

Thinking about it, I realize I can't answer those questions until I come to terms with a more basic one. What in fact *is* "time"? Even the encyclopedia refers to it as a "mystery." The dictionary doesn't help much, because it begins by defining it as "a period. . . ." But a "period" implies the passage of time, so the definition is circular. The one point that stands out is that time involves *change*. An action or a process can exist only because it involves extension through time: extension that includes change from one state or condition to another. That change, however, can occur only within a certain framework that we call space. This is why physicists speak of time as a fourth dimension, complementary to the spatial dimensions of height, length, and depth. For change to occur within those spatial dimensions, it requires time. Time, then, is the measure of changing space: space in the external world, but also space within ourselves.

I'm reminded of a sketch that used to hang in the St Vladimir's Seminary Bookstore. It consisted of a single panel depicting a totally frustrated and bemused Calvin (of *Calvin and Hobbes*), making a point with clenched fists. The caption was something like this: "God put me on this earth to accomplish a few things. Right now I'm so far behind, I'll never die!"

God puts us here for a purpose. He calls us to accomplish a few things, to change the space in which we live, and to do so in specific ways. Some of that change involves other people or things exterior to ourselves. Much of it involves ourselves directly, our interior life that St Paul calls "the inner man." Time is the prerequisite for change I make within myself. Or to be more precise, time is the instrument given me by God that allows Him—with my cooperation—to work those changes within me. That takes time, possibly a lifetime. And right now, I'm so far behind I'm *afraid* to die.

There's a simple but important moral to all this. Time is a gift, granted by God in order for us to fulfill His purpose, to accomplish the few things He puts us here for. Those few things invariably involve change. And that change concerns above all our inner space.

So rather than risk life and limb to arrive somewhere on time, or curse the delays that seem to mean such waste, maybe, by God's grace, I can come to the point where I treasure time as an opportunity rather than resent it as a constraint. Maybe I can come to realize that the time I waste, like the time I covet, is not mine at all, but His.

Nightmares

I DON'T HAVE NIGHTMARES VERY OFTEN, but when I do, I wish I
hadn't.

Waking up in a cold sweat, heart pounding away, feeling totally
vulnerable—but to what? Often I can't even remember what I was
dreaming about, or if I do, it seems insignificant, silly, or absurd.
Sometimes, though, it's terrifying.

Some nightmares recur frequently enough that I've become
almost used to them. Falling dreams, for example, or standing in
front of a classroom full of students without the vaguest idea as to
what I'm supposed to be lecturing about. Then there are those that
evoke sheer dread, like being pursued by a giant spider, or running
from a hit squad and finding I can only move in slow motion.

These are the worst, really: horrifying dreams of unnamed pur-
suers, demons of the night that are determined to get me. Again,
thank God, they are rare. But the daytime stress all too easily translates into a nighttime panic, as those demons, in myriad form,
chase me down the highways and byways of Morphean uncon-
sciousness.

Bad dreams aren't just psychological. They're not just an emotional safety valve that lets out the built-up steam of stress, anxiety,
guilt, or whatever. They represent a profound spiritual malaise, an
inability to turn all that stress, anxiety, guilt, and such over to God.
As unwanted and unwelcome as they are, nightmares are in some

way self-inflicted. They symbolize a powerful and demonic rejection of the first gift the Risen Christ bestowed on His disciples: the gift of Peace. A major struggle in the spiritual life is to allow God Himself to transform our night sweats into peaceful repose, confident that His will governs all things, and that the Cross of Christ is an invincible weapon which has once and for all destroyed the might of Satan and his minions.

Like every struggle in the Christian life, this one derives its energy and direction from the Holy Spirit. Our "synergy" or cooperation with the Spirit, though, is essential. What can we do to take on effectively the struggle against the demonic, against ourselves and our own nighttime vulnerabilities?

Years ago a friend shared with me a tactic in the warfare against nightmares that actually works. At least it works in cases of "pursuit" dreams, when we find ourselves in a panic, running—or trying to run—from some person or beast that's chasing us down to do us in. That tactic, simplistic as it may sound, is to stop, turn around, and face the enemy. As impossible as that sounds, it is learned behavior that we can practice and train ourselves to adopt.

The place to start is that in-between state when we know we're dreaming yet can't coax ourselves into wakefulness. With a little practice, we learn to recognize that we are dreaming, that we can extract or abstract ourselves just enough from the unfolding nightmare scene to take control. It's scary at first. But gradually we really do acquire the ability to rewrite our bad dreams (the good ones, too, I suppose, but there's no need to do that).

The other night, for the first time in a long while, I dreamt I was being chased by something that threatened my very life. It was, as usual, about stress: too many overdue phone calls to make; too many loose ends tripping me up at every turn; too much chaos. And it was after me. Finally the threat took concrete shape. It became a raging tiger, fangs bared, vicious claws exposed, ready to tear my flesh to shreds.

As a gift of pure grace, my friend's advice came back to me. I stopped the frantic running, turned around and faced this thing. It terrified me. But the object of my terror was suddenly transformed into Calvin's Hobbes: a stuffed tiger with a silly grin on his face. And I woke up laughing.

It doesn't always happen like that. Yet I've heard enough friends and parishioners talk about their bad dreams to realize that on some level we're all in this together.

We are everyone and everything in our dreams, they tell us. This means that Pogo's insight is still valid: "We have met the enemy, and he is us."

Stop, turn, and face the enemy. If it's not a stuffed tiger, at least it won't be any worse than looking in the mirror.

19

A Special Friendship

O N OUR FRIDGE there's a magnet with a picture of the back of two little bears gazing into the sunset, their stubby arms draped over each other's shoulders. The caption reads: "Happiness is being married to your best friend."

Ordinarily I'm allergic to feel-good refrigerator messages ("Let's put the *fun* back in 'dysfunctional'!"), and even more so to those that make me feel guilty ("Maid's day off: clean up after yourself!"). This one, though, always has been a reminder of what really matters in our life. In the midst of a great deal of clutter, business, and stress, it's a welcome call to return to the most basic of basics: deep and abiding friendship between two people who have committed themselves to each other for life and for eternity.

A quotation attributed to the fourth-century Cappadocian saint, Gregory the Theologian, reads: "Marriage is the key of moderation and the harmony of desires, the seal of a deep friendship. . . . For marriage does not remove God, but brings us all the closer to Him, for it is God Himself who draws us to it."

Among the virtues of marriage Gregory lists here, the most important is the last: the "seal of a deep friendship." Insofar as marriage is sealed with that particular seal, then moderation and "the harmony of desires" follow naturally, spontaneously. This doesn't mean that there will never be quarrels. Or that lust is forever overcome and that we won't ever be attracted to some other person. It's no guarantee against the temptations that pursue married people as much as those we naively used to call "celibates." There can be little doubt, though, that a conjugal union sealed by the bond of genuine and deep friendship possesses unique inner strength, purpose, and, more pragmatically, staying power.

What so often destroys marriages is precisely the lack of this kind of friendship. A couple may marry because of shared infatuation, strong mutual interests, even a common spiritual vision. They may be on the same career track or like the same distractions or share the same love for children. Then again, they may be drawn together because of a similar woundedness: the legacy of an abusive childhood, for example, or loneliness because they have already lost a spouse through death or divorce.

But if the element of friendship is not there, the marriage has little chance to last. If it does endure, it will most likely be conventional and suffocatingly dull.

When clergy counsel young couples who are planning to marry, they usually prioritize their advice. First of all, they stress the importance of shared faith and prayer, urge that the children be brought up in the church, and perhaps even recommend that the couple take periods of retreat, either together or individually. Then they move on to the quality of the relationship the couple should strive towards, in the realms of sexuality, finances, health, and so forth. Finally they may recommend that the couple seek out common interests: anything from theater to books to sports that can spark mutual interest and keep the two from drifting apart. They rarely speak about the importance of friendship.

There are no formulas for creating friendship. There are no manuals that can teach it, no exercises that will systematically strengthen it. Friendship is a gift.

This means that perhaps we clergy should begin by seeking to discover if the couple has this gift or not. More than compatibility in matters sexual or spiritual, a deep and genuine friendship provides the basis, the bedrock, for any enduring relationship, including conjugal union.

If it is really God Himself who draws us to marriage, He does so most effectively—in the way that is most blessed—by bestowing on the couple the inestimable gift of friendship. With their common life grounded in this gift, they can then work out other aspects of their relationship, including growth toward shared faith and prayer.

"Every good and perfect gift is from above, coming down from the Father of lights" (Jas 1:17). Conjugal friendship is that kind of gift. And we can ask for it, pray for it day in and day out, from the One who desires from the depths of His heart to bestow it on us.

The little bears have got it right. Happiness is being married to your best friend.

20

What Price Renewal?

*I*N THE EARLY 1980s a Russian expatriate whom I knew slightly
made a remark that at the time sounded preposterous. This
man was born and brought up in Moscow. By some means, he had
made his way to the United States and settled with his family in an
urban area outside of Manhattan. He traveled a good deal and came
to know his adopted country as well as one can in half a decade. He
was intelligent, observant, and deeply committed to his Orthodox
Christian faith.

His remark came offhandedly one day while we were talking
religion. "You know," he said, "it's really much harder today to be a
Christian in the United States than in the Soviet Union."

At first I was a little offended. This sounded like a gratuitous slap
at the great majority of Americans who consider themselves believers, and especially at those among them who clothe the poor, feed
the hungry, visit the sick, and otherwise take the gospel seriously.

As we talked further, the point he was trying to make became
clearer. Authentic Christianity thrives under hardship and persecution. In a society driven by consumerism and an obsessive fixation
on individual "rights," it suffocates.

In Russia at the time, Christians who acted on their faith risked
losing their jobs, their lodgings, and in extreme cases, even their
children (Baptists, far more than Orthodox, knew the horror of
having their children kidnapped by State security agents). In
the United States, Christians didn't risk a thing, except possibly

boredom. The heady days of the civil rights movement were all but over, the economy was turning around after the Carter years, and we were able once more to forget that many of our fellow citizens had no health insurance, were unable to survive on the minimum wage, and found themselves generally excluded from the "new prosperity."

For most of us, things were looking up, at least materially. The spiritual cost, though, was horrendous. Mainline Protestant denominations were seeing substantial losses in their numbers and influence; Catholic clergy were leaving the priesthood, if not the Church, in droves; and many Orthodox were settling comfortably into ethnic enclaves that preserved social identity and little else.

Compartmentalization was the order of the day. So many hours per week were devoted to earning a living, so many to caring for the kids, so many for "leisure time activity," and, if there was any time left over, an hour or two for God. The upshot was that God became domesticated and the gospel became banal. Protestant theologians such as Barth and the Niebuhrs had left the scene, together with their proclamation of the all-powerful and all-righteous God of judgment. With the deaths of Maritain, de Lubac, and Merton, Catholicism lost eloquent voices that for decades had powerfully proclaimed the nature and meaning of faith, Church, and spiritual life. And the untimely death of Fr Alexander Schmemann deprived us of one of the most vibrant and profound contemporary witnesses to genuine Orthodoxy. Great theologians, speaking out of their respective traditions and faith-experience, were gone, and with them there disappeared a clear image of God, Church, and the human person.

More than twenty years later, little seems to have changed. Our lives are still compartmentalized and God is still domesticated, at least in the popular mind. Despite the WTC attacks and the economic crisis, Christians in America (are you ready for this?) have succumbed to consumerism. We take what we want and we leave the rest. We fashion for ourselves the image of God that is most comfortable, most appealing, most entertaining. Religious commitment is reduced to emotional fervor ("Jesus Rocks!", a *Newsweek* cover shouts), morality is reshaped to accommodate our basest passions, and people like me who complain about it are dismissed as archaic, irrelevant, and intrusive.

Even today it may be harder to be a Christian in the United States than in Russia.

If we look at it the right way, though, that may be a blessing. The challenge we face here today is not external persecution, although that is a growing threat in other countries and may soon be here as well. Our challenge, as it always has been, is to hear the gospel of Christ and to shape our lives in terms of it. It is to declare our faith in God's presence, love, and saving power, and to do so in the face of mockery and harassment from our peers, the media, and those in authority. It is to join with people of other faiths, or of no faith, who labor to serve and to care for the poor, the sick, the suffering, and the marginalized members of society. It is to unite with other Christians, including those we disagree with, in offering to God's world words and gestures that inspire hope and a sense of purpose in what to so many people seems to be a meaningless existence. It is to live so simply, joyfully, and fully that it is no longer we who live, but Christ who lives in us.

This is easy to say. Left to ourselves, there is no way we can make it happen. But if Soviet Russia could raise up countless martyrs—living witnesses ready to die for their faith—we can do the same. If prophetic voices such as that of the martyr-priest Alexander Men can emerge to breathe life and passionate faith into the contemporary Russian soul, we can hope and pray that God will raise up such voices here as well.

As in Russia, it requires one most basic element in our life as Christian people. It requires what St Paul described to the Philippians as the will and the desire to "know Christ and the power of His resurrection." That knowledge requires of us that we share Christ's sufferings—on our behalf and for a tortured and fragmented world—"becoming like Him in His death, that if possible [we] may attain the resurrection from the dead" (Phil 3:10–11).

Here, perhaps, lies the ultimate significance of September 11, 2001—not simply to shake us out of our complacency, but to remind us once again that the way to salvation passes inevitably by the way of the Cross.

Genuine renewal doesn't depend on stirring up evangelical fervor or holding revival meetings across the country. It means that we—each of us, to the measure of our capacity—take up the Cross of Christ, to witness, to serve and, if need be, to die for the sake of those around us, in the full knowledge that if we suffer with Christ and for Christ, we will also be glorified with Him (Rom 8:17).

21

"No One Comes to the Father, But by Me"

S HORTLY AFTER JACK LEMMON'S death last year, ABC did a special
showing of "Tuesdays with Morrie," with Lemmon in the title
role, giving what was arguably his finest performance.

In many ways the film was even better than the book, because
in Lemmon's face we could see the beauty and tragedy of a thoroughly good, wise, and compassionate man as his life slowly ebbed
away under the withering effects of ALS, "Lou Gehrig's disease." A
retired professor from Brandeis University, Morrie Schwartz
imparted insight and hope to Mitch Albom, a former student whose
life and love were increasingly threatened by his pressure-filled
profession as a sports columnist for a Detroit newspaper. Mitch's
Tuesdays spent with his mentor and friend transformed more than
his relationship with the woman he loved. They also taught him the
truth of Auden's poignant reflection: *either we love or we die.*

Morrie was a Jew, brought up in conditions of poverty and prej-
udice. His humor and good cheer gave way at times to fits of early
morning anguish and anxiety, in part, a legacy from his childhood.
As his disease progressed, those emotions were joined by others:
fear, anger and bitterness, the familiar syndrome of "Why is this
happening to me?" Yet the dominant mood was brightness, and
above all, love. Love, affection, and compassion that called forth the
same attitudes, the same gifts, in other people.

After watching that film with my wife, I made some remark
about its one aspect that I found disappointing. "Here this man is,

facing death—and doing so with an extraordinary amount of grace and peace. Yet there's no transcendence to it at all: not a word about God, about the hope of salvation and eternal life."

With Morrie-like astuteness, she replied, "Not overtly, in any case." Then she smiled.

Sometime before dawn I woke up and started thinking about people like Morrie. Ever since church school I had wondered and worried about Jesus' assertion in John's Gospel, "No one comes to the Father, but by me." I believed that then and I still do now, half a century later. What does it mean, though, about people like Morrie? Or other Jews who could not and can not accept Jesus as their Messiah, yet live lives that radiate goodness, kindness, holy wisdom, and love? What does it mean about Buddhists, Hindus, Muslims or any other members of "the world's great religions," who have never really heard the gospel—or if they have, have never been able to shape their lives and their beliefs according to its promise?

Christians disagree very much among themselves about how we are saved. For some, it's enough just to stand up and say that they accept Jesus Christ as their personal Lord and Savior. For others, including the Orthodox, the way to salvation requires ongoing repentance, struggles against our worst inclinations, and acts of charity ("Faith without works is dead," the apostle James reminds us). In any case, the indispensable condition is nevertheless Jesus Christ and His saving grace.

But does salvation in and through Christ necessarily require conscious and active *belief* in Him? For Christians, the answer is without any doubt, "Yes." Yet faith itself is a gift ("For *by grace* you have been saved through faith," St Paul insists, "and this is not your own doing, it is the *gift* of God"; Eph 2:8). Is conscious, active "faith" in Christ, then, still a requirement for the multitudes who have never been able to hear the gospel? Or is their salvation perhaps founded on the indisputable truth that God desires, from the depths of His heart, that every person, as a bearer of His image, know the joy of eternal communion with Him?

Jesus Christ is and always will be the unique Way, Truth, and Life. Apart from Him, no one comes to the Father. But just how conscious does every non-Christian soul have to be of His specific, unique, and indispensable role in leading us along that pathway?

Many Orthodox would take me to task for even raising such a question, and some would probably think I should be defrocked. But if Christianity is inclusive rather than exclusive, if the real criterion for salvation is not the cry "Lord, Lord," but rather the acts of charity Jesus Himself calls for in Matthew 25, then it is a question that must be raised.

St Paul declared that three great virtues abide forever: faith, hope, and the greatest of them all, love. Many people are saved by faith. Yet I can't help hoping and praying that many more—like the Morries of this world—are saved by love.

22

The Missing Ingredient

THERE'S AN IMPORTANT ELEMENT of the Gospel narratives that we all too easily overlook. It is the reaction on the part of people who hear Jesus' teachings and witness the extraordinary signs or miracles He performs. In a word, that reaction is one of *awe*. It is a response of wonder, tinged with fear, in the face of what has been called the *mysterium tremendum*, the unfathomable mystery of divine presence and power.

In Christian experience the wonder remains, but the fear is transformed into a profound reverence. When Christ heals people, the Gospels tell us, bystanders react with "amazement." They are "astonished," sometimes even "overwhelmed," by what they see and hear. When the experience is powerful enough to plunge them into silence, it provokes feelings of awe. Like Moses, they take off the shoes of their soul, for they find themselves on hallowed ground.

This, in any case, is how it should be. In today's reality, awe has been reduced to "awesome!," a reaction that's just a notch above "cool!" We have so domesticated God that we no longer feel awe in His presence, we are no longer shaken to the bones by His overwhelming power and glory. Yet any God who is devoid of the capacity to evoke awe is no God at all. It is an idol of our own making, a pitiful caricature of all that is genuinely holy.

Awe is the missing ingredient in American religion, including Christianity. It is the absence of awe that has transformed traditional faith and worship into "American popular religion," with its feel-good therapy services offered up to a Big Buddy in the sky. For those who are looking for something else, something more, the question is: How do we recover an authentic experience of *awe* in the presence of the true God of infinite might and majesty?

Often, it seems, we look for such an experience in the wrong place. We look for it in earthquake, wind, and fire, rather than in "the still small voice." The deepest sense of awe in fact requires silence.

This was brought home to me in a very striking and marvelous way not too long ago. I was finishing a biannual teaching period at our seminary in Paris and planning to leave the next day for the States. On my last afternoon, I walked through traffic noise and mid-week bustle from the Latin Quarter across the Seine to the Right Bank, ending up near Les Halles in the very heart of the city. There amidst luxury apartment buildings and trendy shops rose a magnificent medieval stone church I had never noticed before, apparently of mixed Gothic and Romanesque architecture. I entered through a heavy wooden door toward the back and came into an atmosphere of nearly total silence. Several people were sitting here and there, praying or just being. A few tourists walked quietly outside the huge pillars on either side of the nave. Those gigantic columns, topped by intricately carved capitals, rose to meet the vaulted ceiling: earth rising to heaven, heaven descending to earth.

In that stillness praying came as naturally as breathing. For a long while I sat on one of the hundreds of straight-backed wicker chairs facing the main altar. Candles of every size and shape burned before statues and shrines throughout the church, their flames barely able to hold back the shadows.

Then suddenly the setting sun poured its rays through the stained glass windows to my right. The columns, then the entire edifice became suffused with brilliant, golden light: the Joyful Light of the Holy Glory we celebrate each evening at Vespers. The scene was one of transfiguration. All of us there, like Motovilov with St Seraphim in the Russian wilderness, were bathed in that light, transfigured by it, yet unaware that we ourselves reflected the beauty and splendor of that moment.

In that radiant stillness, God was present. He is present everywhere, of course, no matter what the circumstances or receptivity on our part. But for a brief while I was aware of His presence to the point of *awe*. And with that awe there came a profound sense of joy.

Thinking back on that experience, I feel a certain sadness, a tightness in my throat and chest. Awe is a gift. And more often than not it's missing in my life.

But for a few moments it had returned. It was fleeting, but it was real. It appeared in the silence and beauty of that church, to restore something precious I had lost. It confirmed once again what I have so often wanted confirmed: that God is the Lord, and that He appears to us, in our humility and fragileness, as the source of infinite power and grace, to fill us with His own love and glory.

Through the gift of awe, God reveals Himself as He truly is. He reveals Himself as *God*.

23
Divine Conversation

> "The fruit of theology is perfect love."
> —St Gregory of Sinai

*H*OW FAR WE HAVE COME from that understanding of the purpose of "theology" in the life of the Church! The term implies a divine word, one that derives from and speaks with awesome wonder of the God who is beyond all language because He is beyond all human comprehension. Yet God reveals Himself to us. He makes possible our understanding and articulation of His presence and purpose within our own immediate experience. He calls us to formulate and to speak the language of theology, for our own edification and that of those around us, so the world might "hear and believe." That language, however, is unique, because its referent is unique. Accordingly, the great theologians of Eastern Christian tradition will describe the language of true theology as *theoprepeis*, "worthy of God."

Theology in the first instance is less our words about God than God's Word addressed to us. "In the beginning was the Word," the evangelist John affirms, and that Word was the source of revelation, of all true *theologia*. By it God made Himself known to us as Person, as One who seeks communion with us in love. That divine Word came to its most sublime expression in the Person of Jesus. It is He who reveals, makes known, and renders accessible the very Person of God the Father. He is the source of all true theology, since He is the eternal Son and Word of God who dwells eternally in the "bosom of the Father," yet who comes to us, to dwell among us, and to "interpret" the Father to us (*exēgēsato*, Jn 1:18).

It is only derivatively, therefore, that "theology" came to signify our response to God's self-revelation. "Theologians" or "doctors of the Church" were acknowledged and venerated as spiritual guides, mentors in the faith, who received the Word of God in and through the person of Jesus, and elaborated that Word in human language. That language they offered to us for our edification, to provide us with a saving, life-giving "knowledge of God." At the same time, they offered the fruit of their meditation and insight back to God as a "sacrifice of praise." Theology for them was nothing other than divine conversation: communication and communion between God and those whom He created in His own image. Thus everyone, without exception, is called to engage in "theology," even if the Church venerates only three great teachers—John the Evangelist, Gregory Nazianzen and the Byzantine mystic Symeon—as true Theologians.

During the patristic era, theology was understood to be by its very nature the fruit of prayer. The Western tradition spoke of stages or levels in the creation of authentic theology that correspond to ways or levels in the reading of Scripture: *lectio, meditatio, oratio, contemplatio*. The first stage involves spiritual reading of biblical passages and their ecclesial interpretation; the second, rational reflection or meditation on the overall body of tradition; and the third, internalization of the fruit of that meditation through intense and focused prayer. In rare cases, the Holy Spirit leads one finally to *contemplatio*, known in the East as *kathara proseuchē*, "pure prayer," or "prayer of the heart," by which the language of theology and the knowledge it conveys are transformed into a deep and intimate communion with the Divine. At this stage, theology fulfills its true purpose by bearing the fruit of perfect love.

The true theologian, Evagrius tells us, is one who prays. The same may be said of those who have so internalized the Word of

God that they become capable of that perfect love. They, too, are true theologians.

Patristic tradition made a distinction between "theology" and other forms of discourse. Theology spoke of God: the inner being, the interpersonal relationships, and the saving purpose of the Holy Trinity. Other matters fell outside the realm of genuine theology: anthropology, worship, mission, and so forth. Gradually the term "theology" came to embrace all aspects of human life and destiny in relation to God. Theologians now distinguished theology *ad intra* from theology *ad extra*, the former referring to the inner life of the Godhead and the latter to the divine "economy," or plan, for the world's salvation.

What we call "theology" today seldom corresponds to what true theology is meant to be. Every discipline from psychology to literary criticism makes a claim on the term. Would-be theologians speak, or used to, of a "Death of God" theology, which is an oxymoron. Many develop liberation or feminist or gay-lesbian "theologies" built upon a particular social or political agenda. While some of these may to some degree correspond to God's purpose in the divine economy, they are not "theology" in the true sense. They are our words about God and the world, rather than God's Word addressed to us "for the life of the world."

Even within Orthodoxy the term "theology" is often misused, and the "theological disciplines" often fail to speak in a language that is both "about" God and "worthy" of God. Why does this matter? Because theology—derived from Scripture and patristic tradition, then elaborated anew in each generation within the Church—is more than language. It is, in its purest form, communion: a communion in perfect love between God and ourselves.

Some years ago an Orthodox bishop from an East European country participated in a discussion at the World Council of Churches on the "problem" of prayer. Most of those in attendance complained about how difficult and frustrating it is to pray in our day and age, how much social, psychological, and other pressures militate against prayer. Finally, with an air of mild incomprehension, the elderly bishop stood up and spoke. Humbly and rather apologetically, he admitted that he could not understand why others found prayer so difficult. "It's really quite simple," he said. "In the morning, you get out of bed, make the sign of the cross, then begin: 'Our Father, who art in heaven . . ! .'"

Naïve as he may have seemed to the others in their grappling with the existential "problem of prayer," this bishop understood the simplicity, the beauty, and the strength of genuine prayer—prayer which, according to the Scriptures, is a gift of the Holy Spirit (Rom 8). He, perhaps more than any of the others, was by that very fact a true "theologian," one who had, in the quiet of his daily meditation, come to commune with God in all the joy of perfect love.

24

Silence as Sacrament

"For God alone my soul waits in silence."
(Ps 61:1)

"When the Lamb opened the seventh seal, there was
silence in heaven for about about half and hour."
(Rev 8:1)

"Silence is the sacrament of the world to come."
(St Isaac the Syrian)

S ILENCE IS NOT JUST *the absence of ambient noise. Nor does it mean
the lack of laughter or music or shared reflection.*

*Silence is a state of mind and heart, a condition of the soul. It is inner
stillness.*

Silence in heaven reigns amidst joyous song and ceaseless celebration. It is awe in the presence of the Divine.

*Silence in this world leads us beyond earthquake, storm and fire,
beyond stress, anguish and pain. It makes audible, words of ineffable
beauty.*

Silence lets us hear the still, small voice of God.

Hidden in the mountains of south-central France is an ancient
Carthusian monastery that dates, in part, from the eleventh century. The "new" section was completed some two hundred years
later. Referred to as "La Petite-Chartreuse," it is the smaller—yet still

massive—sister structure to "le couvent de la Grande-Chartreuse," founded by St Bruno in 1084. The Carthusians follow the Rule of St Benedict. They were perhaps the only medieval monastic body that preserved the Rule's strictness, including its emphasis on silence.

Chapter six of the Rule includes the following admonition: "Since the spirit of silence is so important, permission to speak should rarely be granted even to perfect disciples, even though it be for good, holy, edifying conversation; for it is written, 'In much speaking you will not escape sin,' and in another place, 'Death and life are in the power of the tongue.'"

This strictness regarding silence may seem severe to most Orthodox Christians, even to those who have devoted themselves to the monastic vocation. A lack of rigidity is a great blessing in Orthodox monastic life, but it too often goes together with an equal lack of silence.

(An Orthodox bishop once shared with me an unhappy impression: "Our monastics talk too much. . . . ") To recover a sense for the sacramental quality of silence, we would do well to spend some time in a community of Carthusian monks—or in any case, to live for a while among monastics whose life and calling have been shaped by strict observance of the Benedictine Rule.

Many years ago I had such an experience, and it left a mark on me that I hope and pray will never be totally lost. With my wife and children I visited a community of contemplative Roman Catholic sisters who, with their bishop's blessing, had taken up residence in the then vacant Petite-Chartreuse. Although their liturgy and spiritual pathway had been very much influenced by Orthodoxy, they owed their gift of silence to St Bruno and to the environment he created.

One moment of that visit stands out above every other. After an early morning climb through the hills surrounding the monastery, I arrived back at the heavy, carved wooden gate leading into the main cluster of buildings. Crossing the courtyard, I stood in front of the huge stone walls of the first building, then entered one wing by an arched doorway at the rear.

In front of me was a long corridor, some fifteen feet wide, stretching into the darkness ahead. Sunlight poured through a row of small windows to my left, illuminating myriad particles of dust suspended in the air. As my eyes became accustomed to the semi-darkness, I made out the shape of a tall figure standing at the end of the corridor, dressed in monastic garb, with the cowl pulled down over his face. A moment later, I realized I was looking at a large, carved wood statue, one that had stood in that place for hundreds of years.

The silence was palpable. Walls of sand-colored rock closed it in, and me with it, to the point that I could hear my heart beat. The floor was a bed of crushed rock, so that each step broke the silence with a quiet crunch.

Standing still in that sacred space, I felt the walls permeated with prayer. Countless monks, unknown to the world but cherished by God, had passed along that corridor, moving with measured steps toward the chapel and the communal office. For a moment, I longed to be with them, to pull a cowl down over my head and spend long moments or hours in a silence broken only by the solemn beauty of Gregorian chant.

I left that place with a feeling of regret, knowing full well that I could never acquire the depths of inner stillness that authentic monasticism, of East or West, requires. I, too, talk too much, am too distracted, too spoiled by the glitter of this world, too impatient, too vulnerable, too weak, too proud. . . . And above all, I lack silence — silence of the kind that comes with genuine inner struggle against all I have just named, and so much more that I dare not mention outside of confession.

I still feel that regret, and for the same reasons. But by the grace of God, I have tasted the beauty and the power of silence, at least a little. And I am grateful.

If there is one gift I could offer to our monastics, indeed to all of us including myself, it would be the gift of silence. Silence in the outward conditions of our life, that encourages the growth of deep inner stillness. Silence that stifles the perpetual noise, which fills the mind and tenses the nerves. Silence that opens both the mind and the heart to otherwise unattainable heights of prayer.

Silence that lets us hear the still, small voice of God.

"God Is With Us!"

*T*HESE BRIEF MEDITATIONS on ethical, biblical, and doctrinal themes have led back repeatedly to one of the most fundamental tenets of Orthodox Christian faith. This is the truth we experience daily and celebrate with special fervor during the Great Compline services of Nativity and Theophany, the truth that indeed *God is with us.*

This affirmation is to be understood in two complementary ways. On the one hand, it expresses the fact that the Triune God, who is infinitely beyond all created reality, nevertheless enters our own time and space, to participate fully in our life, both individual and corporate. God upholds and sustains the entire created order; He participates fully in every aspect of human existence and experience. The Son and the Spirit are present and active within the Church and the world as the "two hands of the Father," to bring us "from non-existence into being," to create us, sustain us, and lead us toward our final end or *telos*, which is everlasting communion with God in the kingdom of Heaven. First of all, then, God is with us in actual presence, to work out His "economy," His divine purpose for the transfiguration of the cosmos and the salvation of mankind.

On the other hand, to affirm that "God is with us" is to say that God *personally* shares our every experience, including suffering and death. He does so completely and with utter faithfulness, as an expression of His limitless love. That love defines His very being and existence ("God is love," the apostle affirms (1 Jn 4), using the term *agapē* ontologically and not just metaphorically). Through the indwelling Spirit of Christ we have access to God the Father at every moment and in every circumstance. Christ is and remains Lord of the Church, Head of the universal Body of those who live "in Him." As Author of Life, He raises up with Himself those who also die "in Him"—through baptism as well as through physical death—and grants them to share eternally in His own glorified life.

Jesus can declare that for those who endure persecution, betrayal, hatred, and even death for His sake, not a hair of their head shall be lost (Lk 21:18). God cares for every living thing, the birds of the air and the grasses of the field. How much more does He care for those who, through their faithful commitment to Him, become "children of God," "a chosen people, a royal priesthood, a holy nation" (Mt 6:25–32; Jn 1:12–13; 1 Pet 2:9)! That care entails actual participation by God in our life and our destiny. Insofar as we place that destiny into His hands, through constant prayer and works of love, He makes of us His own "special people," and leads us "out of darkness into His marvelous light" (1 Pet 2:9). Silently, invisibly, yet with unyielding purpose, He leads those who seek Him and long for Him toward the ultimate fulfillment of their life and being in the plenitude of the communion of saints.

There is a significant realignment occurring these days within mainline Protestant churches, one that is due largely to different ways of conceiving God's being and presence within the world. It is no longer particularly meaningful to speak of "Presbyterians," "Episcopalians," "Lutherans," "Congregationalists," "Methodists," and so forth. Each denomination today is characterized by such a broad spectrum of beliefs and practices, that often the only way to know in what church one presently is worshiping, is to look at the signboard out front. An individual congregation can swing from "liberal" to "conservative" or vice versa, with the arrival of a new pastor whose beliefs and practices are radically different from those of his (or her) predecessor.

The realignment presently going on cuts straight through church bodies, even through individual parishes. It is dividing those who hold to "traditional" faith, practices, and values from those who have by and large discarded them. The most positive effect of this dynamic is to lead many Protestants—theologians and pastors, as well as committed laity—to reexamine their faith and patterns of worship, and in essence to return to a more orthodox form of Christianity.

The impetus behind much of this development among contemporary Protestants consists of powerful and convincing experiences of the presence and activity of God within their personal and ecclesial life. This does not mean "charismatic" experiences as we usually define (or caricature) them, although the experience of healing, for example, or of some striking spiritual awakening can often be the catalyst that works a significant change in their life. More often, it appears that the major influence leading to this "return to the sources" is exposure to Scripture from a new perspective, especially one shaped by the insights of the ancient Church Fathers, theologians of the Latin West and Orthodox East. That patristic perspective may be filtered through modern writers on "spirituality." But if the spiritual vision of those writers is genuine, and it is conveyed with conviction, then the effect is the same. Protestant Christians discover that their true lineage goes back well before the Reformation, to the orthodox teachers and spiritual masters of the ancient Church.

Throughout the twentieth century, working on a legacy dating at least from the Enlightenment, many leading Protestant thinkers moved away from that ancient tradition, largely under the influence of secular literary analysis applied to the Bible (historical-critical methodology, reader-response criticism, deconstruction) and of the relativizing tendencies intrinsic to highly pluralistic societies ("all pathways lead to God"). Among German theologians especially, the concept of "the Word of God" tended to be restricted to "the Bible and its interpretation." God was "present," but only through "the Word," the written testimony of the canonical

Scriptures—and even then selection was usually made, consciously or not, of a "canon within the canon" (largely limited to preferred portions of the few letters attributable to the apostle Paul). The result was to discard as irrelevant elements in the New Testament that were judged to be products of a "Frühkatholizismus," the developing doctrinal teachings emerging from the early "catholic" Church rather than from what they judged to be the original and authentic apostolic tradition.

A dramatic consequence of this tendency in the area of biblical study was the sharp distinction made between "the historical Jesus" and "the kerygmatic Christ." The former was seen as a human being through whom God spoke His Word, while the latter amounted to a virtual invention of the post-apostolic Church that sought to transform Jesus into a god, a divine figure shaped mainly by pre-Christian mystery religions, as well as by the doctrinal conviction that "only God can save us."

This is, admittedly, a minority view among Protestants. The powerful influence of certain German, British, and American theologians who thought this way, however, clearly conditioned the atmosphere of a great many mainline Protestant congregations throughout the last century, and it did so chiefly via their pastors' seminary educations.

Reaction in recent decades on the part of conservative Evangelical Protestants has created the present conditions that are leading significant numbers of Western Christians to recover their theological and spiritual heritage. They acknowledge the very real value in much of the scientific work that constitutes an historical-critical approach to biblical studies. Yet they are gaining ever new appreciation of the patristic perspective which enables the reader of Scripture to move from a purely literal interpretation to one that is genuinely "spiritual," that is, informed by the presence and activity of the Holy Spirit through the very process of hearing the Word of God. At the same time, many are returning to a more patristic (and biblical) christology, seeing in Jesus of Nazareth not simply a man through whom God spoke, but the very embodiment of God's self-revelation: the eternal divine Son who is also the *Logos*, the creating, sustaining, revealing, and life-giving Word of God.

This leaves me with a simple and very basic point—an evangelical truth—that I wish beyond all else I could convey to Christians and non-Christians alike. It is the truth that "God is *with* us," that He knows us better than we can ever know ourselves, that He shapes our life and our destiny, that He loves us beyond all measure.

Equally important, though, is the truth that "*God* is with us." The one who shares our life and suffers our death, who accompanies us through every situation we face and, insofar as we desire it, shapes each situation in view of our salvation, is none other than *God*.

When I first entered an Orthodox church and experienced the beauty of its worship and the power of its teachings, when I beheld the faithful venerating with tears the image of their crucified Lord and shared their joy at the proclamation of His resurrection, I knew I had come home. Since that time—despite heartache over jurisdictional problems, heresy-hunting by the overly zealous, ethnic exclusiveness, and countless sins for which I'm personally responsible—every day, every service, every evening spent reading in the realm of Orthodox theology reconfirms that initial impression. "Where your treasure is," Jesus reminds us, "there your heart will be also" (Lk 12:33–35).

For a growing number of us, both heart and treasure are in what we know as Holy Orthodoxy. No triumphalism, no proselytism—for God knows that everything that Orthodoxy represents for us is pure, unmerited gift. But it is a gift we wish to share. In the most poignant moments of our life, in worship or in serious conversation, we want to extend the invitation to "Come and see." Come and experience the quiet joy of knowing, through genuine faith and worship, that indeed "God *is* with us," that in very truth He is closer to us than our own heart.